KIDS, THE LAW, AND YOU

KIDS, THE LAW, AND YOU
Understanding and using the legal system to protect our children

Robert Craig Waters, Attorney

Self-Counsel Press Inc.
(a subsidiary of)
International Self-Counsel Press Ltd.
U.S.A. Canada

Copyright © 1994 by Self-Counsel Press Inc.

All rights reserved.

No part of this book may be reproduced or transmitted in any form by any means — graphic, electronic, or mechanical — without permission in writing from the publisher, except by a reviewer who may quote brief passages in a review.

Printed in Canada

First edition: July, 1994

Cataloguing in Publication Data

Waters, Robert Craig.
   Kids, the law, and you

   (Self-counsel legal series)
   ISBN 0-88908-939-6

   1. Children — Legal status, laws, etc. — United States.
2. Minors — United States.   I. Title.   II. Series.
KF3735.Z9W37 1994   346.73101'35   C94-910275-X

Self-Counsel Press Inc.
(a subsidiary of)
International Self-Counsel Press Ltd.

1704 N. State Street
Bellingham, Washington
98225

1481 Charlotte Road
North Vancouver, British Columbia
V7J 1H1

CONTENTS

PREFACE xiii

**PART I
OVERVIEW**

1 CHILDREN'S LAW — A NEW WORRY FOR PARENTS, TEACHERS, SOCIAL WORKERS, AND OTHER CHILD CARE PROVIDERS 3
  a. The American family under the microscope 3
    1. Children "divorcing" parents 4
    2. Children switched at birth 4
    3. Unusual custody battles 4
    4. Reproductive technology 4
    5. Other issues 5
  b. Understanding preventive law 5
  c. The development of children's law in the United States 6

**PART II
BASIC PREVENTIVE LAW**

2 THE NEED TO PLAN AHEAD 11
  a. When the parent or caretaker gets sick or dies 11
  b. When the parent or caretaker is incapacitated 12
    1. Someone to care for the child 12
    2. Someone to care for you 13
  c. When the parents die prematurely 20
  d. What if no plans were made? 22

3 WHAT HAPPENS WHEN THERE IS A DIVORCE? 24
  a. Each member of the family suffers 24
  b. Preventive planning to meet children's needs 25
    1. Fear 25
    2. Counseling or psychological care 26
    3. Fear of court proceedings 26
    4. Guardian ad litem or adult guardian 27
    5. Fear of testifying or appearing in court 28
    6. Child abuse allegations 30
    7. Public knowledge of a divorce 31
    8. Divorce involving public figures or sensational allegations 32

	c.	The financial needs of adults	33
		1. Make sure you get the support you are entitled to	33
		2. Hidden assets	33
		3. Pensions, retirement savings plans, and health insurance	34
		4. Taxes	34
	d.	The emotional needs of adults	35
		1. Support and counseling groups	35
		2. Special emotional needs of fathers	35
	e.	Custody of children	36
		1. Custody issues during the divorce	36
		2. Mediation	37
		3. Custody issues after the divorce	37
		4. Uniform Child Custody Jurisdiction Act	38
	f.	Grandparents	38
	g.	Other adults who know the child	39
	h.	Child support problems	39
4	**WHAT DOES THE LAW SAY ABOUT CHILD ABUSE?**		**40**
	a.	The battered child syndrome	41
		1. Symptoms	41
		2. Levels of acceptance	41
		3. Understanding the battered child	42
	b.	Sexual abuse of children	44
	c.	Children abusing children	47
	d.	Other criminal violence against children	47
	e.	When should you suspect child victimization?	48
	f.	Children suing abusive parents or adults	51
5	**WHAT SHOULD YOU DO IF YOU SUSPECT A CHILD HAS BEEN ABUSED?**		**53**
	a.	Avoid confrontation	53
	b.	Parents	53
	c.	Other family members	55
	d.	Guardians and foster parents	55
	e.	Teachers	56
	f.	Social workers	57
	g.	Others	58
6	**USING THE LAW TO HELP THE VICTIMIZED CHILD**		**60**
	a.	Get help for the child	60
	b.	"Street-proofing" your child	61
		1. Street-proofing programs	61
		2. Teaching children emergency telephone services	62

      3. Teaching children about sexual abuse   63

7 THE PROBLEM OF CORPORAL PUNISHMENT   65
    a. Parents   65
    b. Teachers   66
    c. Foster parents and social workers   67
    d. Court-appointed guardians   67
    e. Other adults   67

8 FALSE ACCUSATIONS OF CHILD ABUSE   68
    a. Investigation of a false accusation   68
    b. What if you are arrested?   69
        1. The right to an attorney   69
        2. The right to remain silent   69
        3. Securing your release from jail   69
    c. The trial   69
    d. Getting your name dropped from state child abuse registries   70

9 CHILD NEGLECT AND ABANDONMENT   71

10 HOW CAN THE LAW PROTECT CHILDREN WITH DISABILITIES?   74

PART III
THE STATE AND THE CHILD

11 WHEN DOES A CHILD BECOME AN ADULT?   79
    a. The general age of consent   79
    b. Marriage   80
    c. The drinking age   80
    d. Medical care   81
    e. Testing and treatment for venereal disease   81
    f. Contraceptive services   82
    g. Abortion   83
    h. Withholding treatment on religious grounds   83
    i. The terminally ill child   83
    j. Emancipation of children   84

12 WHAT HAPPENS IF A CHILD BREAKS THE LAW?   85
    a. The juvenile justice system   85
    b. Juvenile status offenses   86
    c. What should the parent or adult do?   86
    d. Improper treatment of detained children   87

13	**WHEN CAN CHILDREN "DIVORCE" THEIR PARENTS?**	88
	a. "Divorce" versus termination of parental rights	88
	b. The outcome of the *Gregory K.* case	89
	c. What does the *Gregory K.* case mean?	90
	d. Children switched at birth	90
14	**ADOPTION**	92
	a. Adoption procedures	92
	b. Problems in adoption	93
	c. Rights of adoptive children and biological parents	96
	d. Inheritance by adopted children	96
	e. Stepparent adoptions	97
	f. Biological grandparents' rights over adoptive children	97
	g. Rights of other biological relatives	97
	h. Adoption of older children and adults	98
15	**CHILDREN BORN OUTSIDE OF MARRIAGE**	99
	a. The situation today	99
	b. Paternity problems	100
16	**WHAT IS THE LAW DOING ABOUT MISSING, KIDNAPPED, AND EXPLOITED CHILDREN?**	101
	a. Parental kidnapping	101
	b. Other missing children	102
	c. Exploited children	103
17	**WHO CONTROLS A CHILD'S EDUCATION AND RELIGIOUS TRAINING?**	104
	a. Public versus private schools	104
	b. Home schooling	105
	c. Gender-based discrimination in the schools	106
	1. Gender-based discrimination in general	106
	2. Sports opportunities	107
	d. Students who are also parents	108
	e. Sexual harassment in schools	108
	f. Sex education	109
	g. Prayer in the schools	109
	h. Religious training of children	110
18	**BENEFITS AVAILABLE TO CHILDREN AND THEIR FAMILIES**	111
	a. Family leave	111
	b. Social security	113
	c. Public assistance	114
	d. Tax breaks	114

19	**OTHER LEGAL PROBLEMS INVOLVING CHILDREN**	116
	a. Seat belt laws	116
	b. Injuries to visitors	116
	c. Gun laws	117
	d. Dangerous instrumentalities	118
	e. Child labor laws	118
	f. Legal liability for children with serious disabilities	119

PART IV
MEDICAL ISSUES INVOLVING CHILDREN AND THE LAW

20	**SURROGATE PARENTING AND REPRODUCTIVE TECHNOLOGY**	123
	a. Surrogate parenting	123
	b. Gestational surrogates	126
	c. Semen donations	127
	d. Frozen or stored embryos, eggs, and semen	128
	1. Frozen embryos	128
	2. Frozen semen	130
	e. Using medical technology for sex selection	130
21	**WHEN CAN SOMEONE SUE OVER BIRTH-RELATED PROBLEMS?**	132
	a. Birth-related injuries	132
	b. Birth defects and wrongful birth	133
	c. Wrongful life	135
	d. Wrongful pregnancy	135
	e. Wrongful conception	135
	f. Lawsuits for the sterilization of a minor	136
22	**WHAT IS THE LEGAL STATUS OF THE UNBORN CHILD?**	138
	a. Abortion	138
	1. Abortion law in general	138
	2. Minors and abortion	139
	b. RU 486 — The "French abortion pill"	141
	c. Abortion-related lawsuits	141
	1. Abortion malpractice	142
	2. Abortion racketeering	143
	3. Accidents or negligence injuring unborn children	143
	4. Toxic injuries to unborn children	144
	d. Criminal attacks on pregnant women	146
	e. Sex selection of fetuses	147

ix

23 WHAT DOES THE LAW SAY ABOUT CHILDREN AND SUBSTANCE ABUSE?   148
    a. Children who abuse drugs   149
    b. Children who abuse alcohol   150
    c. Substance abuse by pregnant women   151
        1. Drug abuse by pregnant women   152
        2. Alcohol abuse by pregnant women   153
        3. Pregnant women who abuse other drugs   154
    d. Lawsuits against pregnant mothers who abused drugs   154
    e. Children who turn in drug-abusing parents   155
    f. Children of alcoholics   155

APPENDIXES

1   Resources   157
2   Private child welfare organizations   162
3   Private child welfare organizations for missing children   166
4   State child labor agencies   167
5   State child support enforcement agencies   171
6   State child service agencies — general services and child abuse and neglect programs   175
7   Major government agencies investigating missing, kidnapped, and exploited children   179

SAMPLES

#1   Nomination of preneed guardian for minor child (under Florida law)   14
#2   Declaration of guardian in the event of later incompetence or need of guardian (under Texas law)   16
#3   Living will (under Illinois law)   17
#4   Health care proxy (New York law)   19

NOTICE TO READERS

Laws are constantly changing. Every effort is made to keep this publication as current as possible. The author, the publisher, and the vendor of this book make no representations or warranties regarding the outcome or the use to which the information in this book is put and are not assuming any liability for any claims, losses, or damages arising out of the use of this book. The reader should not rely on the author or publisher of this book for any professional advice. Please be sure that you have the most recent edition.

PREFACE

This book is intended to give parents, teachers, social workers, and caretakers of children a broad overview of the rapidly changing law affecting child care. A resource of this type is of great use in today's world, where the law affecting children and their caretakers is in great upheaval. Many adults simply do not know where to turn when they have questions about the new "children's law" or the so-called children's rights movement that is now affecting all of our lives. Almost every day, newspapers bring new and disturbing headlines about some troubling legal issue involving children.

However, much of the law in this area is quite new. The law also changes constantly and differs dramatically from state to state. Every effort is made to include up-to-date and significant material in this book. But it is impossible for any one book to cover all issues in every American state. Only a treatise containing many volumes could do that.

For that reason, this book cannot address the specific legal problems of individual readers, nor should anything in this book be viewed as legal advice. This book will help alert readers to important issues and show ways to avoid legal problems before they happen. This book also will show readers how the law may affect them and when they should seek further help and advice from professionals. But readers with specific legal problems should obtain help from support agencies in their own states or cities, or should contact a qualified local attorney. This book cannot substitute for one-on-one help and sound advice addressed to the particular needs of the individual, which may involve laws not discussed here. Please consult the Appendixes at the back of this book for agencies and contacts that may be of assistance.

Chapter 2 shows documents that you might want to have in order to use the law to protect children and yourself. These forms are samples only and are valid only in certain states and only for people who do not have unusual legal problems. Different states may require that different forms be used other than those shown in this book, and it is impossible to reproduce all of these forms in the limited space available here. If you need a particular form that addresses your own state's laws or your own special legal problems, you should consult local child welfare organizations, your local libraries, or an attorney in your city.

Note: If you are involved in an ongoing legal problem involving a child, take the time to consult a qualified local attorney. Many lawyers will not charge you for a first visit, in which they will assess your case and give you some preliminary advice. You may be able to find lawyers who will help you for free or at a reduced charge. Call the Bar Association or child welfare agencies in your city or state for more information. (See Appendix 1 for more information.)

PART I
OVERVIEW

1
CHILDREN'S LAW — A NEW WORRY FOR PARENTS, TEACHERS, SOCIAL WORKERS, AND OTHER CHILD CARE PROVIDERS

Today, the law regulates child care with an intensity no one could have foreseen 10 or 20 years ago. Our grandparents and even our parents could never have dreamed it possible, yet each day there are stories in the news about final adoptions that are revoked, children who "divorce" their parents, and teachers and other child care providers who face unusual legal problems and public embarrassment. Families and adults are spending hundreds of thousands of dollars in legal fees over problems like these, which their own parents would never have encountered. Many adults are very disturbed by what happens when the American legal system deals with children.

a. THE AMERICAN FAMILY UNDER THE MICROSCOPE

State agencies now hold the American family under scrutiny. As just one example, the new reproductive technology has made headlines out of the most personal aspects of family life. The once absolute privacy of the family is being torn away by a society increasingly concerned with the way children are born and reared. Many adults are afraid — afraid they might run afoul of the law no matter what they do with the children in their care. It is a genuine and understandable concern.

There is an obvious reason for these intrusions into our lives. The failures of a few parents and child care providers have resulted in widespread public outrage. Hardly a month passes without horrific headlines about child abuse and neglect. Many of the stories are unquestionably horrible, even outrageous. For example, Americans were shocked in 1993 when 12-year-old Polly Klaas of Petaluma, California, was kidnapped during a slumber party in her own house when a stranger knocked on the door and abducted her. The child's body was not found for two months. Few of us have ever even imagined that such terrible things are possible when children are involved, but today's headlines say otherwise.

There are other reasons as well for these new intrusions into family life. The theories are still controversial, but some experts now argue that a bad childhood can lead to an adult life riddled by crime, addiction, mental illness, and violence. In response, a growing children's rights movement has arisen. Among its most prominent advocates is Hillary Rodham Clinton, wife of the President of the United States. This movement is pressing state and federal agencies to provide ever greater protections for all children.

Caught in this social tug-of-war is the American family and all other child care providers, because greater protection also means greater intrusion and responsibilities for adults caring for children. Even good parents, teachers, and care providers fall under the government's watchful eye. For example, parents or other adults have been investigated for "child abuse" based on accusations that proved ridiculous. In one notorious Florida case, a neighbor reported a woman for child abuse, and state agencies launched an investigation, only to discover that the neighbor had overheard the woman spanking a naughty dog. More seriously, some men and women involved in child care have had their reputations ruined by government investigations of groundless and bizarre charges.

The bottom line is that every parent, teacher, social worker, and child care provider must now be aware of the growing new body of law governing child care. This book is meant as a resource to help fill the need. It is a frank "adult-to-adult" discussion of what every parent and children's caretaker needs to know about today's complicated legal issues. Tough problems are not glossed over. In the real world, none of us can afford to blind ourselves to the things that might hurt us or the children we love and care for. And many of today's problems are far more difficult and troubling than those we remember from our own childhoods.

In fact, only a few years ago a book of this type would not have been necessary. But today, every parent, teacher, social worker, and care provider must be aware of what the law requires. The "bad parenting" and abuses of a few have resulted in new legal requirements that bind all of us. Failing to honor the law — even when the law seems unreasonable — can lead to costly legal expenses, damaged reputations, imprisonment, ruined careers, or broken families.

Potential problems are not confined merely to alleged child abuse. Other traps also exist to snare parents and child care providers as well as the children in their care. Many of these have resulted in dramatic newspaper headlines, some quite recent. These headlines have frightened child care and service providers throughout the nation, and with good reason.

1. Children "divorcing" parents

One of the most visible "children's rights" cases was the lawsuit filed by a Florida boy identified as "Gregory K." The boy made international headlines when he sued his own parents for "divorce" because he believed they were unfit. In the pages that follow, this book helps show why the *Gregory K.* case is not as troublesome as it sounds, and how most parents and other caretakers can easily avoid being legally "divorced" from their children.

2. Children switched at birth

Another highly visible Florida case involved a teenage girl named Kimberly Mays who had been switched at birth by the hospital where she was born. Her biological parents discovered the truth many years later and sued to obtain custody of the girl, even though the girl was bitterly opposed to the idea. This case alarmed parents throughout the United States, who were left to wonder whether a stranger someday might make a similar claim against their own children. Later, this book takes a look at the law governing cases of this type.

3. Unusual custody battles

A large number of other cases have arisen throughout the United States in which biological parents have tried to win back the custody of children. Often the problem involves a man who is proven to be the biological father of a child but had never previously been recognized as such by the law. At other times, biological parents have tried to revoke adoptions or take biological children away from foster parents. These cases have been a serious worry for many families, especially adoptive and foster parents. Chapter 14 examines this issue and shows how to use the law to the best advantage.

4. Reproductive technology

Other attention-grabbing cases in California, New York, Michigan, and New Jersey have involved the problem of surrogate motherhood (where a woman agrees to bear a child for another couple). Such arrangements have often resulted in lawsuits, sometimes because the surrogate mother decided to keep the child, and sometimes because the child was born with a physical or mental disability and no one wanted to keep it. Yet another highly visible case involved a custody dispute over frozen embryos that had been stored for possible future use — a scientific miracle possible through the new reproductive technology. See chapter 20 for a discussion of these issues.

5. Other issues

Other medical and legal problems parents and caretakers must face today are also quite new. Before 1980, everyone thought that modern medicine had defeated most of the life-threatening diseases that once killed too many of our children. Many parents and grandparents still remember breathing sighs of relief when polio was finally defeated through the invention of new vaccines. Now, we face ailments such as AIDS, herpes, and other sexually transmitted diseases (STDs) that can create profound problems for children and those who care for them. Parents and caretakers need to understand how the law can be used to protect themselves and their children.

Before 1973, there was little possibility of a pregnant teenage girl getting an abortion without her parents' help. Now, some states allow girls to have an abortion without their parents or caretakers even knowing. Likewise, children with an STD — often including AIDS — can be tested and treated without anyone else being aware. Control of a child's medical treatment is not always the sole decision of a parent or care provider, a possibility many people find very disturbing.

Traumatized children often suffer serious emotional disorders that are only made worse when the children are asked to confront their abusers in police or court proceedings. Sometimes these children are subjected to intense publicity in newspapers and on television, causing problems for the child and the caretaker. In response, the law has developed new methods to protect children and their families and care providers from some of the harmful effects. Parents and children's caretakers need to know how these laws can help them.

b. UNDERSTANDING PREVENTIVE LAW

It is important to understand how to prevent problems before they even arise. For that reason, the emphasis throughout this book is on *preventive law*.

Many people have heard of preventive medicine, where you go to your doctor for regular checkups so that any health problem can be spotted before it gets serious. In the United States, there is a growing trend toward preventive law, which means regularly examining certain aspects of your life, including your relationship with your children and your family, to make sure you are avoiding the legal pitfalls that have caused serious problems for others. Just as many parents keep medical reference books to help rear their children, today there is a need to keep a legal reference book handy for the same reason. (For more information on preventive law, see chapter 2.)

There are many precautions that you can take as a parent or child care provider to protect yourself and your child. This book gives you an awareness of some of the troubles that have plagued other parents and care providers — and tells you to avoid them.

Some of the material in this book deals with problems that every parent should consider, though few will ever face them. Cases like Gregory K.'s effort to "divorce" his parents, for example, are so far rare. But there are other problems that every parent must confront at some point. This includes questions like "Who gets custody of my children if I cannot take care of them?" and "How do I set things up so that my child is cared for if I die?"

Once again, the law provides ways to deal with such problems. In many instances, a little forethought and preparation is all you need to protect you and your child. This is why preventive law exists: to help you plan for your child's future and protect your rights.

c. THE DEVELOPMENT OF CHILDREN'S LAW IN THE UNITED STATES

Both children's law and the children's rights movement are new developments. Until quite recently, the legal system operated under some very simple presumptions about families and their children. Up until the early part of the 19th century, a child was considered to be the property of his or her legal father. Divorce was rarely allowed, and the father was given custody of the child unless he waived that right by word or action. The legal system was unwilling to intervene in child care issues. Questions such as corporal punishment or alleged child abuse were viewed as private matters in all but the most extreme cases.

Much the same situation existed in public institutions such as schools, orphanages, and other care facilities. In public and private schools, well into the 20th century, school personnel often beat pupils severely for misconduct that we might think minor today. Yet the law regarded such punishment as merely a routine part of growing up.

By the beginning of the 20th century, these views began to gradually shift. The change began with divorce and child custody. Around the turn of the last century, the law started to believe that very young children — those thought to be "of tender years" — were better off with their mothers in the event of separation or divorce. This development occurred primarily because of evidence gathered by the new sciences of psychology and psychiatry.

As divorce laws became more concerned with children, the idea that the legal father "owned" his children fell into disfavor. Mothers almost automatically started getting custody of children under what judges called the "tender years doctrine."

However, the tender years doctrine never regarded children as being the property of the mother. To the contrary, the doctrine was based on what then was thought to be the best interests of the child. Mothers, in other words, were regarded as better care providers.

Many fathers still tried to get custody of their children, and they sometimes succeeded. But this almost always involved a battle of expert psychologists and psychiatrists, who had to appear in court to say which parent could best rear the children. Through the years, a steady stream of such cases made the legal system more and more familiar with the mental and medical needs of children. This was an education that the legal system would later expand into many other areas.

After World War II, American society became more and more aware of the impact a person's childhood had on adult life. During this period, popular books on child development could be found in almost every family home. By the late forties and fifties, this awareness resulted in efforts to improve the lives of children throughout the United States. In the 1960s, a vast number of federal and state government programs were set up to help children. President Lyndon Johnson helped sponsor these programs; their aim was to improve the quality of education, food, and medical care for children.

With these new programs, the public became more aware of a variety of other problems. In the early sixties, a group of medical experts first realized that a surprisingly large number of children treated in hospital emergency rooms showed signs of repeated and severe abuse. Likewise, civil unrest, riots, and rising juvenile delinquency raised concerns about children's home life.

Some efforts were made to increase government regulation of child care at this time, but these were minor steps compared to what would come later. However, several reforms were begun in the sixties that had a lasting impact. Among these were efforts to improve the conditions of children in state-run facilities and efforts to severely restrict the use of corporal punishment in public institutions such as schools.

In the 1970s and early 1980s, the United States entered a period when many social issues — especially children's issues — were put on the back burner. Some new programs were started and new laws were passed. But these were stopgap measures. Instead, the nation focused on other social issues, such as abortion, international "human rights" under President Jimmy Carter, and "down sizing" the federal government under President Ronald Reagan. Most children's issues became low profile.

All of this began to change around the mid-1980s when a vocal group of advocates started pressing for "children's rights." This was partly a response to some people's perception that the Reagan administration wasn't doing enough for children. Hillary Rodham Clinton was one of these early advocates, but others included law professors, child welfare officials, doctors, and judges. These advocates began publishing articles and conducting studies on the way American children lived. In only a few years, they managed to convince a number of politicians that children were being neglected, abused, and psychologically injured in larger numbers than anyone had thought.

Starting in the mid- to late-1980s, states began passing laws designed to increase the vehicles for protection for children. Among the most noticeable were so-called "child abuse registries." These provided toll-free numbers where child abuse could be reported, and usually all reports were followed up by a state investigation. Other programs included "guardians ad item:" adults appointed to help children who have become involved in the legal system, such as when their parents are divorcing.

The many programs are too numerous to name here, but together they resulted in something that had never happened before: an intense awareness of children's rights.

By the late 1980s and early 1990s, the results of all of this activity were clear. Cases such as Gregory K.'s effort to "divorce" his parents were a direct result of all the work done by child advocates a few years earlier. Gregory K.'s lawsuit would have been impossible a decade earlier. And now, the children's rights movement seems to have developed a momentum all its own.

Newspapers are reporting a considerable number of other children who are trying to "divorce" their parents. With each one of these cases, the legal rights given to children seem to grow. At the same time, the legal authority of parents, teachers, and care providers becomes more uncertain. The law in this area obviously is changing rapidly, and still other developments are likely in the years ahead. For this reason, today's parents, teachers, and child care providers now are being called upon to understand legal issues they have never encountered before.

Today, no parent, teacher, or child care provider can afford to be unaware of the new children's rights movement and the laws it has helped enact. This book is for you.

PART II
BASIC PREVENTIVE LAW

2
THE NEED TO PLAN AHEAD

a. WHEN THE PARENT OR CARETAKER GETS SICK OR DIES

Few of us like to think about what will happen after we are gone from this world. This is an understandably human feeling. Yet those of us who love and care for children must look out for their best interests. Our children are too important to let simple emotion prevent us from making these important plans. Consider what might happen if adequate plans are not made.

In Texas, a married couple were tragically killed in a freak shooting incident. Both had children by prior marriages as well as children of their own. The husband had prepared a will several years earlier, prior to his present marriage, but the wife had no will at all. The husband also owned part interest in a small but profitable family business. However, his will only said that his property would now go to his "children."

As a result of this couple's lack of planning, the children ended up in a complex and lengthy lawsuit over who would have custody of them, and who would control the husband's share of the family business. Under Texas law, as in every state, minor children are legally not allowed to control most major kinds of property they might inherit. An adult must be appointed to do so. And in this situation, several relatives of the husband saw this as an opportunity to gain greater control over the family business. Greed was their primary motive, not the best interests of the children.

Worse still, the husband's will itself was subject to a legal challenge because it had not been updated after his latest marriage. The children of the latest marriage were not even born when the will was signed, which meant that they now might have to sue to claim a portion of their father's estate. And the wife's children by a prior marriage were left with the possibility they would inherit nothing from their stepfather, even though this is probably not what he intended. Neither parent dreamed that they both might die so suddenly, so they never made a proper plan for the children's custody.

This case illustrates what many lawyers tell thoughtful parents: "Hope for the best, but plan for the worst." We all have a moral duty to make sure our children are never caught in a trap we could have avoided with advance planning.

Fortunately, laws exist throughout the United States to enable adults to engage in this type of preventive planning to help children. All that is necessary is a little forethought and awareness of the legal "tools" that are available for our use. This book can help you become aware of these tools, how they work, and how you can use them to best advantage.

A few points should be emphasized. It is never enough to plan just once for your children's protection. The husband in the Texas example did sit down and have a will drawn up. He made at least one attempt to plan for his children's future. His mistake was in failing to update his planning after the circumstances of his life changed — his remarriage and the birth of new children. The result was a catastrophe for the children he loved.

All parents and children's caretakers need to update their preventive law plans whenever a major change occurs in their lives. Major changes can include the following:

- Marriage, divorce, or remarriage
- The birth of a child
- The death of a spouse or child
- Obtaining substantial property, wealth, or a business
- The discovery that you or your spouse has a life-threatening disease
- The discovery that a child may have a serious disability for all or most of his or her life
- The death of anyone named in your will or anyone who would have received your property if you had died

The reason you should reexamine your planning in these situations is obvious. Each one of them is an event that substantially changes your priorities and the legal consequences of your earlier planning.

For example, a will should *always* be updated after a marriage, divorce, or remarriage. If this is not done, it could be challenged in a lawsuit, especially if the new spouse or children born of the marriage are not named in the old will. Likewise, buying new property means you need to decide exactly how that property would be divided among your spouse and children. And if you learn a child will suffer a serious disability, you need to provide for special care for that child to the best of your ability.

You also should update your planning as soon as you learn that you or your spouse are suffering a life-threatening disease. *Always* avoid waiting until you are on your deathbed to update your plans. Everything you do when you are extremely sick might be challenged on the grounds that you were too feeble to understand your own actions. This could lead to lawsuits, which will harm your children's interests.

Always keep in mind the possible need to update your plans in the future. Never assume that you can plan once in a lifetime and then forget about the issue.

b. WHEN THE PARENT OR CARETAKER IS INCAPACITATED

All of us like to think that so long as there is life in our bodies, nothing is going to stop us from looking out for our children. In the real world, however, parents and caretakers sometimes suffer illness or injury that leaves them unable to act or make decisions. They are legally "incapacitated." This is not a big problem if another parent or adult relative is available to care for the child. In that case, the law recognizes that this other adult can step in to care for both the child and the other parent.

As well, there are increasing numbers of single-parent families in the United States. If the single parent becomes incapacitated and no other adult is available, then the law must step in to say who will care for the children and who will care for the incapacitated adult. Obviously, underage children cannot make decisions for an incapacitated parent.

To plan for such a problem, the adult must make sure that someone will look out for the children and the incapacitated adult. Perhaps the same person will fill both roles, or perhaps it would be wiser to have different people. Many states allow parents or caretakers to express their wishes in advance, and at a future date a judge weighs these wishes.

1. Someone to care for the child

Obviously, the most pressing problem is finding a competent adult to look out for your child if you became sick. Fortunately, most states give you the authority to express your wishes. Some state laws even say that a parent or caretaker's wishes are binding unless a judge finds them contrary to the child's best interests or finds some other legal reason to disregard them.

Florida, for example, allows parents to fill out a document called a Declaration of Preneed Guardian naming an adult to care for a child if the parents are unable to do so. This declaration must be honored by the Florida courts unless the adult named in the document is unfit. Florida, however, is unusual in the degree of control it gives to parents.

In many other states, the process of making your wishes known is called *nominating a guardian* or making a *declaration of guardian* for the child. Some states prescribe particular legal forms that must be used in making a nomination, while others will consider any evidence of what the parents wishes were. In many states, the judge will take into account written statements by the parent or testimony by other persons as to what the parent intended. Sample #1 shows a Nomination of Preneed Guardian for a Minor Child in Florida.

However, most states only require the judge to hear the evidence. Usually, the judge is not bound by it. Many states also require the judge to take into account the child's wishes if the child is 14 years of age or older. In a few states, the judge is bound by the child's wishes unless the child chooses a guardian who is unfit.

If you are a single parent and you have no relative who could care for your child if you became ill, you should make sure that your wishes about your child's future guardian are known. Even writing down your wishes on a piece of paper, then dating and signing the document, is a step in the right direction. This document may not be binding on the judges in your state, but at least it will make your wishes known.

Make sure the document is kept in a safe place or entrusted to someone so it will be readily available if you became sick.

An even better step is to contact child welfare agencies, support organizations, or attorneys in your area. They can help you understand how the law in your state works and what documents you need to fill out. Some provide blank documents for you. If you go to an attorney, a wise step is to ask him or her to take care of all your preventive law planning in one session, which will save money.

2. Someone to care for you

The other problem you must confront is who will look out for you if you become incapacitated. Obviously, poor planning on your part will be detrimental to your child, particularly if your chosen guardian is untrustworthy. For example, suppose you failed to make any plans before you became sick, and a judge then appointed an irresponsible brother or sister as your guardian. The guardian might have control of all of your money and could steal it, leaving you and your child penniless. To avoid future problems, plan wisely.

Many states allow adults to express their wishes in advance concerning who should be their guardians or make decisions for them if they become incapacitated. State laws vary, but five main types of legal "tools" exist:

(a) a nomination or declaration of a guardian,

(b) a voluntary guardianship,

(c) a living will,

(d) a durable power of attorney, and

(e) a separate document authorizing another adult to make health care decisions for you. (In some states this may be called a "durable power of attorney for health care," a health care "proxy," or a "health care surrogacy.")

SAMPLE #1
NOMINATION OF PRENEED GUARDIAN FOR MINOR CHILD
(UNDER FLORIDA LAW)

I, Sue Smith, residing at 14 Tropical Way, Miami FL 33313, the only surviving parent of the minor child named herein, make this declaration to nominate a preneed guardian and alternate preneed guardians for the said child. I make this declaration willfully and voluntarily on the 14th Day of January, 19--, in the County of Dade, Florida.

1. This document governs the guardianship of the following child:

   a. Name of child as it appears on birth certificate or as changed by court order: Terri Jo Smith

   b. Date of birth of child: 25 May 1990

   c. Social security number of child: 467-00-000

2. I do hereby nominate my best friend, Jean Friendly (the "Preneed Guardian"), who resides at 911 Sunshine Avenue, Miami FL 33313, as the Preneed Guardian of the child named herein. I direct that she serve as the guardian of my child in the event I die or become incapacitated and am unable to care for the child.

3. If the person named above is unavailable to serve as guardian, I nominate my uncle, Bobby Relative, who lives at 1456 Central Lane, Ocala FL 32600, to be the preneed guardian under all the terms and conditions stated herein.

4. My unequivocal wish is that the persons nominated in this document be given preference over any other person, including relatives by blood or marriage not named herein, whenever a court appoints a guardian for my child. By not naming such other persons, I do not imply any disrespect or disapproval. I only express a sincere belief that the persons nominated above are best able to act as guardian and that the best interests of the child will be most fully served if the desires expressed herein are honored.

5. This document supersedes and revokes all prior nominations of preneed guardian for minor child executed by me.

6. Should any word or combination of words herein be found unenforceable under the law, that word or combination of words shall be deemed severed from this document and void, and the remainder of this document shall be given effect as nearly as possible.

IN WITNESS WHEREOF, I have executed this declaration, on this 14th day of January, 19--, in the County of Dade, Florida.

_____
DECLARANT

_____, residing at _____
WITNESS   ADDRESS

_____, residing at _____
WITNESS   ADDRESS

[NOTARY AFFIDAVIT]

(a) Guardian named in advance

A nomination or declaration of your own guardian usually works much the same way you might nominate a guardian for your child. Some states require that you use special legal forms, while others say that your wishes will be honored if there is proof. Sample #2 shows a declaration of this kind for the State of Texas. However, most states give a lot more weight to your wishes about your own guardian than to your wishes about your child's guardian. As a result, the person you nominate is likely to be named your guardian if you became incapacitated. This means your guardian might be given authority to make all decisions about you and your property. (The guardian could make decisions about your child only if a judge also named the same person as the child's guardian.)

(b) Voluntary guardianship

The second legal tool is the voluntary guardianship. A voluntary guardianship means that you voluntarily go to a judge and ask that a guardian be appointed for you. Obviously, this means you must already know that something will happen that will leave you incapacitated. An example might be major surgery that could be life-threatening. Voluntary guardianships are a good planning tool, because judges in most states will honor your request and appoint the guardian you choose. Then you can rest assured that the person you want will act as your guardian, not someone you do not want or a total stranger.

(c) Living will

The third planning tool that is available is the living will. Living wills are a kind of legal document in which you say what you want done if you become permanently unconscious or so hopelessly ill that only artificial life support will keep you alive. Living wills typically are plain, easy-to-understand forms that simply say that the persons who signed them do not want to be kept alive artificially after they are permanently unconscious or once death becomes unavoidable. Many people overlook living wills as a device in planning for their children's futures, but living wills can be very useful in this regard.

For example, suppose you failed to express your wishes about artificial life support and, as a result, your doctors kept you alive through medical machines for many years. This type of extraordinary or "heroic" medical care is very expensive and could eat up all of your money and property, leaving your children with nothing after you finally died. Many people do not want to be kept alive by machines after they are permanently unconscious, especially if this means leaving their children in poverty. A living will is useful because it can help you avoid this possibility.

Living will forms are easily available. Most major hospitals will provide you with a standard blank form at no cost. Some state Bar associations (see Appendix 1) and medical associations will provide you with copies. Many office supply companies stock standard forms that you can buy for a few dollars. Sample #3 shows an example of how a living will can be worded in Illinois.

Attorneys will draft living wills for you. However, as a general rule the forms are so easy to obtain that it often is a waste of time and money unless the lawyer prepares the living will as part of a package deal. This would not be true, however, if you want a special living will drafted or have unusual legal problems that need to be addressed in the living will.

(d) Durable power of attorney

The fourth planning tool is the durable power of attorney. Many people think the label "attorney" is given only to people licensed to practice law, but the word actually can be used to describe people authorized to make certain decisions as the agent of another person. The latter are called "attorneys in fact" to distinguish them from

SAMPLE #2
DECLARATION OF GUARDIAN IN THE EVENT OF LATER INCOMPETENCE OR NEED OF GUARDIAN (UNDER TEXAS LAW)

I, John Jones, make this Declaration of Guardian, to operate if the need for a guardian for me later arises.

1. I designate my sister, Aileen Jones Arken, to serve as guardian of my person, and my friend, Michael Dove, as alternate guardian of my person.

2. I also designate my sister, Aileen Jones Arken, to serve as guardian of my estate, and my friend, Michael Dove, as alternate guardian of my estate.

3. If Aileen Jones Arken dies, fails or refuses to qualify, or resigns, my alternate guardian succeeds and becomes my guardian.

4. I expressly disqualify my brother, Dory Jones, from serving as guardian of my person or estate.

Signed this 14th Day of January, 19--.

John Jones
John Jones, Declarant

Jane Lee
Jane Lee, Witness

Brenda Lee
Brenda Lee, Witness

SELF-PROVING AFFIDAVIT

Before me, the undersigned authority, on this date personally appeared the Declarant, and Jane Lee and Brenda Lee, as witnesses, and all being duly sworn, the Declarant said that the above instrument was his Declaration of Guardian and that he had made and executed it for the purposes herein expressed. The witnesses declared to me that they are each 14 years of age or older, that they saw the Declarant sign the declaration, that they signed the declaration as witnesses, and that the Declarant appeared to them to be of sound mind.

John Jones
John Jones, Declarant

Jane Lee
Jane Lee, Witness

Brenda Lee
Brenda Lee, Witness

Subscribed and sworn to before me by the above-named Declarant and affiants on this 14th Day of January, 19--.

J. O. Ewe
Notary Public in and for the State of Texas
My Commission expires:

SAMPLE #3
LIVING WILL
(UNDER ILLINOIS LAW)

This declaration is made this 14th Day of January, 19--. I, May Jones, being of sound mind, willfully and voluntarily make known my desires that my moment of death not be artificially postponed.

If at any time I should have an incurable and irreversible injury, disease, or illness judged to be a terminal condition by my attending physician who has personally examined me and has determined that my death is imminent except for death-delaying procedures, I direct that such procedures which would only prolong the dying process be withheld or withdrawn, and that I be permitted to die naturally with only the administration of medication, sustenance, or the performance of any medical procedure deemed necessary by my attending physician to provide me with comfort care.

In the absence of my ability to give directions regarding the use of such death-delaying procedures, it is my intention that this declaration shall be honored by my family and physician as the final expression of my legal right to refuse medical or surgical treatment and accept the consequences from such refusal.

May Jones
May Jones, Declarant
In the City of Chicago, Cook County, Illinois:

The Declarant is personally known to me and I believe her to be of sound mind. I saw the Declarant sign the declaration in my presence (or the declarant acknowledged in my presence that she had signed the declaration) and I signed the declaration as a witness in the presence of the declarant. I did not sign the Declarant's signature above for or at her direction. At the date of this instrument, I am not entitled to any portion of the estate of the Declarant according to the laws of intestate succession or, to the best of my knowledge and belief, under any will or Declarant or other instrument taking effect at Declarant's death, or directly financially responsible for Declarant's medical care.

Ellen Simmons
Ellen Simmons, Witness

Sue Stone
Sue Stone, Witness

"attorneys at law" who engage in legal practice. A durable power of attorney is a legal document that names an "attorney in fact," who can be anyone you choose, whether a lawyer or not, to make decisions for you if you cannot do so yourself. (However, health care decisions are usually subject to special requirements and often are not included within a standard durable power of attorney.)

Durable powers are most useful if you have a business, assets, or property that would need to be supervised by a competent adult if you became ill. This might be true if good supervision is necessary for the welfare of a child. For example, a durable power of attorney could name a trusted friend to run your business if you became too ill to do so, and to see that your children and spouse have sufficient money from the business's profits to meet their needs.

A durable power of attorney can be more complex than other documents like a living will. If your business or assets are more complicated, have a durable power of attorney drafted by a lawyer. You also might need to consult with your accountant regarding any possible tax problems. For less complicated situations, you may be able to use standard preprinted forms available at office supply or stationery stores. Keep in mind, however, that a durable power of attorney is a binding document that can have important consequences. Choose your "attorney in fact" carefully, because a poor choice could result in the loss of a business or assets.

(e) Health care decision makers

The fifth planning tool goes by many names in different states, but the more common names are *durable power of attorney for health care* (in California), *health care surrogacy* (in Florida), or *health care proxy* (in New York). These types of legal devices exist so you can name another person to make health care decisions for you if you are unable to do so yourself.

Many states impose special conditions on these "surrogate" health care decision makers because of the unique problems at stake. For example, a poor decision by your surrogate might cost you your life, whereas a poor choice under a durable power of attorney might only mean a loss of assets. Surrogates commonly are forbidden to authorize certain "radical" medical procedures like lobotomy, abortion, or commitment to mental hospitals.

State laws differ, and quite a few states have no clearly set-out procedures. In some states, a durable power of attorney can include health care decisions, while other states have very strict rules about how health care surrogates can be appointed. Usually, major hospitals and medical societies in your area will have information on how you can appoint a health care surrogate for yourself.

A health care surrogate will be making decisions affecting your health. Every parent and child's caretaker should consider appointing a surrogate. Even if you only name your spouse as your surrogate, the fact that the signed document exists and is readily available will speed the process of getting medical treatment and make your doctors and nurses feel better about the way decisions are being made. Sample #4 shows a health care proxy for New York State.

A health care surrogate is particularly important if you do not have a blood relative or relative by marriage. In the past, some hospitals have been forced to delay treatment because they could not find an adult authorized to make decisions for someone who was unconscious. Such delays could affect your life or health and, in turn, your children's future. In other words, to look out for your children, you

SAMPLE #4
HEALTH CARE PROXY
(NEW YORK LAW)

1. I, Michael Smith, hereby appoint my friend Sue Jones, who lives at 145 Friendly Avenue, New York, NY 10023, phone number 212-555-1212, as my health care agent to make any and all health care decisions for me, except to the extent that I state otherwise below. This health care proxy shall take effect when and if I become unable to make health care decisions for myself.

2. I direct my health care proxy shall have the authority to make decisions regarding artificial nutrition and hydration (food and water fed to me through tubes).

3. I name the following person as my substitute proxy if Sue Jones is unable, unwilling, or unavailable to serve: Joe Mark, who lives at 137 Friendly Avenue, New York, NY 10023, phone number 212-555-1212.

4. Unless I revoke this proxy, it shall remain in effect indefinitely.

Signed this 14th Day of January, 19--

Michael Smith

Michael Smith
145 Friendly Avenue
New York, NY 10023

We, the witnesses whose signatures appear below, declare that we are 18 years of age or older, that the person who signed this document, Michael Smith, is personally known to us and appears to be of sound mind and acting through free will, and that Michael Smith signed this document in our presence.

Jane Roe

Jane Roe, Witness
150 Friendly Avenue
New York, NY 10023

Darlene Doe

Darlene Doe, Witness
153 Friendly Avenue
New York, NY 10023

also need to look out for yourself as best you can.

c. WHEN THE PARENTS DIE PREMATURELY

The greatest worry many parents and caretakers face is the thought of what would happen to their child if they died prematurely. The Texas couple who were killed in a freak shooting accident (mentioned earlier in this chapter) gives a chilling glimpse of the kinds of problems that are created when parents or guardians fail to plan for the worst.

Part of good planning includes making sure your plan is up to date. Having a proper up-to-date plan can make things much easier for your child. Of course, the emotional loss your child would suffer cannot be eased by anything on this earth. But you can take steps to make sure that children are properly cared for until they reach adulthood and to see that they (and not some greedy or unscrupulous adults) enjoy the benefit of the property or businesses you own.

Your will, or Last Will and Testament, is your most effective legal tool. Younger parents or guardians may feel it is not necessary to have a will, but a good will is absolutely essential for anyone who is parent, a guardian, or a legal caretaker of children. A will can be used to do two very important things in one document:

(a) Name the person you want to be guardian of your children.

(b) Name the person who will be the *custodian* of the property you leave to your children.

Naming your children's guardian and the custodian of your property are especially important if you are a single parent or if you have no trustworthy relative to take custody of the children. However, even secure couples need to do this, if only to plan for the possibility that both parents may die tragically.

Wills are very flexible legal documents. They can range from the very simple to the exceedingly complex. As a general rule, the more complicated your personal and business affairs are, the more complex your will. Complex wills should be drafted by trained attorneys. There is no easy test for what separates simple wills from more complex ones. However, if you have any doubts, take the time to consult with an attorney in your area. Attorneys in most areas will not charge for an initial consultation. Take advantage of this opportunity.

For a simple will, there are a number of good books that explain how you can draft your own will. Make sure you get a book that is respected, that was prepared by a lawyer, and that deals with the law of your state. Some publications advertise wills that are valid in all states, but you should be aware that state laws can differ dramatically. You may be one of those people who needs to be aware of something unique to the law of your state. Finally, make sure you select a book that deals with the special legal problems of the custody and property rights of minor children. Some do not.

One of the most important things to understand is that you cannot give full control of your property to a minor child. Most states now have a Uniform Transfers to Minors Act, which means that you must designate an adult to be the custodian of your estate. If you fail to do so, a custodian must be chosen by the person who is the legal representative of your estate after you die or (in the case of a trust you have created) by your trustee. Children will not be allowed to control the property themselves without adult supervision, nor can the child choose the custodian. In most states —but not all— the custodian will continue supervising inherited property until the child reaches age 21. A few states have reduced the age to 18. (If you want to increase the age, you usually can find a way to do so. However, it is wise to get an attorney's advice first.) Those states that have not yet adopted the Uniform Transfers to Minors Act typically have laws that are similar to it.

Choose an adult custodian wisely because this person will be able to exercise considerable control over your child's inheritance. Select someone who is absolutely trustworthy and who cares for your child. If no such person is available, consider using an established and respected financial institution. Often, the trust department of a respected local bank will supervise your child's inheritance under the terms of your will. Such institutions often have considerable experience in this field. Financial institutions are heavily regulated and supervised by state or federal laws.

The use of a legal trust also is something you may wish to consider. Wills can be drafted so that assets actually are delivered into the trust, not directly to the minor child. A trust is a legal device by which an adult trustee is given authority to supervise property or other assets for the benefit of someone else, including children. Trusts are extremely flexible and can include restrictions. For example, you can specify that assets in the trust be used only for certain purposes, or that your child will not receive the assets until a certain age, or that the assets be used only for living and educational expenses. A "spendthrift trust" can be established if you are worried that a child might squander an inheritance without proper supervision or if the child seems prone to debt.

Most trusts should be established only with proper advice. You can use a skilled trust attorney if you wish, but often banks and financial institutions will help you prepare the necessary papers. You should consult with the trust department of a respected local bank before you start writing your will.

There are special legal requirements that often must be met in order for property to be transmitted into a trust through your will after you have died. State laws vary, so get advice from someone fully aware of your state's laws. Often, trusts also involve special tax problems under the Internal Revenue Code. A skilled lawyer can help you create a trust that avoids creating needless tax problems for your child.

The second major concern in drafting a will is choosing someone to receive custody of your child, usually called a guardian. Almost every state allows a parent to state in a will who this person should be. Some states give great weight to the parent's wishes, though many allow judges to choose someone else for a variety of reasons. A large number of states say that if the child is 14 years of age or older, the child is permitted to say who he or she wants as a guardian. A few of these states require judges to respect the child's wishes if reasonable. You should check with child welfare agencies, local lawyers, or your local library to see which laws apply in your state.

If you are concerned that an unsuitable adult may end up as your child's guardian, you can prevent it from happening. You can use your will to express your desire that this adult *not* receive custody of the child and to specify the exact reasons why that person is not qualified. The judge then would be forced to deal with your reasons at the time your estate is settled.

Several states also provide special legal tools that can help you enforce your wishes. In Florida, a Nomination of Preneed Guardian (see Sample #1 earlier in this chapter), can be recorded in the courthouse like a property deed. The document is binding on Florida judges unless the parent's choice of a guardian is clearly unreasonable. Check with attorneys in your area to see if there are special legal tools you might be able to use in your state.

You can establish a guardianship to meet special needs. For example, suppose the child's grandmother would be the ideal person to care for your child but is completely incapable of managing the property and assets your child will inherit. Under the law of every state, there are ways to designate the grandmother as the guardian of your child's "person," but to give control of property and money to someone else. You might specify, for instance, that the money you leave your child will be managed by the trust department of a respected local bank, with instructions to pay the grandmother a monthly sum to cover the child's expenses. Any attorney trained in writing wills should be able to help you customize a guardianship to suit you and your child's needs.

It is often best to have your will prepared by a lawyer. It is true that simple wills can be prepared by anyone, but legal issues involving children are often complex. This especially is true if you want your child's custody to go to someone other than your nearest relative. Sometimes bitter custody disputes erupt after a child's parent has died. Perhaps the most famous was that of Gloria Vanderbilt, America's "poor little rich girl," whose relatives engaged in a lengthy and hurtful custody battle over her. While most people are not as wealthy as the Vanderbilts, they can still sometimes let their emotions run away from them when a child's custody is at stake. Often the child is the one who suffers most.

Another pitfall to avoid at all costs is a possible challenge to your will. Even if your estate is worth only a few thousand dollars, this can be an incentive for relatives to challenge your will. Your estate's assets could be eaten up by expenses incurred during a lengthy lawsuit, and your child could be harmed by the uncertainty caused. Take the time to consider whether you have a relative who might try to take part of your child's inheritance. None of us likes to think our relatives would do such a thing, but we must be realistic when planning for a child's future. Consider what might happen, then act accordingly.

If you anticipate *any* possibility of a custody dispute if you died or *any* possibility that someone will challenge your will in court, seek an attorney's help. There are ways to make a will as ironclad as humanly possible. In some states, wills can be drafted so they contain a "poison pill," such as disinheriting anyone who challenges your will or making a challenge completely unworthwhile in some other way. (Not all states allow this, however.)

Remember that your child's future is at stake. Seek professional help if needed. Feel free to shop around among attorneys until you find one whose attitude and fee suits you. Ask for a quote of how much you will be charged. If you cannot find a qualified attorney in your area, call your state's Bar Association for a referral (see Appendix 1).

Yet another reason for seeking an attorney's help involves federal and state tax laws. Estates sometimes are subject to inheritance taxes, and an improperly drawn will may create unnecessary federal income tax problems for your child. This is especially true with larger estates. Tax laws are very complex; they can change suddenly and dramatically. A trained attorney can help you avoid tax problems. Always consult a qualified attorney if there is any possibility of a tax problem affecting your estate.

d. WHAT IF NO PLANS WERE MADE?

In many cases, the failure to make plans for your child may not cause a problem. This is true if there is only one obvious close relative who could care for the child (or for you, if you are incapacitated). For example, if you are married and not separated, your spouse almost certainly would be able to take charge of things, care for your child, or care for you. The law itself would recognize this is the correct result. Likewise, if your only close relative was your own mother, then few would doubt that she would take charge of things.

Other situations are not so clear, however. This especially is true for single or widowed parents, or divorced parents who are estranged from the child's other parent. In some cases, the closest relative may be someone you do not trust. In other cases, you may have no close relatives at all, or no relatives who would want to take custody of your child or care for you when you were incapacitated. In these situations, advance planning is absolutely essential.

The failure to plan could result in your child's custody going to someone you do not want, or in someone being appointed as your guardian who you personally would not want. In the worst case, your child's custody might be given to the State itself, which would usually place your child in a foster home. The foster care system throughout the United States has many good features, but unfortunately children in the foster system are often placed with several different homes until they reach adulthood. This can result in an unsettled childhood. Most parents who have a trusted frend would rather avoid the foster system and would want their child to go to their friend instead.

The other problem with the failure to plan has been discussed throughout this chapter. If your planning is inadequate, lawsuits can result and harm your child. The more money you have, the more temptation there is for someone to sue your child and your estate. Even less wealthy families have endured lawsuits when different relatives sued each other over a child's custody.

The little bit of time and effort involved in making and updating plans is far less worrisome than the thought that a child might suffer because plans were never made or were not updated when necessary. It is the children's future that is at stake.

3
WHAT HAPPENS WHEN THERE IS A DIVORCE?

All of us know that divorce is far more common today than it was in our parents' and grandparents' day. Estimates in some parts of the nation show that as many as one in every two first-time marriages will end in divorce. As a result, divorce has become one of the most common legal problems that confront children and the families who care for them. For that reason, every parent or guardian of a child needs to give some thought to what will happen to that child during and after a divorce. In other words, preventive law requires a little forethought about the possibility of divorce and how it will affect the children both directly and indirectly.

a. EACH MEMBER OF THE FAMILY SUFFERS

Studies show that divorce affects children, wives, and husbands differently. In the late 1980s and early 1990s, a series of studies were conducted in many states on the subject of how gender bias affects the legal system. One special focus of these studies was divorce. The researchers documented the sad fact that every member of a family suffers in a different way when there is a divorce. Children, for example, often are ignored or pushed aside while adults decide their futures. Partly as a result, too many children suffer permanent emotional scars during a divorce.

Typically, wives end up with far less financial security after a divorce. This is worsened by the added responsibility of being the primary child care provider. Men, however, are denied meaningful rights to visit their children or to share in parenting decisions. Many men complain that they are permitted to see their children far too little after divorce.

These problems arise from two facts: men usually earn more than women do, and women usually are perceived as better nurturers of children. Ironically, "no fault" divorce laws have made the problem worse. These laws were meant to make divorce less bitter because no one had to be blamed for ruining the marriage before a divorce would be granted.

Bad as the old divorce laws were, they did have one feature that now has largely been lost: husbands most often were blamed, and as a result ended up paying very substantial alimony to their wives. The wives thus maintained a good standard of living after the divorce. Husbands, meanwhile, could often get far more visitation time with their children, because they could threaten to sue for a reduction in alimony if wives did not agree. The money, in other words, gave the husband a lever to finagle better visitation privileges.

Today, however, the typical American divorce is far different. Both husband and wife usually have jobs, but the husband's job pays better. When the family is split up, the husband goes his separate way — with a job that frequently pays far more than the wife can earn. While some husbands chafe at being alone for the first time in many years, the fact remains that their earnings are greatly enhanced while their responsibilities are reduced. Alimony is far rarer today, and if granted often is only temporary so that the wife can get better job training. As a result, the husband has little means to force more visitation time with the children.

The typical divorcing wife also goes her separate way, but she does so with a shrunken income *and* primary custody of the children. Her resources are reduced and her responsibilities are greater. Worse still, she must provide daily care to growing children, but without the help or support of a mate. Many psychologists note that this situation often breeds resentment, which increases the wife's desire to prevent the husband from visiting the children. If the father is unscrupulous and takes advantage of the situation to rid himself of responsibility for his own children, the wife resents this even more. Some newly divorced wives find their incomes reduced to the poverty level or below, while their former husbands live quite well.

From a legal, emotional, and financial standpoint, all members of the family should keep in mind three things:

(a) the emotional needs of the children must be cared for, even if the children seem all right,

(b) the wife must take all steps she can to make sure she will not suffer a substantial loss of financial resources, and

(c) the husband must make sure he continues to have a satisfactory role in the rearing of his children.

If the husband and wife are divorcing on friendly terms, they should sit down and make a conscious effort to avoid the problems outlined above. After all, if everyone suffers in a different way from a divorce, then everyone has something to gain by cooperating in a way that will avoid these problems. Men, for example, can agree to provide greater financial support in exchange for more meaningful visitation with the children. Women, meanwhile, can agree not to try to isolate the children from the father if he will help out with financial and parenting problems.

Unfortunately, there are many unfriendly divorces. Advance planning is all the more important here because each spouse may not be able to trust the other. Emotions run high, and husband and wife start doing or saying things that will be harmful to everyone, especially the children. If this is a possibility, then both spouses must take steps to protect themselves and the children as best as they can.

Fortunately, there are a few tools that will allow people to exercise preventive law in this area.

b. PREVENTIVE PLANNING TO MEET CHILDREN'S NEEDS

Throughout the United States, the law is beginning to recognize and prevent the various ways children are harmed during and after a divorce. These can be many, but the most common are —

(a) the child's general fear over what will happen when the family breaks up,

(b) trauma caused when the child must become involved in court proceedings,

(c) trauma caused when there is a possibility that child abuse has occurred or when a child is being "coached" to falsely accuse a parent of child abuse, and

(d) trauma caused if news about the divorce becomes public knowledge or creates a scandal.

1. Fear

Every child experiences fear at the possibility of a divorce, even if the child will not admit it. Before the 1970s, very little was done to help children through the natural process of grieving over the family's breakup. Today, both legal and mental health professionals have come to understand how disturbing a divorce is to a child.

Many children not only have overactive imaginations, but also an overactive sense of guilt. They may actually think that they have done something to cause the divorce. More sensitive children can find this thought highly disturbing. Other problems can arise, especially if children come to believe that their future well-being is at stake or they may never see one of their parents again.

As a result, a growing number of divorce courts in the United States now refer people to counseling programs or provide special courses or counseling sessions to help out. Some courts, for example, offer or even require divorcing parents to attend lectures or taped seminars on the impact divorce will have on them and their children. Many other court personnel can provide parents with the address and phone number of public mental health clinics in their areas, which often provide counseling at little or no cost to those who cannot afford the fee.

These services can be very important. One good way to help lessen the fear a child feels is to take advantage of these opportunities and to see that the child undergoes counseling before, during, and after the divorce — even if the child seems all right. This way, a trained professional will be there to see if the child is working through the process normally or to take proper action if the child needs special help. Some children, after all, are more sensitive than others, as most every parent knows. Preventive help early in the divorce process may save more grief later on.

2. Counseling or psychological care

One fairly common situation is that the spouse who has custody of the children immediately before or during the divorce cannot afford the cost of psychological child care. That spouse should seek the help of a qualified local divorce lawyer with a good reputation. (Contact the Bar association in your state if you need a referral to such a lawyer; see Appendix 1.) To one degree or another, every state will get the spouse with enough money to pay for the expenses of the less well-off spouse until the divorce is final. This can include expenses for the children's care.

Usually the attorney will go to a judge and explain the kinds of expenses that must be paid. The other spouse's attorney will be present and will respond. If the judge agrees that one spouse can pay and the other cannot and that the expenses are reasonable, then the judge can order the spouse with money to pay the expenses. Laws vary significantly from state to state. You will need an attorney's help if you intend to take advantage of this opportunity.

Keep in mind that the judge can also order the other spouse to pay for your attorney's fee if you cannot do so yourself. This is an often misunderstood aspect of divorce law, but one that can be very important. If you don't have enough money, feel free to say so when you have your first appointment with a lawyer. Many lawyers will not charge for a first visit and will take your case even if you cannot meet their fee on the understanding payment will occur only if the judge orders the other spouse to pay for such costs. This is an important tool both for making sure both spouses have good legal advice and for seeing that the children are properly cared for until the divorce becomes final.

Take advantage of this opportunity if it can help you. Most important, do not be afraid to talk to an attorney about making your spouse pay for these costs. In many states, the law gives you a right to this kind of support. Use it!

3. Fear of court proceedings

The second major problem children face when their parents divorce is fear of the court proceedings. Some experts call this "legal process trauma." It happens because children do not understand how our legal system works. If children are forced to be interviewed by lawyers or to give testimony in court before strangers, they may assume they have done something terribly wrong. Children may already be blaming themselves for the divorce and they may suffer even greater trauma from their involvement in the legal proceedings. Unfortunately, some lawyers and judges may make the children's pain worse by treating them in the cold professional manner common in a lawsuit. Children cannot understand why people act this way.

Studies show that children face serious problems when they become involved in legal proceedings:

(a) They are anxious when there is no one to look out for them.

(b) They suffer chronic anxiety when legal proceedings drag on for a long time, and especially when proceedings are unexpectedly postponed at the last minute.

(c) They can suffer trauma if they are repeatedly questioned by lawyers or forced to testify in court many times.

(d) They can suffer trauma if they are forced to talk about unpleasant or embarrassing subjects in front of strangers or are afraid to testify in court, even though they must do so.

(e) They can experience needless trauma if they are forced to confront people who may have hurt them.

(f) They can suffer trauma if they receive little or no age-appropriate support during their involvement in the legal proceedings.

Children cannot be completely sheltered from all of the problems described here, but the law has developed several special tools that can help lessen the child's trauma.

4. Guardian ad litem or adult guardian

Because children can be harmed when no one looks out for them in a lawsuit, many states now authorize judges to appoint an adult called a *guardian ad litem* to represent the child. *Ad litem* in Latin means "for purposes of the legal proceeding," so a guardian ad litem is a type of guardian who helps children solely for purposes of a legal proceeding in which they have become involved. However, a guardian ad litem does not actually receive custody of a child and does not have the powers of a regular guardian. The guardian ad litem is simply a person who helps and speaks on behalf of the child in court, but no place else. If a guardian ad litem is appointed for your child, your own custody and rights over the child will not be affected, unless the judge says otherwise.

The guardian ad litem will be present during court proceedings to look out for the child and to help avoid the problems noted above. The guardian ad litem has no other responsibility. Unlike the divorcing parents, the guardian at litem has no personal stake in the divorce lawsuit and thus can devote one hundred percent of his or her attention to the interests of the child. Many states allow the guardian ad litem to speak on behalf of the child at any time. Thus, if the parents are about to do something that is not good for the child, the guardian ad litem can speak out against it.

A word of warning: sometimes a parent or both parents become quite aggravated with guardians ad litem who are present during a divorce. Under the law, the guardian ad litem is not beholden to either of the parents. Guardians ad litem have sometimes been quite vocal in opposing what the parents want to do and may even be able to block some of the parents' plans about the divorce. The advantage here is the divorcing parents sometimes do lose sight of their children's best interests, and the guardian ad litem can at least speak up when this happens. However, some parents have come to believe that their child's guardian ad litem was only acting as a third adversary during the divorce.

If you think a guardian ad litem might be useful in your divorce, you should talk the matter over with an attorney beforehand. Sometimes, a guardian ad litem will be appointed during a divorce if a parent requests it, and it is useful to have a guardian ad litem if the other spouse has abused or injured the child.

A few divorce lawyers have found that guardians ad litem in cases of this type can be very helpful in seeing that the abusive spouse is denied custody or visitation rights or is ordered to pay for the child's medical or psychological care. Judges sometimes regard guardians ad litem as a neutral third party, whereas parents can be seen as biased about the alleged child abuse. In other words, the guardian ad litem's statements about child abuse may be more believable to the judge.

Nevertheless, the parents' wishes about a guardian ad litem are not necessarily binding on the judge. In some states, judges can appoint a guardian ad litem simply because they think it is the right thing to do, even if the parents disagree.

The problem of children being exposed to lengthy legal proceedings is a hard one to avoid. Sometimes divorces drag on for a long time because the husband and wife cannot reach an agreement. Many parents will feel a strong urge to get the matter behind them, so the children's suffering will end sooner.

However, a few spouses have allowed the proceedings to drag on because they know the other spouse is worried about the impact on the children. Delays can be a deliberate effort to force the other spouse to cave in because the children are suffering. This is nearly the same as holding the children hostage.

When this happens, you need an experienced attorney who can bring the problem to the judge's attention. Document every time the other spouse threatens to delay things or hints that the delay will end if certain conditions affecting the children are met. Each side in a divorce has the right to be treated fairly and to receive a fair settlement of the issues. No one should be forced to give up money or property in order to end the suffering of the children. Judges have punished people who tried to manipulate their spouse this way. Your attorney should be able to help you. Likewise, guardians ad litem can also help protect children in this situation.

If possible, avoid last-minute delays or postponements of proceedings in which the child will be interviewed or will testify. Psychological studies show that children can be gravely traumatized if they believe they must appear in a proceeding at a certain time, only to have the time changed unexpectedly. As a result, many skilled lawyers or guardians ad litem do not even tell a child about proceedings very far in advance. That way, if the dates must be changed, the child will not be needlessly traumatized. Some lawyers even tell judges that a request to change a date should not be allowed because of the harm it may do to the child.

5. Fear of testifying or appearing in court

Another problem for children is when they are repeatedly subjected to interviews or asked to be witnesses in court more than once. There is seldom any reason why children must undergo repeated intrusions of this nature. Usually once is enough.

Many attorneys or guardians ad litem ask the judge to issue an order limiting the number of interviews a child must give. Most often, the judge will authorize a single interview only (often called a deposition). The judge can also issue an order saying that the child will only be required to testify once, if the testimony is absolutely essential. In other words, everyone involved in the case is put on notice that they must have all of their questions ready to ask on the one occasion they will be allowed to interview the child or to call the child as a witness in court. If you are worried about your children, ask your attorney to request an order of this type.

Occasionally a child can be particularly sensitive and suffer horrible trauma even at the thought of being interviewed or appearing in court. Whenever this is so, the best policy is to make sure the child receives proper psychological therapy throughout the process. Attorneys and guardians ad litem also are increasingly successful in getting the judge to allow the child's therapist to be present during all proceedings. The therapist can help make sure the child is not needlessly traumatized.

The child can be traumatized by being forced to talk about unpleasant things. This might happen because the child has been abused by a parent, or because the child is afraid to be interviewed or to testify. Until quite recently, little was done to help such children. Children were brought into a room full of strangers without any preparation or counseling.

Today, nearly every state permits three major legal tools to help make things easier for children:

(a) Children can give their testimony on videotape.

(b) Children can testify in another room via closed-circuit television.

(c) Children need not testify if a reliable adult can testify about what the child has said.

(a) Videotape testimony

Usually, the child is brought into a small room where he or she feels comfortable. Only the judge, the court reporter, the attorneys, and sometimes the guardian ad litem or the parents may be present. The child gives testimony, which is videotaped for later use in the courtroom. The child does not have to sit on the witness stand in front of strangers.

(b) Closed-circuit testimony

Another legal tool is the use of closed-circuit testimony. The child is in a room some place distant from the courtroom, sometimes in the judge's private offices. There, the child is questioned and gives testimony. Everything the child says and does is transmitted by closed-circuit television into the courtroom, where the jury and all the spectators listen. For the fearful child, this avoids the problem of testifying with strangers present.

Closed-circuit testimony is most commonly used when there is some suspicion that one parent may have abused the child. The judge can order that parent, for example, to remain in the courtroom and watch the proceedings only on the closed-circuit television. This helps prevent the child being further traumatized by the presence of the parent who may have been abusive.

(c) Have another person testify

This third legal tool prevents the child from having to testify at all. One principle of American law is that hearsay statements are not allowed in court. In the past, this rule often meant that children would be forced to testify, because adults could not testify about things they heard the child say on earlier occasions. Many states have changed this rule so that adults can repeat the child's hearsay statements, provided there is reason to believe the statements were reliable. For example, the child's therapist or pediatrician may be able to describe statements the child made about being abused. If you can use this rule, it may mean your child will not have to testify at all. This can significantly diminish the child's trauma.

Finally, it is important to see that children receive age-appropriate support. Guardians ad litem often are trained in such matters. Likewise, a child's therapist can assist in seeing that the child's needs are met. Consider obtaining help from these people so that your child does not suffer in silence during your divorce.

Even if you do not have a therapist or guardian ad litem, you should ask for help from an adult whom your child trusts. For example, the child may have a special relationship with a grandmother. If so, the grandmother could be asked to accompany the child at all times during the legal proceedings so the parents can worry about their own legal problems. Many children are far more comfortable in many situations if a trusted adult is present to help them.

6. Child abuse allegations

The most serious and disturbing charges that arise during a divorce are allegations of child abuse. Sometimes the abuse is minor, but at other times the abuse can be as serious as repeated incest. A 1990 study showed that somewhat less than 2% of custody or visitation disputes involve allegations of sexual abuse of a child. Most disturbing, the study also suggested that about 50% of all sexual abuse allegations in child custody or child visitation cases are actually proven to be true. About 33% were false. Another 17% resulted in no satisfactory conclusion of the issue.

Both legally and psychologically, charges of this type are of the most serious order. In many states, sexual abuse of a young child can carry a penalty of life imprisonment. The scandal can be devastating, even to innocent members of the family. Nearly every year, newspapers carry stories of people who suddenly have found themselves subjected to intense public attention because they were accused of molesting children. Even innocent family members have suffered terribly, and it is not uncommon for families to lose major sources of income as a result of the allegations.

Nevertheless, child sexual abuse is a serious matter. A 1987 study showed that a parent who has sexually abused a child is likely to commit a repeated offense between 16% to 60% of the time. Even after treatment, a substantial percentage of abusers — as high as 38% — are likely to be unchanged or more abusive even after receiving appropriate psychological counseling. Some studies indicate that one of the most promising treatments for an abusive parent is arrest, conviction, and court-ordered treatment in a prison environment. Criminal conviction seems to drive home the serious nature of the offense.

Not surprisingly, child abuse allegations have a way of completely changing the focus of a divorce. What might have been a simple end to marriage suddenly takes on the tone of something involving secret and ghastly crimes. The allegations take on a life of their own, overshadowing every other legal question at stake. Judges can be swayed even by unfounded allegations.

For that reason, there is an unfortunate tendency among some attorneys or parents to use allegations of child abuse as a kind of legal battering ram to force the other side into submission. Few people relish the idea of seeing their reputations and careers destroyed by the label "child molester." It thus is all too possible to force someone to concede rather than be accused, because even an unfounded accusation can be costly. Nevertheless, child abuse allegations in the context of a divorce deserve some special attention. (For a full discussion of child abuse, see chapter 4.)

If a divorcing parent suspects that the other spouse has abused a child, it is very important to have the child evaluated by a trained psychologist or psychiatrist, especially one who specializes in children's care. Sometimes suspicions prove unfounded. The parent needs to know if this is so before making public accusations.

An unfounded accusation could seriously jeopardize your own legal position during the divorce and might raise questions about your own fitness as a parent. The other spouse's attorney, for example, might accuse you of suffering delusions or of psychologically abusing the child.

Never consider encouraging a child to make up an accusation, or to make less serious abuse seem worse than it was. If the judge ever thinks you have done so, your credibility may be badly damaged. The judge may not believe anything you say afterward. Truthfulness is essential in court, and the law in every state says that a single lie can be grounds for a judge to assume that you were untruthful in other matters too. Whatever advantage you think you may gain from being less than truthful is not worth the risk of being discovered.

Also keep in mind that your children could be needlessly harmed or traumatized if they are encouraged to lie. Many psychologists have noted that children feel guilty even when telling the truth that a parent abused them. Imagine how much worse the guilt would be if the accusation is a lie. (See chapter 8 for more about false accusations of child abuse.)

If your worst fears prove true and a professional believes your child was abused by your spouse, immediately get an attorney's help. If you cannot afford a lawyer, you should contact the agency in your state that investigates child abuse. (Appendix 6 lists the agencies in each state.) These agencies usually investigate immediately and will contact local law enforcement agencies at the proper time. However, if you are not satisfied with the agency's response, you should feel free to contact the proper law enforcement agency yourself.

Child psychologists and psychiatrists almost uniformly advise that an abused child should be put in therapy as soon as the abuse is discovered. Remember that you may be able to make the other spouse pay for therapy. If you cannot afford to pay, most communities have mental health facilities that can provide therapy at little or no cost. Likewise, many cities have professionals who specialize in children's psychological problems. Check the Yellow Pages of the phone book. Your local child welfare agency can also refer you to qualified specialists.

7. Public knowledge of a divorce

Another source of trauma for children is public knowledge of the parents' divorce. Most divorces receive no publicity, but sometimes even the divorces of ordinary people make headline news. This is especially true if child abuse is involved — a fact that compounds the child's anguish. Classmates and other young friends of the child can make the situation far worse by teasing, shunning, or engaging in other hurtful behavior. Many of us know that children can be especially cruel to each other. Moreover, some especially sensitive children can be traumatized by gossip about the parents' divorce. Some psychologists call this kind of behavior "environmental reaction trauma."

Parents should try to anticipate in advance how news of the divorce may affect the child. If you are involved in a simple divorce unlikely to make the news, you should sit down with your child and discuss what is likely to happen. You could ask how he or she thinks friends and classmates will react. Perhaps you could even coach the child on how to respond to particular kinds of responses or questions from other children, emphasizing that there is nothing shameful in the divorce. Ask how many of the your child's friends have divorced parents, and find out how they reacted when the divorce happened.

Above all, you should gauge how your child is going to be affected in everyday social settings, including at school, at religious activities, at the playground, at Scouting programs, and so forth. The overall purpose is to try to street-proof your child as best you can by helping him or her prepare strategies to cope with stressful situations when socializing with peers. Some children are naturally better than others at handling these things. Obviously, the child least able to cope must receive the most help and preparation.

Occasionally, the parent realizes that the child is going to encounter serious troubles dealing with the fallout from the divorce. If this is so, consider starting the child in therapy as soon as possible, hopefully before news of the divorce has leaked out to the child's friends. Many child therapists are especially skilled at helping children prepare coping strategies. Again, support services of this type may be available at little or no cost in local public mental health centers. Or you may be able to get a court order requiring the other spouse to pay the cost of the therapy.

8. Divorce involving public figures or sensational allegations

The child's trauma will be especially severe in highly public divorces involving public figures or where the divorce involves something sensational such as child molestation, murder, or other events that already have received press attention. These cases can be the most difficult to deal with, but there are a few legal tools available.

(a) Guardian ad litem

First, consider asking the judge to appoint a guardian ad litem for the child. If the case is highly sensational, an attorney can be the guardian ad litem, or an attorney can assist the guardian ad litem. The guardian ad litem can watch over the child throughout the legal proceedings, especially where the parent or other responsible adult will be too busy dealing with the legal issues. Guardians ad litem usually have special training in the various kinds of legal tools that can help the child.

(b) Gag order

Second, your attorney can ask the judge to take several actions to protect the child. For example, in some instances a judge can issue what is often called a "gag order" forbidding the press to print certain kinds of information. However, do not count on a gag order as the sole means of protection. Under the First Amendment of the U.S. Constitution, gag orders almost always are considered improper, and usually are dissolved once the news media's lawyers challenge it. Gag orders rarely are a permanent solution to your problem.

Another possible tool is for the judge to order that the child's full name — and sometimes the names of the parents — not be used in any court proceedings or documents. For example, the child could be identified only by initials or as "John Doe" or "Jane Doe."

Yet another tool is that the judge could order the courtroom closed to the public and the news media whenever highly sensational or embarrassing information will be discussed that may harm the child if made public. You also may be able to allow the child to testify without ever having to come into the courtroom. As we discussed in section 5. above, judges can use videotaped testimony from the child or testimony by closed-circuit television, or permit reliable adults to report what the child has said to them in hearsay statements.

(c) Get the media to cooperate

In a sensational case where children may be traumatized by public exposure, your attorney may be able to get voluntary cooperation from the news media in your town. Many local attorneys are on friendly terms with people who work in the news media. An attorney can sit down with these people and get a promise, for example, that the child's name will not be published or broadcast. News media workers are human, and many are parents. They may sympathize with the child if they understand the problem. Reporters may even voluntarily agree not to do things that would hurt the child.

Some news workers may want a concession: for example, a chance to interview the parents or the child. If so, you and your attorney will need to discuss the pros and cons of agreeing to the request. If a single short interview means the child's name will not be published, then the bargain may be a good one. If the particular news reporter is not trustworthy, however, avoid making a bargain.

As a last resort, you can go over the news reporter's head and talk directly to the editor, publisher, or director. However, many news workers may resent being treated in this manner. Your attorney should know when it is a good idea to talk to a reporter's boss and when it is not.

c. THE FINANCIAL NEEDS OF ADULTS

Meeting children's needs is often the most pressing concern for parents facing a divorce, but parents must also keep in mind their own needs. Every divorce is different, and every parent has different needs. However, most adults suffer because of the emotional and financial demands brought on by the divorce.

The most serious problem facing many divorcing parents is the grim fact that the family's finances will be divided. Everyone knows that two can live better than one. Money is stretched thinner when a married couple splits up, leaving one of the former spouses with primary care of the children. Studies in the 1980s and 1990s show that one of the largest single groups living at or near the poverty level in the United States is divorced mothers who have custody of their children. For that reason, every divorcing woman needs to give serious thought to how she can avoid falling into this same trap.

The same applies, though not as frequently, to husbands who receive primary custody of the children or whose wives are wealthy. Such men often face an even bigger problem in court because many judges and attorneys assume that the man is better able to fend for himself than the woman. Prejudice can come into play because some old-fashioned judges may think a man is "not worth his salt" if he wants financial support from his divorcing wife. This can happen even where the only fair thing is for the wife to help support the children or to divide her assets fairly with the husband.

1. Make sure you get the support you are entitled to

If you are in this situation, you must face the fact that you need a skilled attorney's help, especially if your spouse has a lawyer. The law on dividing marital assets can be complicated, and differs dramatically from state to state. There are even a handful of nations, states, and territories called "community property jurisdictions" in which you may be entitled to split the bulk of your spouse's assets half-and-half, no matter what. These jurisdictions include Arizona, California, Idaho, Louisiana, Nevada, New Mexico, Texas, Washington State, the Commonwealth of Puerto Rico, and many parts of the world where Spanish or French is the chief language.

As a result, you should get an attorney's help if you presently live in one of these jurisdictions, or if during the marriage you once resided in one of these places. This is the only way you can make sure you will get what you are entitled to and that your child will be properly cared for after the divorce.

2. Hidden assets

Another way an attorney can help is if you suspect your spouse has hidden assets or property from you. Good attorneys will know how to deal with this possibility and usually can hire private detectives to find hidden assets. For example, your spouse may have business dealings across state lines or international borders. It would be very easy for him or her to hide assets from you.

A trick that came into vogue in the 1980s, for instance, involves placing property or money in the name of a corporation created in one of the Caribbean island nations such as the Netherlands Antilles or the Bahamas. The laws in these places make it easy to hide who actually owns the corporation and thus who owns the corporation's property. However, there are ways to find out, and an experienced attorney should know how to help you.

3. Pensions, retirement savings plans, and health insurance

You may also be entitled to a share in other assets or benefits. For example, some states allow the judge in a divorce to divide one spouse's interest in a retirement account with the other spouse. Likewise, judges sometimes order a spouse to continue to provide payroll-deduction health insurance to the other spouse and children after the divorce. If you have children, getting coverage under your spouse's health plan can ease your financial burden; health care can be expensive. Again, good attorneys will be able to ask you questions and give you advice on exactly what kinds of assets your spouse must share with you and your children. Take the time to ask because it is difficult to change things once the divorce is final.

4. Taxes

There is another problem that faces some married couples after a divorce. Under federal law, the Internal Revenue Service may be able to force you to pay some taxes actually owed by your spouse *if* you were filing a joint tax return at the time in question. This seems unfair, but it is based on the fact that both spouses must sign, and are thus responsible for, a joint tax return.

Because the divorce rate is so high these days, carefully study a joint tax return before signing it. Consider the possibility of filing separate returns, especially if you suspect your spouse is cheating on federal income taxes. It also may be best *not* to file a joint tax return with your spouse once you realize divorce is a possibility. You may end up liable for your spouse's taxes, which could mean the loss of money you need to support your children.

Finally, another word of caution is in order. As soon as you realize that a divorce is possible, *do not* —

(a) make any major purchases,

(b) accept substantial gifts from your relatives,

(c) enter into any business transactions involving your spouse, or

(d) sign any document (such as a loan agreement) that makes you liable for your spouse's debts.

Generally, the law tries to protect you from abuses by your spouse, but it isn't always able to do so.

A Florida woman, for example, purchased her own home after separating from her husband but before the divorce was final. The down payment for the home was a gift from the woman's mother. Despite Florida law to the contrary, the divorce judge awarded the woman's husband a one-half interest in the home. The result was a serious and expensive legal problem that could have been avoided by not accepting the gift of money or purchasing the home after the divorce was final. Judges sometimes make mistakes, as this Florida judge did. It is best to avoid any situation that might make a judge's mistake more likely.

Always remember, the best way to care for your children is to look out for your own interests. A little forethought and planning can save you from an expensive legal problem later on. Always seek an attorney's help if you have any doubts, because the attorney's fee will usually be less than the cost of a bungled divorce. Your spouse sometimes can be ordered to pay your attorney's fee. Contact your state Bar association for the name of a qualified lawyer to represent you (see Appendix 1).

d. THE EMOTIONAL NEEDS OF ADULTS

Along with children, parents involved in a divorce often suffer psychological trauma. This is especially true when the circumstances of the divorce involve deceit, adultery, or some other abuse. Sometimes the parent's emotional problems interfere with his or her ability to look after other matters, including seeing that they do not give away their rights during a divorce and that the children are properly cared for. If you are facing emotional problems, remember that it is best to seek professional help rather than let your emotional problems cripple you when you must be alert and careful.

1. Support and counseling groups

Support groups of various kinds exist in almost every community. These include groups of divorced or divorcing persons, people who have suffered abusive relationships, people who are codependent, and so forth. Ask around until you learn how to contact these groups. Some local newspapers carry a weekly list of support organizations. Also, local mental health clinics keep lists of support groups.

Often it helps to learn how others have coped with problems like yours. Ask whether there are free or lost-cost counseling services available at mental health facilities in your community. If you can afford a therapist, get the name of one who specializes in dealing with the problems you are facing. Help is usually available if you only ask.

Keep in mind that depression, anxiety, and withdrawal are entirely predictable results of being caught up in a divorce. Fortunately, these symptoms are treatable with medicine or with a combination of medicine and therapy. Consult a physician. Many medications are available today to treat depression or anxiety without interfering with your ability to work or take care of children. Do not let yourself suffer silently when help is so easily available. Seek out the support you need.

Once again, sometimes the cost of providing you with therapy or medical care during your divorce can be charged to your spouse. Consult with an attorney about the possibility of getting a court order requiring your spouse to pay or to continue providing you with insurance coverage that will pay for it. In many states, you have a right to these things. Use your legal rights to the fullest.

2. Special emotional needs of fathers

Fathers and their emotional needs are often completely overlooked in today's divorce courts. Part of the reason is that fathers have an image problem. The few irresponsible fathers who forced their wives to give up property in exchange for child custody, or abandoned their children completely, are to blame for this poor image. Most fathers are not like that. Yet many judges and lawyers feel they have an obligation to assume the worst about fathers. All too often, fathers come into court with a ready-made problem.

For men, the problem is usually not money, as it often is for women. The problem men face is that a divorce often means they will lose meaningful contact with their children or will not be allowed to take part in major parenting decisions. This is what divorced fathers complain about most. If you are a divorcing father, you must take some special precautions so that you can maintain meaningful contact with your children.

One of the best ways to do this is to recognize what is often true: husbands are more financially secure than their wives. Before the present era of no-fault divorce, men usually ended up paying a good deal more to their ex-wives, but this also gave them an important legal lever to make sure they could participate in child rearing. If the mother interfered with the father's rights, the father could go to court and threaten to cut off some of the money the wife was receiving. In other words, rights over children also mean a duty toward those children.

Fathers who refuse to pay their fair share toward supporting their children also forfeit the one thing most likely to guarantee them a role in their child's lives. Obviously, fathers should not necessarily agree to pay whatever the wife wants, no matter how extravagant. But fathers should recognize that the failure to pay a fair share means the children will suffer and the father will have a less meaningful role in child rearing.

An attorney can help make sure that the trade-off is fair, that the father does not give up too much, and that the father will have meaningful contact with the children. Moreover, if the mother ever interferes with the father's contact, the father can go to court to modify other arrangements, including financial ones.

e. CUSTODY OF CHILDREN

One of the most divisive issues in many divorces is child custody. As noted earlier, there is a strong tendency in the United States for judges to give primary custody of children — especially younger children — to their mothers. However, fathers in every state can challenge the mother's effort to get custody. When the parents disagree, the result can be a difficult, long, and sometimes expensive court battle over who gets the children. In a few instances, child custody disputes can become horrible struggles in which the parents accuse each other of sexual indiscretions, crime, or lack of fitness to be a parent.

1. Custody issues during the divorce

Across the United States, judges routinely say that the best interests of the child are the sole concern in custody disputes. In other words, the child should be put in the primary custody of the parent who can do what is best for the child. However, state laws vary widely on the factors that determine a child's best interests. In all states, judges can take into account truthful evidence of serious misconduct of a parent, such as crime, drug abuse, or child abuse. Judges often take into account factors that prove a parent is unable to provide proper care for a child, such as when the parent is seriously ill.

The most serious legal problems, however, arise when the parents begin making poorly supported allegations of unfitness against each other. Common accusations include child abuse, child sexual abuse, and adultery. Some very creative lawyers have recently developed entirely new kinds of allegations. These have included accusations that a parent has an unorthodox lifestyle or commonly engages in conduct that might harm the child's health.

A few highly publicized cases have involved parents denied custody of a child because they were nudists. Some parents had their custody rights limited because they smoked tobacco and might expose the child to secondhand smoke. As a general rule, these new types of cases all revolve around a single question: is the parent's lifestyle mentally or physically unhealthy for the child? Judges generally believe that if the answer is yes, then the parent's access to the child should be reduced. However, reaching that conclusion involves an individual judge's peculiar biases or moral beliefs. Many decisions of this type are challenged on appeal for that reason.

These novel cases are hard on everyone involved, and the outcome also is difficult to predict. The law is quite new in these areas, and there is little doubt that lawyers will invent other ways of challenging parental custody. Parents who are about to divorce should take stock of their own and their partner's habits and lifestyles. If one parent believes the other's behavior truly will harm the child, the other parent's custody rights can be challenged. Likewise, parents with unorthodox lifestyles or unhealthy habits should give serious thought to how they would defend themselves in court if the issue arose and whether they should rid themselves of these habits.

As a general rule, parents who cannot agree on child custody should get independent legal help. Custody disputes are difficult even when both parents have led model lives. But when one or both parents live outside the mainstream of American life, *even to the slightest degree*, the legal and emotional problems can be even more intense. A child custody dispute could become a legal nightmare, and might result in publicity that could emotionally scar the child and ruin the parents' reputations. If you believe you may become involved in a custody dispute in your divorce, consult Appendix 1 for information on how to find a qualified attorney to represent you.

2. Mediation

Before hiring an attorney, however, see if you can resolve the dispute with your spouse. There may be programs in your community to help you. Many states now have special mediation programs help divorcing parents resolve child custody problems and other disagreements. Most of these states make mediation mandatory if the parents cannot resolve their differences.

Mediation means the parents sit down with a trained mediator, usually a lawyer or retired judge, who tries to help the parents work through their disagreement. In many cases, mediation can be helpful, though it cannot resolve every dispute.

Contact your local family court clerk or local public mental health service officials to see whether mediation or other programs are available to assist you in dealing with a child custody problem. Such programs can save you all or much of the cost of a lawyer or an expensive court hearing.

3. Custody issues after the divorce

Child custody can continue to be a problem even after a divorce becomes final. In today's world, it is increasingly common for parents to go back to court because they start disagreeing over some aspect of child custody. Whenever one or both parent's circumstances change, it is always possible to convince the judge to reconsider a prior custody order. For example, an ex-wife may ask for more child-support money if her ex-husband strikes it rich. Likewise, an ex-husband might ask that he be given sole custody of the children because his ex-wife has been imprisoned or has become addicted to drugs.

If both parents can agree on changes to child custody, they probably only need to contact the judge who signed the original custody order. A meeting with the judge may be necessary, but many states allow parents to make these alterations if both can agree. However, if any dispute arises, you should get an attorney's help — preferably the same attorney or law firm that handled your original case. Child custody disputes after divorce can be just as difficult as a dispute before divorce.

A special warning is in order if a parent who has custody of a child wants to move to another state. Advance permission from the judge is necessary, especially if the move would make it more difficult for the other parent to exercise visitation rights. As a general rule, the parent should talk with an attorney first. The other parent must at least be told of the intended move and must have a chance to object. Everyone involved may have to have another meeting with the judge to get a change in the child custody arrangements.

Failure to do this could result in trouble. The judge might consider the move a violation of the court order finalizing the divorce. This could result in the parent being held in contempt and possibly going to jail. Worse still, the parent could be accused of parental kidnapping, which is a felony offense in some situations. Taking a child across state lines without permission could involve the FBI in the case. The best policy is to avoid trouble by taking the time to contact a lawyer.

4. Uniform Child Custody Jurisdiction Act

Other problems can happen once a parent has legally moved to another state with the child. Suppose a parent was divorced and obtained a child custody order in Florida, then legally moved with the child to Illinois after getting the other parent's and the Florida judge's permission. If a new dispute arises about child custody, the parent in Illinois might be tempted to try to move the entire custody case into the Illinois courts.

However, every state has adopted some version of a law called the Uniform Child Custody Jurisdiction Act. Subject to some exceptions, this law means that the parent living in Illinois still has to raise any new custody problems in the Florida court, even if this means traveling back to Florida.

The exceptions to the Child Custody Jurisdiction Act are complex, but some are common sense. For example, the parent in Illinois could bring the case into the Illinois court if both parents and the child have not lived in Florida for a long time. There are exceptions dealing with serious inconveniences, hardship, and other factors. The Child Custody Jurisdiction Act can be a problem for parents who have moved. In our example of the Illinois parent, it is possible that a parent still living in Florida would be able to force the Illinois parent to return to Florida to resolve their custody dispute.

The bottom line here is that whenever parents start having a custody dispute across state lines, they need an attorney's help. The attorney can determine where the case must be heard and may be able to take advantage of the Child Custody Jurisdiction Act's exceptions.

In any event, a parent who has moved to a new state should be very cautious about trying to move the case out of the old state. Some parents have convinced a trial judge in the new state to take the case, only to have the entire matter thrown out on appeal. This can be a big waste of time and money, so it is wise to make sure the case is brought to the right court.

f. GRANDPARENTS

Until the latter half of this century, the law recognized few rights that grandparents had over the children of divorcing parents. In fact, some courts even said that the only right grandparents had was the moral duty to step in to care for children abandoned by their parents. Beyond that, grandparents were entitled to almost nothing. If child custody was granted to a daughter-in-law or a son-in-law who disliked the grandparents, nothing could be done to fulfill the grandparents' natural desire to visit with their grandchildren. Parents generally had the ability to refuse to let grandparents visit.

That situation has begun to change dramatically. A few states now even give grandparents the right to seek custody of children in extreme cases, usually where both parents are deemed unfit to take the children. However, as a general rule, any effort by a nonparent to deny custody to a biological or adoptive parent's children rarely succeeds. The United States Supreme Court has said that parents have a constitutional right to the custody of their children, except when one parent gets custody rights against the other parent during a divorce. As a result, a divorce judge can seldom take a child away from a parent who wants custody and is not clearly unfit to be a parent.

Nevertheless, all states now give grandparents the right to at least ask for visitation rights. These laws vary considerably, and some states are far more generous than others. In many cases, the grandparent can contact the parents' attorneys and ask that grandparental visitation rights be included in the final divorce settlement papers. Sometimes grandparents can go into court and ask the judge for visitation rights.

However, the law on grandparents' rights can be complex in some states. If you are a grandparent and there is a possibility one or both parents will oppose your request, seek help from a divorce lawyer. If you want to take custody away from the parents, you *must* consult a lawyer.

g. OTHER ADULTS WHO KNOW THE CHILD

Often, children become very attached to people other than their parents and grandparents, such as aunts or uncles, close friends of the family, or neighbors. A few states now allow judges to take into account these kinds of emotional attachments when making child custody arrangements. The judge may be able to order the parents to allow another adult to have regularly scheduled visits.

However, the rights of these adults are generally thought to be weak compared to the rights of parents and grandparents. Any visitation granted is far less than what a parent or grandparent would receive. Anyone hoping to get visitation rights of this type should seek an attorney's help before going to court.

h. CHILD SUPPORT PROBLEMS

One of the most common post-divorce problems today is the failure of one parent to make adequate and timely payments of child support or alimony to the other parent. Previously, little was done to force payment, although some judges might summon the delinquent parent into court to be threatened.

Today, however, many states take these lapses very seriously. This has come about because a substantial amount of state welfare payments could be traced one way or another to a father or mother's refusal to pay child support.

Every state now has a special agency to enforce child support agreements. Some states have established novel enforcement procedures. The parent may have to pay child support into a special account managed by the state agency. The agency can take immediate action if the payments are not made.

Late payments may be converted into a judgment against the delinquent spouse, which could give the other spouse authority to repossess or seize assets to pay the debt. Sometimes the state can order that money be deducted from the nonpaying parent's paycheck.

Every divorcing parent should carefully consider the problem of future nonpayment of spousal or child support. If support payments will be made for many years to come, it is very tempting for one parent to stop sending the check, or to send it late. An attorney can set up a way to make sure that payments are made on time.

4
WHAT DOES THE LAW SAY ABOUT CHILD ABUSE?

Nothing is more disturbing to parents, teachers, social workers, and other adults than the thought of a child being the victim of abuse, neglect, crime, or other violence.

Every day there are news stories about children who are harmed by an adult's negligent and criminal misconduct. A good deal of child abuse is by strangers, but too much of it comes from people who know the child, and some abuse comes from close relatives or trusted friends. State laws now pay close attention to child abuse and neglect.

This new focus on child abuse and neglect has resulted in an explosion of new laws. State legislatures and even the United States Congress have been influenced by the findings of child psychologists.

Some psychologists' studies have become very influential. Whether you agree with the studies or not, every adult involved in providing care or services to children needs to be aware of what experts have said, as well as the new laws they helped to create.

Adults in some states could face criminal charges or a lawsuit if they fail to report evidence of child abuse. Teachers, physicians, day-care workers, social workers, and foster parents have been common targets of these accusations. In a few states, parents can be sued by their own children — even if their children are adults — for failing to try to stop their own or another parent's or adult's abusive conduct.

The new laws are not perfect, and occasionally adults have been accused of child abuse or neglect based on absurd complaints. Now there are rules about areas of child care that were once left entirely to the discretion of parents, teachers, social workers, and other adults.

The new child abuse and neglect laws center around three conclusions that child abuse experts have reached:

(a) Child neglect and abuse are more common than previously thought.

(b) Abuse and neglect are not nearly so noticeable or easily detectable as some people have assumed.

(c) Abused or neglected children often react in ways people do not understand; sometimes children act in a manner that conceals the abuse or neglect they are suffering, but this is *not* because the child wants to cover up the truth.

While aspects of this research remain controversial, some of the details are supported by evidence and common sense. This chapter outlines the major theories of child abuse researchers, and highlights those that have the most supporting evidence or are the most influential. These theories are helping to shape the new children's law throughout the United States.

This chapter focuses on what every adult needs to know to prevent and detect child abuse and what to do if a child is abused. Adults also need to know how to protect themselves from false and unfounded allegations that they are abusers.

There are preventive law steps that can help you avoid these problems or deal with them if they occur.

a. THE BATTERED CHILD SYNDROME

Modern research into child abuse and neglect really began in 1955 when two medical researchers studied a large number of X-rays taken of children. Their report showed that a surprisingly large number of the children had prior healed bone fractures.

While some children may have suffered accidental injuries that would explain the fractures, a substantial number had no sound medical explanation or even a record of being treated for the prior injuries. Moreover, the number of healed injuries was too large to be explained entirely by accidents. This suggested that some of the children were being neglected (in that they did not receive needed treatment for an injury) and that some of the children were being abused by their caretakers.

Then in 1962, a group of researchers published a comprehensive medical look at child abuse and neglect in the United States. These researchers identified something they called "battered child syndrome" — medical evidence thought to create serious suspicion of abuse and neglect. The researchers concluded that the syndrome existed in more children than people imagined possible at the time. In fact, the researchers believed their study supported the conclusion that child abuse and neglect were not rare events, but were a widespread but hidden secret of the American family.

1. Symptoms

Under the battered child syndrome, abuse is suspected, but not conclusively proven, if one or more of the following symptoms are present that cannot be explained.

(a) The child has died suddenly.

(b) The child has a serious head injury and swelling called a subdural hematoma.

(c) The child has multiple unexplained bone fractures at different stages of healing.

(d) The child suffers from a "failure to thrive" (stunted growth or inability to develop properly for the child's age).

(e) The child has multiple bruising or skin swellings.

(f) The child has other serious injuries for which no adequate explanation exists.

Perhaps the most surprising idea put forward by the 1962 researchers was that battered child syndrome was not confined to households headed by the poor or the mentally ill. The researchers found that children exhibiting the syndrome could be found at every level of society. Evidence of this type of abuse existed in families whose parents were well-educated, apparently stable, financially secure, and regarded as pillars of the community.

Finally, the researchers also reached another controversial conclusion contrary to popular beliefs at the time: people who were in a position to stop the child abuse often failed to do so. Some mothers did not stop their husbands from abusing their children and continued to insist that no abuse was happening, even when confronted with evidence that their children truly had been abused.

2. Levels of acceptance

The 1962 study was greeted at first with shock and disbelief, especially from lawyers and judges. For much of the sixties the theory of battered child syndrome was not generally accepted by the legal community because there was little evidence of abuse other than the syndrome the researchers created to describe their findings. Many people thought that no loving parent or child caretaker would fail to stop an abusive adult.

Likewise, many supposedly abused children, including those who exhibited evidence of battered child syndrome, denied that they ever suffered ill treatment. Judges and lawyers pointed out that these children often gave inconsistent stories that made it seem as though they were lying or just imagining things. When these denials were coupled by another parent's statement that no abuse was happening, many lawyers and judges concluded that the early studies were wrong.

The evidence of battered child syndrome was rejected during the 1960s because the abuse could not be confirmed by the people actually involved — the adults and children. The denials by the children and the entire family almost always meant that no charges of child abuse or neglect would hold up in court.

Through the years, researchers continued to study the baffling inconsistencies they were finding in their studies of child abuse and neglect. The injuries researchers found in children were too common and too numerous to be explained by some sort of widespread childhood clumsiness. Yet, if abuse really was happening, why would the children *and* the "nonabusive" parent or adult deny the abuse was happening?

Beginning in the 1970s and into the present decade, researchers began to piece together reasons why children and parents might deny the existence of abuse. Psychological experts began to discover, for example, that children are often threatened by their abusers or can even be "brainwashed" when abusers take advantage of the psychological immaturity of children. One common tactic used by some abusers is to tell the child that the entire family will be split up, the children put in foster homes, and every one of them impoverished if the abuse is revealed to others.

Sadly, this kind of threat is all too likely to happen once child abuse is revealed to the authorities. For example, most abusers are fathers, stepfathers, or male guardians or relatives; but the entire family is usually dependent on the income or security this man provides. If the man was arrested, there is a distinct possibility the children might be placed in a foster home at least temporarily, and the abusive male would be jailed and would lose his job. The result could be a disaster for the entire family.

Researchers also realized that this same problem explains why the other spouse often denies that any violence has happened. The nonabusive spouse may face an impossible choice: reveal the abuse and lose both family and income, or else just keep quiet and hope things get better.

Another tragic aspect of child abuse can also be explained in the same way. In the 1960s, researchers were baffled by the fact that children who accused an adult of abuse — especially a parent — frequently recanted by withdrawing the accusation or saying they lied. This led many people to believe that the children were too confused to be reliable or were too young to know what the truth was. For many years, prosecutors were very reluctant to bring criminal child abuse charges against a parent because the children were so likely to change their stories later. The legal system, in other words, was unable to do anything because the children made poor witnesses in court.

3. Understanding the battered child

Psychological researchers, however, studied what prosecutors and judges seldom got to see — what happened to the child *outside of court* after that child made an accusation of abuse. In nearly every situation, two things occurred. First, the accused parent or other adult was arrested or faced possible arrest. And second, the child was either put into a foster home or was left in the care of another parent who faced a virtual catastrophe because of what the child had said. Children naturally feel guilt at the idea of sending their own parent or other trusted adult to jail, and this guilt will be increased if the child feels punished as a result. Many children assume that being put in a foster home is a punishment, because it is something that disrupts their lives and feels very unpleasant to them.

Even if the child is left in the care of another nonabusive parent or adult, other kinds of guilt come into play. For example, if the father has been or may be arrested, the family's income and their position in the community are under threat. Often, the mother cannot provide for the family without the father's contribution. Loss of money, adequate food, and housing are very real possibilities. As a result, the mother may be tempted to pressure the child to recant, perhaps even without intending to do so.

Researchers found, for instance, that many mothers in this situation were visibly worried and wondered aloud, "What are we going to do now?" Children always notice when their parents worry; many children assume that their parents are worried because they have done something terrible to the family. As a result, some children convince themselves that the abuse never happened or retract the accusation out of fear. The nonabusive parent may have a powerful incentive to believe the child's retraction of the accusation. In a few cases, a child may even be pressured to say he or she lied, or may become so confused that the accusation of abuse looks like the product of an unstable and immature imagination.

Through the years, researchers have documented hundreds of cases in which this sort of thing has happened. On the whole, the psychology of the situation is not difficult to understand, once the realities facing many families are understood. All of us would like to think that adults are more altruistic toward children, but a threat of poverty or public disgrace can be a strong incentive for whole families to hide abuse and neglect. It is a more extreme version of refusing to air dirty laundry in public. Ironically, the incentive may only be stronger for families that are wealthier or better educated because they have more to lose.

Over the years, the courts and state legislatures have been influenced by the studies of child abuse outlined above. In particular, state legislatures and courts have been more willing to accept the researchers' conclusion that child abuse is a crime that is very easy to hide.

As a result of reforms like these, many courts will allow the use of battered child syndrome as evidence against persons accused of abusing children, especially where the children were killed, were unable to say what had happened to them, or have recanted their accusations. Most legal experts continue to believe that battered child syndrome by itself is not enough to result in a criminal conviction or the loss of rights over a child. However, combined with other evidence, battered child syndrome can create a strong case of child abuse and can help lead to justice in cases that previously would have been ignored by the legal system.

Many people regret that the legal system now intrudes into these kinds of family matters. However, there is no doubt that some children have suffered abuse, and this is the problem the law is trying to remedy. The evidence shows that the justice system is stopping abuse that would have gone on unhindered.

However, all of us now face new uncertainties because of child abuse laws. For example, how do adults draw the line between permissible "corporal punishment" on the one hand and improper "child abuse" on the other hand? In many states, the act of punishing a naughty child could result in the entire family being investigated for child abuse if a busy-body reported the incident to state authorities.

That is one reason adults today must become better educated about what the law allows and requires, since we all have to live with the fact that child rearing and child care are now regulated by law. (For a full discussion on corporal punishment and what the law allows, see chapter 7.)

b. SEXUAL ABUSE OF CHILDREN

By far the most disturbing form of child abuse involves sexual acts. Many of us do not even like to think about the possibility of such a thing happening to the children we love, but in today's world it is one of the hard facts every adult must face. Sexual abuse of children is one of the hardest and most unsettling problems facing the legal system. Strong steps must be taken to protect children. Legislators, judges, parents, and concerned adults throughout the United States are taking these steps.

The failure to act is far too costly in the long run. Researchers have strong evidence that children subjected to child sexual abuse suffer horrible problems throughout their lives. They are far more likely to grow up to abuse children themselves, to become substance abusers, to commit suicide or suffer serious mental illness, or to be unable to form lasting relationships such as a good marriage. Some researchers who have studied traumatized children report that they repeatedly "relive" the abuse they suffered when young. They relive it in the problems they create for themselves and in the problems they create for others.

There is a growing body of evidence that child sexual abuse is far easier to hide and far more difficult to detect than many people assume. Many parents, teachers, social workers, and other adults think they would know if something so terrible was happening to a child they love because they assume the child would immediately show some telltale sign or tell what has happened. Many researchers, however, report that the kinds of reactions children typically show are not what adults expect. As a result, many adults simply misread the signs and think everything is all right. In some cases, it is possible for a child to be abused for years without anyone knowing except the child and the abuser.

In 1983, an influential study of child abuse was published that detailed how this can happen. The study described what it called the "child sexual abuse accommodation syndrome." Although this syndrome is controversial, it is gaining increasing acceptance in legal communities throughout the United States. Legislatures and judges are beginning to use knowledge of this syndrome in trials of persons accused of child molestation and to create laws. Parents and other adults who work with children need to be aware of what the syndrome means.

The syndrome's chief importance is that it helps describe and explain how children are abused over long periods of time without the abuser being caught. This is very important in convicting the abuser of a crime because judges and juries in the past often assumed the children would have tattled to a responsible adult if the abuse actually happened. By the same token, the syndrome can help an adult understand, and possibly how to detect, child sexual abuse. To do so, the adult must understand how children react to this kind of abuse.

Psychologists believe that child sexual abuse accommodation syndrome shows itself in five ways that adults often do not understand:

(a) Sexually abused children have a tendency to keep secret the fact of their own abuse.

(b) Sexually abused children are overwhelmed by a sense of total helplessness, no matter how strong the children may seem, when they are sexually abused.

(c) Sexually abused children usually are psychologically entrapped by their abusers, resulting in the child actually giving in to the abuser's demands.

(d) Sexually abused children often disclose their abuse only after a long delay, and their disclosures often are conflicting and apparently unconvincing.

(e) Sexually abused children often retract their accusations even though the accusations are true.

How are such things possible? Children who react this way seem to be helping the very people who have abused them by hiding the truth.

As adults, we often make the mistake of thinking that children's minds work like ours, even though psychologists have been telling us for the last century that children think quite differently. Children do not understand cause and effect the way adults do. They have yet to develop a concept of right and wrong that is strong enough to withstand pressures from a strong-willed adult.

As a result, children may not actually realize that an adult is wrong to sexually abuse them, especially if the adult tells them it is okay. Even if children understand that the sexual abuse is wrong, they may think they have done something to provoke it and thus are at fault for what happened. Many children have a natural tendency to assume that adults are always right, that they must give in to what adults want, and that they should be punished if they do not.

The secrecy children tend to show about sexual abuse, for example, must be understood from the child's perspective. Sexually abused children commonly are threatened with horrible revenge if they reveal what is happening. The threats may even prey on the child's natural sense of guilt about the sexual acts.

For example, some abusers tell children through words or actions that the sexual act is illegal (which is true, of course), but that the *child* is responsible for it. Children may actually be told or believe that they will be in terrible trouble if people learn what is happening. Some children may even believe that they will become criminals and will be sent to prison.

Many children have a natural sense of modesty, which only increases their sense of guilt. Children may even feel they could not possibly tell their parents or another trusted adult something so horrible, because they believe the parents or adult would not love them anymore. A considerable number of child sexual abusers have been engaging in this misconduct for years and have learned how to prey on children's special vulnerabilities.

Many adults tend to think that children would immediately tell about sexual abuse as soon as it happened. Once again, child sexual abusers counter the child's tendency to do this. Children often have no experience with sexual matters at all, and they tend to accept the abuser's explanation about what is happening. They assume that the abuser — as an adult — will always tell the truth. And if the abuser says the act is so horrible that other adults will not love the child any more, the child may believe that, too. This is a horrible conflict for a child, because the child hates the abuse but feels powerless to stop it.

As a result, helplessness is a major feature of a child's reaction to sexual abuse. Once again, many adults have to leave behind their own adult sensibilities in order to understand the child's perspective. We adults have spent our entire lives developing a sense of free will, of control of our destinies, and of standing up for ourselves and fighting back against aggression.

But most children have not yet developed these qualities, and they tend to react to abusive situations like any small creature does: they either submit or play dumb. As a result, most abused children do not fight back when an adult sexually assaults them. The children believe (rightly or wrongly) that they lack the ability, so they do not even try. They do not like what is happening, but they do not try to fight it.

Unfortunately, many judges, lawyers, and juries in the past have not understood this aspect of child sexual abuse. Sometimes lawyers hammer away at children in court, demanding to know why they did not fight back. Some adults mistakenly assume that the failure to fight back indicates consent or even a moral failure on the child's part.

A few feisty children may put up a fight, but *the most common reaction is helplessness.* Any child who reacts this way is only doing what is psychologically normal for a child in that particular situation. Adults who think this behavior is abnormal risk harming the child even further because such a reaction makes the child feel at fault for the abuse. Many experts insist that adults should never use words or actions that blame the victim.

Children also tend to become entrapped by their abuser, so that they actually seem to accept the very abuse they are suffering. Researchers believe this happens much the same way that hostages sometimes start to identify with their kidnappers. Often this happens because the child assumes the adult is right, especially if the abuser is a parent or other figure whom the child respects. The adult overpowers the child's poorly developed sense of right and wrong. Some children even come to view giving in to the sexual demands as the price that must be paid for the parent or adult's "love" or protection, and some abusers even will say so to the child.

Some psychological researchers believe that a very considerable number of child sexual abuse cases are never discovered. Those that are, however, often show a troubling pattern: the child's disclosure is delayed and unconvincing. This happens for many of the same reasons outlined above.

Abuse often is discovered not because the child tells, but because something else has happened to reveal the abuse (such as being discovered in the act). Children often give strange and inconsistent explanations because they feel they have done something wrong. Every adult has had experience with children caught in misconduct, who then invent impossible explanations. Much the same thing happens to children who have come to understand that their own sexual abuse is "dirty."

Another common reaction is for the child to retract accusations of sexual abuse. A child does this because of the way adults react to what the child has said. The alleged abuser commonly brands the child a liar or finds some way to threaten the child. If the abuser is a parent, the entire family may be horribly disrupted, even threatened with disgrace and financial ruin. Sometimes the nonabusing parent or other adults may treat the child differently, even though they don't intend to.

Children are quick to perceive these things. As a result, many children retract their accusations because they believe this will make these disturbing new problems go away. Many children think that taking it back will make things the way they were before.

Unfortunately, some adults tend to believe the retraction, even in situations where other evidence of abuse exists. When adults act this way, the child is branded as untrustworthy. Worse still, the child typically is returned to the abusive situation, and any future efforts to detect or stop the abuse are far less likely to happen. After all, the child doesn't understand what the truth is.

The child learns a powerful but disturbing lesson — that telling the truth only makes things worse. As a result, the child may be locked into a pattern of abuse that will continue for many more years. Far too many children will suffer the ill effects for the rest of their lives, long after the abuse has ended and even long after the abuser is dead.

c. CHILDREN ABUSING CHILDREN

Special concerns arise when a child is sexually abused by another child — a form of abuse that is increasing at a disturbing rate. Many state laws say that minors cannot be "excused" simply because of their age, and in some states even a child can be put on trial for "statutory rape." (Statutory rape exists when the victim is under a certain age, typically in the 14- to 18- year range, because youths of this age are thought to be unable to legally consent to sex.) However, a child who molests other children frequently will not be treated as an adult criminal, but will be brought before a juvenile judge for possible placement in juvenile rehabilitation programs. Children rarely receive the same penalties adults would for this crime, except perhaps in those states that allow children to be tried as adults in special circumstances.

One important point in cases of this type is the need to look closely at the history of the child who is victimizing others. It is very common for such children to have been sexual abuse victims earlier in their own lives. The fact that this child now is "acting out," may indicate that a pattern of future child molestation already is developing and could grow worse later in life. Both the child's and the victim's parents would be wise to insist that the young molester be given psychological treatment. Earlier in life, it is easier to stop a pattern of child molestation from becoming permanent.

The victim of any act of child molestation should also be given psychological treatment. Case after case has documented that premature exposure to inappropriate sexual acts can have dire consequences later in life. A wise precaution is to seek professional therapy for the child so that the therapist can help work through the confused emotions that almost always develop.

One tragic case in Florida involved a boy who committed suicide only days before he was scheduled to testify against the man who had abused him. Persons close to the boy said he could not stand the thought of saying in public what had happened to him, and he had not received the support he needed.

d. OTHER CRIMINAL VIOLENCE AGAINST CHILDREN

The battering and sexual abuse of children are a special concern today, but no less so than the criminal violence our children too often face on the street and in the schools. The year 1993 was an especially troubling one. Americans were horrified by the number of serious crimes — even murder — being committed by teens and young children, often directed at other children. Perhaps the worst news event of all was from England, where two ten-year-old boys were convicted of beating to death a two-year-old toddler they had abducted from a shopping complex.

Many American parents, meanwhile, became increasingly disturbed by statistics showing that a substantial number of children and teens were carrying weapons with them to school "for protection." In 1993, the federal government estimated that about 100,000 students carry guns to school on any given day. Other estimates run even higher. Another 1993 study concluded that 36% of children in grades 6 to

12 felt they faced a threat of dying prematurely because of gunfire. In some large school districts, airport metal detectors are commonplace. The State of Texas, meanwhile, has begun stationing law enforcement officers on permanent assignment in some violence-prone schools.

Judges and lawmakers are paying attention to this trend of crimes of violence committed by and against children. At least two states, Colorado and Florida, have enacted tough new laws that place severe restrictions on the ability of juveniles to carry or possess firearms. There is strong indication other states will follow suit.

Meanwhile, a number of states have passed laws that, to one degree or another, attempt to make parents or guardians responsible for certain violent acts by children. Florida, for example, allows parents in some situations to be prosecuted if they fail to secure a weapon and a child then takes the weapon and injures someone else. Some juvenile judges talk openly about publishing the names of delinquent children and their parents as a means of deterring crime.

Parents are far more likely to become aware that their child was victimized, except perhaps for minor crimes the child simply does not or is too embarrassed to report. Serious crime committed against a child by strangers almost always gets immediate and intense attention by child care or school officials and the police.

As a result, parents and other adult caretakers often have a chance to take immediate actions to help the child. This can be far different from family violence or sexual abuse, which often goes undiscovered for long periods of time.

e. WHEN SHOULD YOU SUSPECT CHILD VICTIMIZATION?

The information above will be useful to help adults discover undisclosed child victimization. Knowledge of the battered child syndrome is helpful because adults can use it to develop a healthy suspicion if children show signs of repeated injuries in various stages of healing.

Likewise, knowledge of the sexual abuse accommodation syndrome can help adults understand why this particular type of abuse can go undetected for so long, and why these same adults need to look beyond explanations children may give when adults become suspicious. The fact is that children can't tell anyone, either because they do not know how or they are afraid.

However, there are other clues as well. Child experts have learned that abused children often behave in ways that may indicate physical or sexual abuse by family, friends, or strangers. There are no hard and fast rules here, only indicators that should give rise to a healthy suspicion. And keep in mind that suspicion is not the same thing as legal proof. Suspicion means that an adult should take a closer look just to make sure nothing bad is happening to the child.

Adults must be very careful in how they talk about or react to their suspicions. Remember, you can be sued for falsely accusing someone of child abuse.

To understand the abused child's behavior, adults must try to place themselves in the child's position. Being victimized typically creates a sense of absolute helplessness and shame in the child. Most children can't stand up and fight back. The sense of being completely overpowered by another person can be overwhelming and horrible.

Children have a strong tendency to think in terms of absolute right and wrong. They frequently believe that bad things only happen as a means of punishing something that was wrong. So, when children are subjected to violence or other abuse, they face a serious emotional dilemma while trying to understand what has caused this kind of punishment. Why were they singled out? What did they or others do to cause such a horrible thing to happen?

This problem can result in several distinctive behaviors. Some children tend to blame themselves for the violence they have suffered, no matter how unjustifiably. These children assume they were bad and dwell on unimportant things they said or did before or during the abuse. The child may react with "obsessive-compulsive" habits, such as repeatedly washing parts of their body or repeatedly performing odd rituals that often are accompanied by signs of distress or unhappiness. Other children will blame a parent or someone else for abandoning them to the abuser or for doing something wrong to cause the abuse.

Still others will develop numbed personalities, as though they were trying to escape the pain they feel. The child can withdraw from normal social life and other children, or develop an artificial and overly cheerful personality as a buffer zone to protect themselves from a world they find hostile and unfriendly. Some children show rage or inappropriate aggression, almost as if they are imitating the very people who abused them.

Sexually abused children may show any of these behaviors, or they may start sexually abusing other children. Any sexual behavior that is not appropriate for the child's age suggests the possibility that the child has been sexually abused. This especially is true if he or she hurts others and the child's sexual aggression lacks the quality of being a form of play. Obviously, many children engage in behaviors somewhat like those listed above, though perhaps less extreme. If the behavior is minor or short-lived, adults probably should not be concerned. For example, two children "playing doctor" may be naughty, but one incident by itself does not indicate abuse.

However, if these unusual behaviors become repetitive, frightening to the child or to other children, or hurtful despite efforts to stop them, adults should suspect some form of child abuse. One of the hallmarks of an abused child is a tendency to constantly repeat some odd, dangerous, or frightening behavior that is connected in some way to the abuse they suffered. Often the behavior mimics the abuse, sometimes in actual detail, or sometimes symbolically.

For example, some abused children will invent games that reenact the abuse they have suffered, almost as if they are trying to resolve the problem through their play life. In one study, an expert examined several California children whose school bus had been seized by kidnappers, with the children being held in horrible and isolated conditions for a lengthy period of time. After being freed, many of these children began engaging in a kind of grim, repetitive, and frightening "play."

Several children, for example, developed a dangerous game in which they placed chairs high up on the family's kitchen table and pretended to be the driver and passengers of a bus. Their mother became worried because the children repeatedly played the game, and because there was a real danger the children would fall off the table and injure themselves. This game obviously symbolized the abuse the children had suffered.

If adults see children repeatedly playing games in a way that could be dangerous or that seems to frighten the children more than amuse them, it may indicate child abuse. Children normally take great pleasure in their playtime and in the games they invent for themselves and each other. Abused or traumatized children, on the other hand, may engage in play activities that lack this same sense of happiness.

This occurs because the children's minds are preoccupied with the terrible thing that happened to them, and they use play as a desperate effort to work through the problem. Play, after all, is the way many children learn about and adjust to life's requirements. It is normal for children to play "house" or a game where they act out a future role. For abused children, games are a way to express their feelings and objectify their grief, fear, and trauma.

Other forms of unusual and inappropriate repetitive behavior deserve further investigation. For example, abused children often draw pictures of the violence they have suffered, even if they are unable to verbalize what has happened. (In fact, sometimes child experts are able to learn more from children's drawings than from actually talking to the child.) While it is normal for nonabused children to draw super heroes or soldiers battling the forces of evil, children who repeatedly draw or color pictures of age-inappropriate things may have a problem.

For example, a very young child who draws pictures of naked people in suggestive poses should make you suspect some kind of sexual abuse, because this behavior is not at all appropriate to the child's age. If the child's explanation of the pictures shows that the child is afraid or has strong feelings, you should investigate further.

Abused children often have very bad nightmares about the abuse they suffered. Again, all children have nightmares, but abused children have the same bad dreams over and over. These dreams can frighten the child or cause some other emotional disturbance. The dreams may contain scenes and images inappropriate for the child's age.

For example, if a five-year-old child dreams about being raped, the parent should suspect that the child has been sexually abused or has witnessed a rape. Likewise, if a child has a repeated nightmare about a knife being held to his or her throat, the parent or guardian should ask the child if something like this has happened to him or her.

Another possible indicator of abuse is when children, especially young children, develop a severe and unexplainable fear of certain people or situations that normally should not bother them.

Very young children have a strong tendency to generalize. A young child who gets bitten by a cat could become fearful of all cats, even friendly ones. In the same way, a child may develop a severe and unexplainable fear of everyday activities such as being dressed, being diapered, or being bathed because something bad has happened during these activities. As another example, a young child may develop a fear of all men because at some point a man subjected the child to abuse.

One word of caution is in order here. Because young children generalize, they may show fearful reactions to people who have not abused them. For example, one expert reported a case where a young child developed a fearful reaction to her father diapering her. The mother later learned that the child reacted this way because a different man at a day-care center had repeatedly fondled the child while diapering her, not because her father had abused her. The child generalized her fear onto all men who were diapering her, including her innocent father.

All children go through stages where they work through problems, and they behave in ways that seem illogical to adults. It is normal for children to refuse to do things or be reluctant to do things, such as bathing or going to day care or school. This doesn't necessarily indicate abuse.

However, there are certain aspects of a child's life that should be joyful, not fearful. Children are acutely aware of how dependent they are on adults for care, and almost always show a joyful reaction at receiving daily care from the adults they know. Adults should pay attention when a child reacts with inappropriate fear or emotion to normal daily care-giving.

You must be cautious, though, because children can react this way to any sort of traumatizing event. If the child seems fearful, determine whether there is an explanation for the behavior other than child abuse. For example, children who have endured natural disasters like hurricanes, floods, earthquakes, or fire may react in ways similar to abused children. Other traumatizing events such as the death of a parent, a loved one, or a pet may produce similar reactions, although usually only temporarily. Adults should never assume that odd or extreme behavior always indicates abuse. There may be other reasons for the child's fear.

Finally, a child's sisters and brothers may also behave in ways that show they've been abused or victimized. For example, you might notice that a child's older sister suddenly becomes withdrawn, depressed, or always seems to be badly bruised. Or that the child's sister or brother who was "always having accidents" has died suddenly or vanished mysteriously. In these situations, you may develop a reasonable enough suspicion to take a closer look at the other children of that particular family. However, you must be careful to look into things only to the extent that it is proper; you must not intrude upon the family's rights.

To summarize, any one or more of the following should be enough to create at least a suspicion that some sort of child abuse may have occurred if the behavior cannot be properly explained:

- The child repeatedly shows signs of serious injuries that do not match the child's reasons for how they happened. Remember that often children will not tell the truth about the abuse they are suffering because they are afraid or they have been coached.

- The child describes being sexually attacked, and perhaps later changes or retracts the story.

- The child has nightmares about or repeatedly draws pictures of violent or sexual matters inappropriate for the child's age.

- The child shows signs of serious emotional troubles unusual for the child's age, including groundless fear or shame, withdrawal, or inappropriate aggression, rage, or sexual conduct.

- The child shows inappropriate fear of daily care-giving by an adult the child normally should trust.

- A sister or brother of the child shows any of these symptoms, or has died suddenly or been reported missing without a good explanation.

Once again, child experts believe there is no hard and fast rule for determining when child abuse has occurred or is occurring. Many normal children show some of the symptoms described above for brief periods and in ways that are not significant. You should be suspicious about behavior that is repetitious, extremely odd, or dangerous.

Remember, suspicion is not the same thing as legal proof. Chapter 5 discusses what you should do once you suspect that a child has been abused.

f. CHILDREN SUING ABUSIVE PARENTS OR ADULTS

There is a growing trend in the United States for abused children to sue their abusers for money damages. Some of these lawsuits are filed even while the children are still minors, commonly by the adults or foster parents who now have custody of the children. As a general rule, any abuse of a child is a form of assault or battery, which means a lawsuit for damages is possible. Commonly, lawsuits on behalf of abused children will seek repayment for medical and therapy costs and for intangible damages such as pain and suffering. In many states, the largest single claim against the abuser may be for "punitive damages" — an award of money to punish the abuser.

Under earlier law, judges commonly refused to let children sue their parents. The idea behind this rule was that such suits would injure the family as a unit. However, a number of states now have abandoned the rule in whole or in part, especially where the child's lawsuit is trying to collect money from an insurance policy bought by the parent. Some judges have reasoned that only the insurance company would benefit by refusing to allow the suit. To these judges, the lawsuit should go ahead if it may help pay for the child's injuries and treatment.

There are also an increasing number of adults suing the people who abused them many years earlier. One highly publicized case of this type was filed in late 1993 against a prominent American church official in Chicago. This suit sought $10 million in damages and charged that the church official more than 15 years earlier had sexually abused the person who filed the suit. According to the suit, memories of the abuse had surfaced during psychological therapy. The suit was later dropped, however.

As this case illustrates, these suits often arise because the adult has somehow recovered suppressed memories of being abused as a child — most often of sexual abuse. Until recent years, suits of this type were not possible because a statute of limitations forbade a lawsuit filed more than a few years after the abuse had ended. However, that situation has changed in many states.

A growing number of states have modified the statutes of limitation. Many of these now say that adult victims of certain types of child abuse (especially sexual abuse) can file suit if they do so within a few years after they discover they were abused. This usually means the alleged victim must prove that memories of the abuse had become repressed and were only recently recalled. An expert psychologist almost always must testify whether or not this is what probably occurred.

Suits of this type remain very controversial and are not allowed in all states. Some people have criticized these lawsuits because they have a potential to destroy the abuser's reputation based on very little evidence other than memories the victim supposedly had forgotten for many years. These memories are especially subject to attack if they were recovered through hypnosis because this procedure creates the risk that the hypnotist may "plant" memories that are not real or may modify existing memories. However, those who favor the suits note that child abuse — and especially sexual abuse — is easily hidden and commonly is not discovered for many years.

It is significant that the Chicago suit mentioned above was dropped because the person who filed suit came to doubt that "memories" of the abuse were real.

In any event, the trend in American law is increasingly to allow these suits, provided there is sufficient evidence abuse occurred. Cases of this type are hard to prove and certainly should not be encouraged in the absence of solid evidence. A bad case could be dismissed or lost, and the person who was sued may turn around and file a separate lawsuit for defamation or other injury. Any lawsuit can be a very stressful and draining experience. People should think very seriously whether they want to endure the time and expense involved.

Finally, cases of this type involve novel and complicated legal, medical, and psychological issues. Any adult who wants to file a suit because of childhood abuse always should get help from an attorney.

5
WHAT SHOULD YOU DO IF YOU SUSPECT A CHILD HAS BEEN ABUSED?

a. AVOID CONFRONTATION

If you suspect that a child is being abused, the first thing to remember is **do not play the role of police officer.** In other words, do not launch your own investigation into things that are outside your authority. Don't spy on the suspected person or confront him or her unless you have legal authority. (Some social workers may have legal authority and permission, but few other adults do.)

Second, **do not make an accusation or tell others of your suspicions if you have any doubt that child abuse is occurring.** Groundless accusations of child abuse can result in a lawsuit for slander or defamation, and can make the person you accuse into a lifelong enemy. In the past, neighbors and family members have become bitter adversaries because one of them made an unfounded accusation of child abuse. Some people have had violent confrontations with the people they accused.

However, there are other ways to check into your suspicions. If the child is legitimately in your care, there is nothing to stop you from observing the child's behavior for the telltale signs of abuse. You may ask the child reasonable questions, such as why the child has so many bruises, if you have observed such injuries. Some teachers may develop reasonable concerns when children in their classes start drawing pictures of inappropriate subjects, such as naked people in sexual poses.

Likewise, scout leaders or adults involved in religious organizations are in a position to determine when children are showing signs of serious emotional troubles, and may pull the children aside for appropriate counseling. At that point, they could ask the child what is bothering them. Sometimes children will not talk about abuse, but sometimes they may. There are many cases where abuse was discovered because a friendly adult asked the child, "What's wrong?"

If your suspicions become firmer, you need to think seriously about what you should do. Never act without giving the problem serious thought unless you are absolutely convinced that immediate action is necessary to save the child from further harm. You may need to speak confidentially with your superiors or with other people who have more training in dealing with such matters, such as psychologists, a school principal or head master, social workers, a trained lawyer, or a religious leader. Any further action you take will depend on your relationship to the child.

b. PARENTS

If you are a parent and suspect your child is being abused, you have a legal obligation to take whatever steps are necessary to investigate and stop the abuse. Many states recognize that parents have a duty to protect their children's life and safety. There is a growing trend in the United States to allow abused children to sue their parents for abusing them or allowing abuse to occur, even many years later. These kinds of lawsuits are discussed in greater detail in chapter 9.

If you are not certain abuse has occurred but believe there is a possibility, you need to proceed cautiously. If the abuse seems to have ended, you should take your child to a trained child psychiatrist or psychologist and a pediatrician as soon as possible. Local community health centers may also offer these services. The fee may be reduced if you cannot afford private care.

If you think your child has suffered abuse, get therapy and medical attention for your child. The therapist and pediatrician can help document whether or not abuse has occurred. If it has, you should contact child abuse officials. Afterward, the therapist or pediatrician can play an important role in seeing that the abuser is brought to justice; usually the therapist's testimony will be used as evidence when the abuser is brought to trial.

If you suspect that the abuse is still going on, you must stop it. This may not be so difficult if the abuser lives outside your household. For example, if the abuse occurred in a day-care center, you can remove the child from the center and have him or her examined by experts. You can safely discuss your suspicions with a therapist or pediatrician because they are required to keep your confidences. But remember: do not make a public accusation at this point.

Once you have solid evidence of abuse, immediately contact the agency responsible for investigating child abuse in your state. (See the Appendix 6 for a list of these agencies.) Also contact your local police or sheriff's department so that they can begin a criminal investigation.

You can expect the police or sheriff's deputy to visit you, and it would be a good idea to have available the evidence of the abuse. Law enforcement officers will want to see it and may want to talk to your child. You also should make sure your child receives proper psychological therapy and medical attention during the period of the investigation, which can be especially traumatic.

Special problems can arise if one parent learns that the child is being abused by the other parent. If the family is going through a divorce, the parent who discovers the child abuse should immediately contact his or her lawyer. If the parent does not have a lawyer, he or she should consult a qualified attorney as soon as possible.

Child abuse raises difficult legal questions. Each state handles the question of abuse in a different manner. Never try to handle these matters on your own. Not only is the law on this subject difficult to master without legal training, but as a parent, you may be unable to set aside your own emotional reactions well enough to deal with courtroom disputes. (Consult Appendix 1 for more information on finding a lawyer, including free or low-cost services.)

Child abuse almost always has a tremendous effect on the outcome of a divorce and especially on child custody. Judges will never give custody to an abusive parent if there is any reasonable alternative. Even states that favor joint custody of children seldom allow the abusive parent to have much access. Judges often limit the abusive parent to "supervised visitation" only, meaning that another adult (sometimes a state social worker) must be present. In some states, the abusive parent must pay for the child's therapy or other costs related to the abuse.

If one parent discovers child abuse after a divorce is final, much the same procedure should be followed. Contact the attorney who handled the divorce or another qualified lawyer immediately. If necessary, a lawyer can file an emergency request asking the judge to strip the abusive parent of all visitation rights and take other steps needed to protect the child. The judge may be able to issue a restraining order or injunction forbidding the abusive parent from coming near the child or the child's home or school.

If the child was abused in a school or other institution, you should file complaints with the proper officials. You may complain to the school principal, elected members of the local school board, or other people in charge. The person who committed the abuse will usually be disciplined.

Once again, do not make complaints about abuse unless you are absolutely sure it happened and you have convincing evidence. If someone loses a job because of a false accusation, he or she may be able to sue you (see chapter 8).

If the abuse was done by a neighbor or a stranger who followed the child, you need to be sure that local law enforcement officers know what has happened. The police may be able to arrest the person or make sure he or she will leave your child alone. In serious cases, you can go to court to get a judge to issue a restraining order or an injunction forbidding this person from coming near your child, the child's school, or your house. A lawyer can help you do this.

After the abuser has been arrested or charged with a crime, you usually have the right to call the local prosecuting attorney's office and ask to speak with the attorney handling the case, who may be able to help you with several problems. For example, if the abuser is released on bail, you can ask the prosecuting attorney to make sure that the judge orders the abuser to stay away from you and your child.

The prosecuting attorney may be able to tell you where to go for more help. Many states have victim's advocates who will help you deal with the court system and get other help.

c. OTHER FAMILY MEMBERS

Other family members do not usually owe the same responsibility to the child's care as parents unless they have assumed custody of the child or have taken some action that may contribute to any child abuse. However, many people feel a moral obligation to do something when they suspect a young relative is being abused. Again, caution is in order. False accusations of abuse can cause serious trouble or lead to a lawsuit. Do not make an accusation if you cannot prove it is true.

If you are certain abuse is happening, you should report what you know to state child abuse officials. In serious cases, you may need to report the matter to the local police. Never try to end the abuse by confronting the abuser personally or by making threats. Leave enforcing the law to the police or state child abuse agency (see Appendix 6).

d. GUARDIANS AND FOSTER PARENTS

Children's guardians fall into two categories: general guardians, and *guardians ad litem*. A general guardian is someone other than a parent who is legally authorized to have custody of and make legal decisions for a child. Most often the authority is granted by a judge, but sometimes people are recognized as guardians because the state legislature has given them authority over specific children. Foster parents, for example, are a type of guardian even if no judge has given them this authority. (Adopted parents, however, are treated as though they were the biological parents of the child.)

General guardians can be examined by the state at any time. If a judge has created the guardianship, the guardian usually must make periodic reports about the child's welfare. The judge can even send state officers to the home or any other place to make sure the guardian is performing his or her duties properly.

In most states, a judge can revoke a guardianship if he or she believes it is in the child's best interests. Also, other interested persons (such as close blood relatives) have the right to challenge a guardian's actions in court or to try to remove a guardian. Foster parents are in a similar position, except that they usually report to the state's child welfare officers, not to a judge. Foster parents can also be stripped of their rights over the child if they have not provided proper care.

If guardians suspect a child is being abused, they have a legal duty to try to stop it. If someone else in the child's home is abusing the child, the guardian or foster parent could be charged with criminal neglect, lose custody of the child, and be sued for the child's injuries. The failure to detect and stop serious abuse could result in legal troubles in almost any situation. Even if the guardian or foster parent did not know the child was being abused, if the state believes the guardian failed to investigate suspicious circumstances, he or she can be blamed for allowing the abuse to continue.

If you are a guardian or a foster parent, you should talk with an attorney as soon as you suspect that abuse has happened. This is important if the child was abused in your home. Criminal charges are possible; get an experienced attorney's help.

In some states, child abuse must be reported to the state authority. Let your attorney report the abuse if there is any possibility of further legal trouble or criminal charges.

If the child was not abused in your home, you should act as any responsible parent would. Take immediate steps to end the abuse, and make a prompt report to the state child abuse agency and, in serious cases, to the police. Depending on the laws in your state, the failure to report could result in charges against you. If you have violated the law or any of responsibilities to the child, get an attorney's help as soon as possible.

Guardians ad litem are in a different situation than other guardians. As noted earlier, the guardian ad litem makes decisions for the child only for purposes of an ongoing legal problem. Nevertheless, many guardians ad litem have had children in their care who they suspect are being abused. If you are in this position, first find out if what you suspect is true.

For example, you could ask the child about suspicious bruises or other similar problems. Do not act like a police investigator or spy on the child's family. As a guardian ad litem, you should act only within the authority granted by the judge or by state law.

In a serious situation, a guardian ad litem may be able to ask to have the child examined by a qualified pediatrician or child therapist to find out if abuse occurred. If you are not an attorney, you should get an attorney's help to do this. Often, local attorneys volunteer their time to help children in the courts, and you may be able to get legal help through local volunteer legal organizations.

If abuse has occurred, it may be necessary to get a court order to temporarily take away the parent's custody rights and forbid the parent from seeing the child without supervision until further notice. Ultimately, the state may try to terminate the parent's rights over the child. This is a complex legal situation; if you are the child's guardian ad litem, you should get an attorney to assist you.

e. TEACHERS

Teachers who suspect one of their students of being abused must act very cautiously. By law, teachers in many states must report child abuse to the proper authorities. Failing to report could result in a reprimand from school authorities, loss of a teaching license, or even a lawsuit for failing to help the child. On the other hand, an unfounded or false accusation could cause the teacher serious problems, including a possible lawsuit for slander or defamation. As a teacher, you must be careful how you deal with a situation where you suspect a child is being abused.

First and foremost, if you suspect abuse, but you aren't sure it really happened, get a copy of your school's or school board's written policy on handling child abuse and follow what it says. If no policy exists, you should consult with the principal or other immediate supervisor. As a general rule, the teacher should let the supervisor decide how the case should be handled unless he or she is clearly being unreasonable.

If your supervisor acts unreasonably, you should discuss the matter with a qualified attorney. Many unions and school systems provide teachers with access to attorneys to help them with problems related to their jobs. Take advantage of these resources because they can save you serious legal trouble later on.

The one thing teachers should not do is try to act as investigators when they suspect abuse. Do not try to spy on the child's home or question neighbors or others about the possibility of abuse. You could open yourself to a lawsuit for invasion of privacy or slander. Any investigating should be done by child abuse officials and the police. You are free to observe and counsel the child in the classroom, but any investigation outside of the school setting is not a good idea.

If a teacher finds solid evidence of abuse, many states absolutely require that the matter be reported to officials. To protect yourself, make sure you fully document all the evidence you have gathered. Write out in detail everything you know that indicates child abuse, then sign and date the document. If other school personnel have any knowledge of the matter, ask them to write out their own versions of what happened, then sign and date the document. Keep these documents and all pieces of evidence you have in a safe place in case you need them in the future.

Again, follow your school or school system's policy about making reports if one exists. The actual report probably should be made by your supervisor, not by you, unless the school policy says otherwise. It always is better for you if you and your superiors act together after consultation. That way you are less likely to look like you are acting alone and have no support from other people in your school. The support of your supervisor could be very important if the child's alleged abusers attack your credibility.

Finally, once you have made a proper complaint, let the system take its course. Child abuse officials will need to talk with you, and you should be candid with them. Other than that, do not attempt to interfere with the official investigation. For the child's sake, you need to maintain the image of a concerned but impartial witness to abuse. If you lose your impartiality, people may believe you have a grudge or should not be trusted. Remember that your job is not to investigate and prosecute the case, but to look out for the child's best interests.

f. SOCIAL WORKERS

Social workers — state employees who supervise state-sponsored child care programs — face legal problems different from any other category. Like teachers, they usually are required by law to report known instances of child abuse. There is a substantial risk that social workers and their employers may be sued if they fail to report the abuse or take action to stop it. The social worker who doesn't adequately investigate or report evidence of child abuse can be sued for failing to properly supervise the child's care.

A few headline-grabbing cases have involved children who ultimately were killed by abusive adults. The courts, however, are not uniform in allowing lawsuits of this type. The United States Supreme Court in 1989 ruled that a federal civil rights lawsuit was not the proper means of suing a state worker in situations of this type. Nevertheless, state courts have been far more willing to permit these kinds of suits. And the possibility of a suit means that social workers must be far more careful when they are confronted with evidence of abuse. A surviving relative of the child may be tempted to sue because often the child abuser has no money to pay for damages, whereas a state government does.

On the whole, however, social workers also have far greater powers to investigate abuse. Depending on their jobs, many social workers either have authority to visit with the child in the home or elsewhere, or can contact someone else who does. Many lawsuits arise because the worker has failed to do these things and has otherwise violated the agency's policies on reporting or investigating child abuse. In this situation, the social worker also might be fired or disciplined.

If you are a social worker, you can avoid these problems by being fully aware of your agency's policies. All policies should be followed, and, if you have any questions, you should talk with your supervisor. Lawsuits are a serious problem and can result in bad publicity. Usually the state agency has to pay for the lawsuit, but in some situations the social worker can be held responsible for part of the cost. To deal with this possibility, some social workers join unions or other organizations that will cover legal costs associated with their jobs.

g. OTHERS

Many other adults will come across evidence of child abuse during their lives. They may suspect that a neighbor's child is being abused, or they may witness a stranger engaging in suspicious acts with a child. As a general rule, the law in many states does not impose an obligation on strangers to report suspected child abuse in this situation. Lawyers often say that people have a moral obligation to report, but not a legal one. In other words, it a question of personal conscience.

There are exceptions, of course, which vary considerably among the states. Many states require licensed medical workers or physicians to report child abuse they discover on the job. Some states (including Georgia and Illinois) impose quite sweeping duties to report on a large number of professions, including dentists, counselors, law enforcement officers, nurses, psychologists, psychiatrists, and day-care workers. For example, the duty to report might be triggered where a person who holds one of these jobs has seen a child with injuries that could only have been caused by child abuse or neglect.

However, even where broad reporting statutes of this type exist, there are few means of enforcing them. As a rule, few people are prosecuted for failure to report. Many states complicate the matter further by making it a criminal offense to make a false report of child abuse. Some adults may conclude that they are better off remaining silent than risking being accused of making a false report. If the adult is not entirely convinced that abuse has occurred, this is a reasonable choice.

However, this does not mean that all legal problems can be avoided by remaining silent. First, an adult who has a legal duty to report could be sued by the child or the child's adult representative for failure to make the necessary report. Some states may allow a lawsuit of this type on the grounds that there was a duty to report and the child suffered further harm because the report was not made. Suing someone who has a legal duty to report abuse is even more tempting if he or she has a lot of money or a large insurance policy. Many lawsuits happen because of money, especially against prominent persons such as physicians.

Second, if an adult does anything that might actually contribute to the child's risk, then that adult could be considered legally responsible for anything that happens later. For example, suppose your neighbor asks you if her young son can stay at your house for the afternoon, and your gardener abuses the child without your knowledge. You could be sued for negligence on the grounds that you did not properly supervise the child or the gardener. A state child abuse agency also might investigate you to determine if you have any other legal responsibility.

Although all adults have a moral duty to report abuse, once you make a report, there are legal problems. For example, suppose you publicly accuse a neighbor of abuse, and the state later determines that your report was untrue. Your neighbor could sue you for slander or defamation. (Many states do not allow people to sue you just because you filed a complaint with a child abuse agency, but this will not protect you if your accusation was made public in some other way — which often happens.) Never make a report based only on suspicions that cannot be proved.

Some states accept anonymous reports of child abuse for investigation. Many adults make complaints anonymously because they don't want their name involved. You should keep in mind that anonymous reports can be treated less seriously, although some states do have laws that require every report of abuse to be investigated.

6
USING THE LAW TO HELP THE VICTIMIZED CHILD

Sometimes our best efforts fail and a child we love is victimized. Adults blame themselves when it happens to children in their care. Often adults get so preoccupied with blame that it prevents them from taking steps to help the child. It is very important for a responsible adult to take immediate action once the problem becomes obvious.

a. GET HELP FOR THE CHILD

Apart from notifying child abuse officers or police, one of the first things the adult should do is see that the child gets proper medical and psychological care. The child should be examined by a pediatrician and by a qualified mental health therapist. Psychological therapy can be especially important because abuse affects children in ways that are not immediately obvious but that can cause serious problems later in life. Many experts believe that child abuse — and especially child sexual abuse — can impair the child's later ability to have a good marriage and develop into a normal adult. Therapy soon after the abuse has occurred can help prevent this possibility.

The other thing the adult should do is start taking steps to make sure the child suffers no further trauma once the legal system is involved. Often the child may be required to give a statement to police, to child-abuse officers, or in court. These kinds of things frighten some children. However, a lawyer or trained child advocate may be able to make things smoother. Legal proceedings, if handled properly, can give children a sense of relief and allow them to put the matter behind them. Some experts report cases where children actually benefited from testifying in court because the experience showed them that their abusers were not like other adults, were bad, and were being punished.

If you can afford a lawyer, hire one who can look out for the child's interests during the legal proceedings. However, many other resources are available. In many cases, the prosecuting attorney handling the case will try to make sure the child is treated well. It may be a good idea to arrange a meeting where you, the child, and the prosecuting attorney can sit down and get to know each other. You should discuss special problems with the prosecuting attorney, such as whether the child is likely to be traumatized by testifying in court. Many prosecuting attorneys make every effort to honor the parent's or adult's wishes about how the case should be handled.

Some states provide victim's advocates to help the child. A guardian ad litem can be appointed to represent the child in the legal proceedings. Likewise, child abuse agencies or child advocacy groups can also assist you. Local organizations can give you contact names.

Many states have tried to make the legal system less harsh for the child. To make things easier for the child, some states allow the following:

- Adults can testify in court about hearsay statements the child made about the abuse. This means the child may not have to testify in court.

- Court orders can be granted forbidding the adult accused of abuse from being with the child, or allowing only supervised visitation (with another adult present).

- Children can testify against their alleged abusers on videotape or by closed circuit television, away from the presence of the person who abused them.

- Experts can explain in court why people tend to deny the existence of child abuse and why abused children often recant their accusations.

- An adult such as a guardian ad litem can speak on the child's behalf during the court proceedings.

See chapter 3 for more on this subject.

b. "STREET-PROOFING" YOUR CHILD

Because of the problem of violence and abuse against children, there is a growing movement in the United States to "street-proof" children — to prepare them to deal with problems they may encounter away from home. Actually, the movement is only a more organized version of what many parents have done in the past as routine.

1. Street-proofing programs

Parents in many communities are banding together to prepare special programs for their children. Religious institutions, hospitals, PTAs, scouting agencies, and many other community organizations are actively organizing street-proofing programs.

These programs take many forms and can be custom-tailored to the problems of each particular community and to the needs of the children. The programs involve adults telling children how they should react when they come up against particular problems in or away from home. For example, what should children do if a stranger asks them to get into a car? Or how should children react if they discover that their house is on fire?

A street-proofing program can pose the question to children and suggest answers. Topics can include dealing with accidents, fire safety, water safety, as well as avoiding crime.

Sometimes street-proofing programs use an adult actor to play the role of a "bad guy," while another adult or a child can play the role of the intended "victim" who escapes. This kind of play-acting is especially helpful for small children because it helps them remember what they are being taught. Small children have trouble remembering things they are told. They are much better at remembering things they have seen or done in person.

The only limit to these programs is the imagination of the adults. There are countless resources to help you out. Many police and law enforcement agencies will send trained officers to have a talk with children during a street-proofing program. Some hospitals, mental health facilities, psychological counselors, or pediatricians may donate their time or services to help out. Child advocacy groups and other agencies involved in child abuse issues also may have trained volunteers who can contribute. In some instances, parents organize and plan the program and present it to the children themselves.

Many parents and other adults are now making a concerted effort to make street-proofing an everyday activity. For example, a television program that shows an episode where a child is confronted with a particular problem can be an opportunity for you and your child to talk about these kinds of problems. You can ask the child, "What do you think you would do if that happened to you?" In this way, you can have an entire discussion about the issue, and you can offer suggestions on how the child should react.

A number of parents have volunteered to participate in organizations that help parents of missing or kidnapped or abused children. For example, whole families in the community of Petaluma, California, volunteered their time to assist 12-year-old Polly Klaas's family, whose shocking 1993 kidnapping from her own home made national headlines.

Some parents report that involving their children in this kind of volunteer work not only sets a good example, but also helps teach the children about some of the dangers they may face in today's world. In other words, the children's awareness of these hazards is increased.

2. Teaching children emergency telephone services

Another important aspect of street-proofing a young child is to teach the child how to use the telephone in an emergency. The child should be able to do at least three things at the earliest possible age:

- Know how to dial 911 (if your community has 911 emergency service)

- Know how to dial 0 to get an operator's assistance

- Know how to dial his or her home phone numbers both locally and long distance.

The use of the 911 emergency number is widely known because many television programs and movies feature people using the service. Nevertheless, every young child must be taught about the importance of dialing 911 in an emergency. (If you want to street-proof your child, first check that 911 is available in the community. If not, teach your child how to dial 0 to get the operator.)

Again, play-acting can help the child remember what to do. You can use a toy telephone and ask the child to dial 911. You can play the role of the 911 operator. You could play several different versions of the game with different kinds of emergencies.

Another important aspect of learning about 911 is dialing the number from a public pay phone. Many children may not realize that 911 can be dialed for free from pay phones in most communities that have a 911 service. A child could be involved in an emergency in a public place, so it is important for him or her to know how to use a pay phone.

Be careful, however, about actually letting the child dial 911 from a real phone. Make sure the 911 service in your community knows in advance and gives you permission to dial 911 as part of training the child.

You may also want to contact the local 911 service to see if it offers training programs for children. If so, a group of adults could set up a program to train a number of children at the same time. If no 911 training program exists for children, you may want to help establish one. Learning about 911 is an important part of training a child in today's world. Many other children could benefit. The program could pool resources to get toy phones that look like home phones and pay phones to train the children.

Children should also understand about dialing 0 to get the operator. This is especially important in communities that lack a 911 service. Dialing 0 is easy to remember, and it could be important if the child is ever kidnapped and taken to a strange place. The child may be able to find a phone and dial an operator for help, and the operator then could notify the proper law enforcement agencies.

The other important phone skill a child should have is the knowledge of how to dial his or her own home phone number. Again, young children learn better if they get the chance to practice on a toy phone. You can make a game out of this, and regularly play the game with the child. Memorizing a long phone number is difficult for children, and they forget things easily, so you should repeat the game regularly to test the child's memory until you are sure there will not be a problem.

Don't forget to teach your child how to make a long distance call to your home phone number. This could be important if the child is kidnapped or ends up lost a long way from home. The best approach is to teach the child how to dial a long distance operator to place a collect call.

Practice on a play phone. If the child cannot remember the area code, teach the child how to tell the operator what city and state the call should go to. Then the operator can find the area code and use other information provided by the child to dial the home number.

3. Teaching children about sexual abuse

One final aspect of street-proofing is probably the most personal and private of all — giving the child age-appropriate training about sexual abuse. This can be one of the most important forms of street-proofing.

Experts in child psychology have found that children fail to tell parents and other adults about sexual abuse because they do not really understand that the abuser is a "bad person." The abuser takes advantage of the child's lack of experience, threatens the child, or shames the child into silence. As a result, sexually abused children frequently remain silent because they believe something terrible will happen if they tell. Sometimes these children even believe that they have done something so shameful they cannot tell even the most trusted adult.

Children need to be empowered to deal with these kinds of problems. They need to have some advance understanding that this type of abuse is not all right for an adult to do, and that they can talk with their parent or other adult caretaker about the abuse. This can help the child avoid falling into the trap of believing the lies an abuser may tell them.

However, empowering does not necessarily mean giving age-inappropriate lessons about sex. There is absolutely no need for you to give your child a premature talk about the "birds and the bees" if you feel this is unwise. Instead, you can sit down in a family setting and have a simple discussion in terms your child understands. For example, a mother might say, "You know, if anyone ever tries to touch you under your clothes, you need to tell mommy about it right away so that mommy can make them stop."

The adult should try to empower the child not to believe the threats of a possible sexual abuser. For example, a mother might say, "If anyone starts trying to touch you under your clothes and then tells you not to tell mommy, you should never believe them. You need to tell mommy right away. Anyone who says you can't talk to mommy about anything is telling you a lie, even if they're an adult."

This may help deal with the problem of an abuser shaming the child into silence. Experts have found that some children keep silent because they genuinely believe the parent or other adult will not love them anymore if the truth were known. The adult might reassure the child that nothing is too bad for them to talk about and that the parent really does want to know if something is making the child unhappy.

Parents can also consider organizing group sessions to help empower a large number of children against possible sexual abuse. Again, age-inappropriate matters need not be included. Often, police departments and child psychologists or psychiatrists may be available to help out. Children may be very impressed if a uniformed police officer tells them that it is not all right for a strange adult to touch them in ways they do not like.

Child experts can arrange a special program such as a puppet show or a story lesson to help empower children against sexual abuse. After all, the goal here is to deprive child molesters of the one big advantage they have — the child's lack of experience in dealing with the criminal mind.

7
THE PROBLEM OF CORPORAL PUNISHMENT

Corporal punishment poses serious legal problems in today's world. Both society and our legal system are increasingly less tolerant of anything that resembles abuse, even if it is only intended as corporal punishment.

Our grandparents punished naughty children with hickory switches and razor strops while the community looked on with general approval. "Spare the rod and spoil the child" was an unquestioned truth. Courts followed a "rule of thumb": the father in a household could "correct" children and other family members with a rod, provided the rod was not thicker than his own thumb.

Today we live in a different world. Using a rod against a child today is a criminal act in many states. Our grandparents' method of punishment risks other forms of legal trouble: lawsuits, investigation for child abuse, and having the child taken into custody by the state. This is not to say that corporal punishment has entirely vanished from our lives; far from it. The United States Supreme Court has even said that the Constitution does not prohibit reasonable corporal punishment in "appropriate" situations.

However, the problem is that large numbers of people do not agree on what is "reasonable" or "appropriate." Corporal punishment today has become a much more risky thing to do in a legal sense. Many Americans do not like this state of affairs, but it is the reality all of us must live with.

This book neither advocates nor opposes corporal punishment. Reasonable people have strong feelings on both sides of this issue. The purpose of this chapter is only to describe the legal issues involved in using corporal punishment. In some situations, adults clearly take a grave legal risk by using corporal punishment against a child. Adults must be able to identify those risks and avoid or minimize them. The risks vary depending on who the adult is in relation to the child.

a. PARENTS

As might be expected, biological and adoptive parents have the greatest leeway in using corporal punishment. However, even here the authority is limited. As a general rule, a parent is less likely to run into legal troubles for milder forms of corporal punishment such as a light swat or two to the child's rear with the palm of the hand.

Nevertheless, parents need to understand that any form of physical punishment of a child can conceivably result in the state investigating the parent for "child abuse," however unreasonable this may seem. Investigations of this type are relatively rare, but they do happen.

The likelihood of legal trouble increases if the child is punished more severely. Throughout the United States, parents have gotten into serious trouble with the law for going too far with corporal punishment. For example, a parent faces serious legal problems if punishment ever results in bruising or marking of the child's skin, bleeding, deprivation of physical needs, or psychological illness. Sending children to their rooms for the rest of the afternoon is unlikely to cause problems, but locking a child in a dark closet may constitute illegal child abuse. A swat to the rear often is within a parent's authority, but physically injuring the child almost always is illegal except in those rare cases where a parent may be acting in self-defense.

The line that separates the legal from the illegal is not easy to draw and can vary from state to state. In some states, child abuse laws are so broad that it could be illegal for parents to use a switch or a belt in punishing the child. And if someone else reports the punishment to state child abuse officials, the parents may be investigated for possible child abuse no matter how mild the punishment seemed at the time. Abuse is often in the eye of the beholder. A child abuse report could be made because the adult who witnessed the punishment strongly believes that corporal punishment is wrong. People who dislike the parent could make an exaggerated report of abuse as a means of revenge.

In any event, corporal punishment is controversial. The fact that opinions differ so much among so many people only means that the controversy is likely to remain alive in the years ahead. Over the past three decades, corporal punishment has fallen into disfavor. This trend is likely to continue. If it does, the law will become even less tolerant of corporal punishment than it is today.

Many parents now use methods of training their children other than corporal punishment. These methods include placing the child on "restriction" or sending children to their rooms for the afternoon so that the child cannot play; this is often described as "time out." Parents who are concerned about the legal problems associated with corporal punishment should go to a library or a bookstore to learn more about alternative methods of punishment.

b. TEACHERS

Teachers are the group most affected by the changing law on corporal punishment. Well into the 1960s, corporal punishment was a standard and accepted method of discipline in American schools. As late as 1977, the United States Supreme Court said that reasonable corporal punishment in the schools is not prohibited by the Constitution.

Now corporal punishment is rare, especially in bigger public school systems. This is because parents have sued teachers and schools after their children received corporal punishment. Even though many of these suits were unfounded, they caused substantial trouble and cost for the schools and the teachers. The legal problems have been so significant that a growing number of schools and school systems absolutely forbid teachers to use any form of corporal punishment.

As a result, any teacher who wants to use corporal punishment must be very cautious. The teacher should first read the school or school system's policy on corporal punishment and should follow what it says. The teacher should also make sure there are no state laws that prohibit corporal punishment in any situation. Professional organizations, the school's attorney, or state or school elected officials will have this information.

If corporal punishment is allowed, the teacher should take at least three other precautions:

(a) Get permission in advance from the school principal, master, or other appropriate supervisor.

(b) Make sure the corporal punishment is imposed in the presence of at least one other impartial adult witness, preferably the school principal, master, or supervisor.

(c) Immediately write down a detailed and fair description of the punishment with the witness, making sure the documents are dated, signed, and kept in a safe place.

If the teacher has any doubt, however, the best policy is not to use corporal punishment. Teachers can use other, far safer methods such as detention, suspension, expulsion, demerits, or lowering a student's grades. Many teachers have been dragged into court or charged with illegal child abuse for imposing corporal punishment, sometimes by children and parents who wanted money or revenge.

Many teachers' unions and other professional organizations have attorneys to defend teachers. Nevertheless, the stress of enduring a court dispute can be extreme. It is always better to avoid legal trouble if at all possible.

c. FOSTER PARENTS AND SOCIAL WORKERS

The problems teachers face are similar to those confronting foster parents and social workers, whose activities are often heavily regulated by the state. Foster parents and social workers should never take any action contrary to the guidelines or policies imposed on them. Even if corporal punishment is allowed, the state's policies should be strictly honored.

Foster parents and social workers should take precautions similar to those described for teachers above. "Unauthorized" forms of punishment could result in children being taken away from foster parents, and a social worker could be disciplined.

d. COURT-APPOINTED GUARDIANS

On the whole, a child's court-appointed guardian should not use corporal punishment unless it is absolutely clear the guardian has the legal authority to do so. For example, a judge will sometimes give a court-appointed guardian authority to use mild forms of corporal punishment. Make sure, however, that this authority is contained in the judge's written order appointing the guardian. If the authority does exist, always use mild forms of corporal punishment. The guardian would be wise to make sure the punishment is witnessed by at least one other impartial adult, if possible, and to see that both the guardian and the witnesses write reports of the incident.

Guardians must be extremely cautious in using corporal punishment because they often have to make periodic reports to the judge. Guardians can be subject to inspections or investigation by state officials. Some judges or state officers may strongly disapprove of corporal punishment and could be inclined to dismiss the guardian for punishing a child in this manner. Being stripped of a guardianship could damage the adult's reputation in the community and could result in the adult being investigated for child abuse or being sued.

e. OTHER ADULTS

In today's legal climate, it is probably unwise for other adults to try to impose corporal punishment on a child. Many of us remember a time when certain adults such as neighbors, religious leaders, close friends, or others would spank a wayward child in the parents' absence. At one time, adults considered this "just being neighborly."

However, tolerance for this kind of behavior has vanished from all but a few communities. As a result, adults who are not the child's parent, teacher, or guardian should avoid using corporal punishment against other people's children. Failure to follow this rule only invites serious legal troubles, including being charged with child abuse or being sued for injuring the child.

8
FALSE ACCUSATIONS OF CHILD ABUSE

One of the more disturbing aspects of America's increasing focus on child abuse is that some adults are being falsely accused. False accusations are against the law in all states, but the law isn't very good at protecting innocent adults.

Sometimes, people make false accusations to get revenge, money, or leverage in an ongoing divorce or child custody dispute. In a few instances, people's lives have been ruined. If an accusation is made, the state will usually investigate. Criminal charges, bad publicity, and an expensive and embarrassing trial can follow. People who have been accused may lose a job or be shunned by others in the community even if the charges prove false.

America's "hair-trigger" sensitivity to child abuse allegations is one reason why adults must be cautious in how they handle children, especially other people's children. The best law is preventive law. Just as you protect your health by avoiding harmful situations or practices, you should avoid situations that can harm you legally. Any action that remotely resembles child abuse could get you in trouble you never dreamed possible.

a. INVESTIGATION OF A FALSE ACCUSATION

In almost every state, false accusations must be investigated. This usually means that state social workers or police will come to talk about the accusation. If they are convinced the accusation is false, usually the matter will be dropped then and there. Any good suspicion that the accusation is true, however, will mean further investigation.

The first contact by state workers or police can be unusually distressing to an adult falsely accused of abuse. Keep in mind, however, that these investigators may not really be convinced that abuse has occurred. Most states require that each accusation be investigated at least once, so the initial contact may be a brief confirmation of facts. However, never assume that this will happen. Any contact by state officials about child abuse could lead to very serious legal problems and should be taken seriously.

If you are contacted on suspicion of child abuse, keep in mind your constitutional rights:

(a) You have the absolute right to remain silent or to tell the authorities only what you want to say. Obviously, remaining silent may make authorities more suspicious about you, but silence alone can never be used as evidence against you in any American court.

Note: If you believe you may be facing criminal charges, you should immediately tell the authorities that you do not want to talk to them. Many innocent people have gotten themselves sent to prison because they made a careless statement that some people misinterpreted as a criminal confession. Your silence, however, cannot be used against you in court. Unless you are placed under arrest, the authorities must respect your desire to remain silent and must leave you alone.

(b) The authorities have no right to enter your home without your permission unless they have a warrant or other court order giving them the authority. Often, an investigator or law officer will ask for permission to enter your home "to look around." You have the right to refuse unless they produce a warrant, and the authorities must honor your decision. Again, if you believe you are facing a possible arrest, do not give the authorities permission to enter. Your refusal to give permission cannot be used as evidence that you are guilty.

b. WHAT IF YOU ARE ARRESTED?

1. The right to an attorney

If you are arrested or it is likely that you will be arrested on false child abuse charges, you face a far more serious problem. You should immediately obtain the services of a criminal defense attorney if you can afford one. Some unionized professions, such as teachers, provide legal services for free to their members. If you cannot afford an attorney, the state must provide you with free legal help, although you will often have to wait until an attorney has time to see you. (The state is *not* required to provide an attorney for free to people accused of minor misdemeanor offenses.) Remember, you have a right to an attorney. Never sign a paper that says you are giving up this right, and never tell police you do not want a lawyer's help.

2. The right to remain silent

After arrest and each time police try to question you, you should tell them that you are invoking your right to remain silent and your right to have an attorney "under the Fifth and Sixth Amendments of the United States Constitution." It is important to actually mention both the Fifth and Sixth Amendments because these are the "magic words" that increase your level of legal protection. Never talk with police unless your attorney is present. If police insist, refuse to say anything until your attorney is in the room and consults with you. Never sign any paper that says you are giving up your rights.

3. Securing your release from jail

In most cases, you can be released from jail on bail, although sometimes a judge will set bail at such a large dollar amount that you cannot afford it. Inability to post bail means you will remain in jail until your trial. You may be able to obtain bail through a bail bondsman, but the cost is usually steep and the bondsman often asks that you put up collateral. This can mean signing over your car or mortgaging your property to the bondsman, who then will foreclose on the property if you violate the terms of your bail bond.

c. THE TRIAL

You should let your attorney handle all aspects of your case. If you can afford a private investigator, have him or her uncover evidence that shows you are innocent. It is far better for you if you can get the charges dismissed without a trial, which will occur if you can demonstrate your innocence before any trial.

A criminal trial is very expensive. In the American legal system, people who can afford their own lawyers are required to pay their own legal costs in a criminal trial even if they are found not guilty. There are cases of people falsely accused of crimes who have been bankrupted by their own trials. Sometimes these people have been able to sue and recover money damages for a "malicious prosecution." However, the money you can recover in a malicious prosecution lawsuit is very limited and usually is only possible if you have been found not guilty at your criminal trial or the charges were dropped.

d. GETTING YOUR NAME DROPPED FROM STATE CHILD ABUSE REGISTRIES

One further problem can arise from a false accusation of child abuse. Many states are maintaining data banks or "registries" of known child abusers. These lists are widely used to screen abusers from certain kinds of jobs or positions involving child care, including teaching. A number of states have been notorious for adding an adult's name to these lists even after the charges were found to be false. Some people have even been denied jobs or suffered other problems because their name was improperly added to a list of "known child abusers."

All of this means that any adults falsely accused of abuse should make the effort to see if their names have been added to an abuse list in their state. Contact the state's child abuse agency to see how you can find out if this has happened.

People who learn that their names are on a child abuse list based on false accusations should immediately write a letter to the agency explaining the situation and asking that their names be removed. If the agency refuses or does not respond, contact the office of your local elected state representative, state assembly member, state senator, or governor. These elected officials can usually get a state agency to take action faster than a private citizen can.

If you still cannot get your name removed from the list, you should contact an attorney. He or she may be able to play hardball with the state and make it remove your name from the list. An attorney can be helpful if you have lost a job opportunity or suffered some other injury because your name is on a child abuse list improperly. You may be able to sue the state for damages or possibly reach an out-of-court settlement to pay for your loss. Some attorneys may take cases for a contingent fee, usually meaning that you will pay a specified fee only if the attorney wins the case. Keep in mind, however, that contingent fees are higher than other fees.

9
CHILD NEGLECT AND ABANDONMENT

Every state has laws dealing with child neglect and abandonment. These laws say what will happen when children are deprived of food, shelter, or proper care, or if the parents simply abandon the children. Unlike child abuse, however, child neglect or abandonment is far easier to detect. Most adults can see when a child is malnourished, is not receiving proper health care, or has been abandoned. Reports of child neglect or abandonment are made and treated the same as reports of child abuse.

After receiving a report, the state normally sends a social worker to investigate the situation. The social worker will make a report and, if the case is severe enough, state officials will take the children away and place them in a children's group home or a foster home.

No state, however, will take children away because a family is poor. Today, welfare programs exist to make sure that children have adequate food and medical care. So long as parents are taking advantage of these opportunities, the children will not be taken away. The state steps in only when the children are facing a health-threatening problem caused by abandonment or neglect. However, neglect could exist if the parent fails to get public assistance for the child.

Drug and alcohol-abusing parents pose special problems. Addiction or substance abuse sometimes results in a parent who becomes neglectful or abusive. The special problems of drug-related abuse or neglect are discussed in chapter 23.

Abused or neglect of children can lead to several other legal problems. In milder cases, state workers may attempt to establish a program to supervise the home life and provide training and counseling to the parents or other adults responsible for the abuse or neglect. Most states follow a practice of trying to preserve the family if at all possible. Some states may ask parents to enter into "contracts" requiring them to attend classes or meet certain goals designed to improve their parenting skills. State workers may visit with the family on a regular basis or may make random spot checks.

In serious cases, however, most state laws require that the child be taken away from the parents at least temporarily. Some states — especially larger or rural states — often have a great deal of trouble fulfilling the strict requirements of these laws. State agencies may have too few employees to investigate every case properly. As a result, some instances of serious abuse or neglect in the home may slip through the cracks. There is a growing trend for lawsuits against the state when its workers know about abuse or neglect and fail to do anything. Lawsuits usually involve cases in which children were killed or horribly maimed. Some suits have involved substantial claims for money damages.

In most states, a court hearing will be held soon after the child is removed from the home. The parents will be allowed to speak to the judge, if they wish, and give their side of the story. The judge will consider the report of state workers who have investigated the case. If the judge finds that the child is being treated in a manner prohibited by law, then the child will be declared a "dependent" or a "ward of the state." This means that the child will continue to remain in the care of state employees, agents, or foster parents. This situation is called a "dependency" case or proceeding. Once children are taken from the home, they are usually placed in a group home or foster home, often on a temporary basis.

As a general rule, the state will then give the real parents an opportunity to rehabilitate themselves. Drug-abusing parents might be required to undergo addiction treatment and prove they have stopped using drugs. A neglectful parent might be required to take classes and show better parenting skills. Almost every state will give the parents every possible opportunity to change their ways. And after a parent has met the state's requirements, the child will usually be returned to the home, often with supervision or visitation by state workers for a period of time.

Parents who are unable to change or who continue abusing or neglecting children can be subjected to more extreme measures. Commonly, the child will remain in a group or foster home on an indefinite basis. Some children may remain there until they become adults and can legally go out on their own. In other cases, the state starts a new legal proceeding to "terminate parental rights." The judge in this proceeding must review all the evidence, must hear from the parents if they wish to speak, and cannot take the parent's rights away unless they are clearly unfit and unable to rehabilitate themselves.

Once a parent's rights are terminated, they are legally regarded as having no relationship with the child at all. In the law's eyes they are not even related anymore.

The child will remain in the state's care but will be available for adoption.

Adoption of the child cannot occur until the parents' rights have been terminated, however. This legal requirement has sometimes led to the tragic situation of a child being returned to previously abusive or neglectful parents after spending many years with foster parents who genuinely love the child. In that situation, the rights of the parents over the child usually prevail, unless the parents remain unfit or unless parental rights are terminated.

In addition, most foster parents are contract workers of the state, and so the state can take the child away from the foster parents provided any special requirements of state law are met. Most states make an effort to leave children with a loving foster family, but there are times when foster children are removed for little or no apparent reason. However, there is a growing trend for foster parents to sue the state when a foster child is taken away unreasonably.

Another strategy foster parents have adopted has been to file their own lawsuit to terminate the parental rights of the foster child's parents. In many states, termination proceedings can be brought by any adult who has an interest at stake, including foster parents. (The foster children may also be able to sue for termination, a subject discussed in chapter 13.) Once the parental rights are legally terminated, the foster parents can file papers to adopt the child. Any foster parent who wants to sue the state, however, always should get an attorney's help. The law in this area is new, complex, and changes rapidly.

A large number of children, however, are never adopted because they have special problems or needs, are too old to be attractive to many adoptive parents, or for other reasons. These children commonly remain in group homes or foster care until they become adults. It is very common for these children to be moved to different homes several times — something that has been criticized as "foster home drift." Unfortunately, many of America's foster children lead very unsettled lives inside a system that commonly has too few resources to give the best care to all the children. Many people want to improve the foster care system, but few states have been able or willing to pay the necessary cost.

10
HOW CAN THE LAW PROTECT CHILDREN WITH DISABILITIES?

Millions of children have disabilities of one type or another. Most adults understand that the term "disability" includes conditions such as blindness, being unable to walk, or mental retardation. Most adults may be aware that laws exist to help protect people with disabilities from certain types of discrimination. However, some adults do not know that the term disability in a legal sense includes many other conditions.

In 1990, the United States Congress approved a landmark civil rights law called the Americans with Disabilities Act. This law says that the legal term disabilities includes many physical and mental conditions beyond what many people ordinarily think.

Under the Americans with Disabilities Act, a disability exists when an individual has a physical or mental impairment that substantially limits one or more major life activities. In addition, people are legally considered to have a disability if they have a record of having such an impairment, or if other people think an impairment exists. This is a very broad definition. In fact, in 1990 Congress estimated that there were about 43 million Americans who had a disability by legal definition — almost one-fifth of the total population of the United States.

A child legally has a disability if he or she has any condition that limits his or her major life activities, or if other people think the child has such a condition. This can include practically anything that limits the ability to attend school, to use public or private facilities available to other children, and to engage in most other activities open to children generally.

For example, children who have a serious disease — whether or not it is life-threatening — legally may have a disability. Dwarfism, stuttering, and reading disorders are examples of other conditions that are probably disabilities in a legal sense. Some lawyers even believe that an overweight child may have a disability if the child's obesity limits his or her major life activities. Disability may include some seriously disfiguring conditions, provided the child's life activities are limited in some way.

Under the Americans with Disabilities Act, many forms of discrimination against children with disabilities are illegal. Other state and federal laws also give substantial legal protection to children who have disabilities. All together, these laws provide substantial legal protections for children who have disabilities. As a general rule, these laws prohibit discrimination by public schools, most private schools, state and local governments, federal government agencies, public transportation services, and private businesses.

By law, many of these organizations and businesses must take special measures to assist children and other persons with disabilities. For example, the Americans with Disabilities Act now requires public facilities and many private businesses to provide wheelchair access to their buildings or offices, with some exceptions.

Likewise, public schools must provide special accommodations for children with certain disabilities. As a general rule, children who cannot leave the home because of a disability are entitled to receive a free education in a "homebound program." The federal government supplies funding to assist local school systems in providing these services.

If children with disabilities are able to attend school with the other children, they are usually entitled to do so. The public school system must provide whatever reasonable accommodations or assistance are necessary to help the child.

For example, several highly publicized cases have involved school children infected with the AIDS virus. The federal courts have almost uniformly ruled that these children have a disability and also have a right to attend public school, subject only to reasonable precautions designed to protect the health of other children. These rulings have been based on the federal courts' conclusion that the AIDS virus is unlikely to be spread among children in a school setting. Decisions like these have been controversial in some communities, but the federal government and the federal courts seem almost completely unwilling to allow schools to impose any further restrictions on children with AIDS.

Public school systems may have to provide special transportation to and from school for certain disabled children. This can include school buses with a wheelchair lift or other special devices. However, children with disabilities do not have a right to participate in activities that are clearly beyond their abilities or that could be harmful to themselves and others. For example, a school is not required to allow a wheelchair-bound child to join a contact-sports team where the child or others might be injured as a result.

American disability laws are now well established. There are a considerable number of separate laws, both state and federal, and a huge number of public and private agencies that are involved in enforcing these laws. If a child suffers from disability-related discrimination, the adult helping the child should contact both state and federal elected officials who represent the community in Congress and in the state legislature or assembly. These elected officers can usually refer the adult to the appropriate agencies and can give valuable help in understanding how to file a complaint and get relief.

In some cases, these elected officers may be able to solve the problem with a phone call or letter. Many agencies and businesses are unaware of what the law now requires. If so, an official letter from a state or federal officer may shock the agency or business to its senses. This may be enough to end the discrimination immediately and at little cost to the child — another sound exercise of preventive law.

In addition, many of the federal and state agencies involved in disability discrimination will perform their own investigations of a serious complaint if the discrimination is not immediately stopped. These agencies may be able to order the agency or business to end its discriminatory and illegal activities.

If these methods do not work, the adult helping the child may wish to contact an experienced civil rights attorney. Contact your state Bar association for the names of qualified civil rights attorneys. Sometimes an attorney may agree to take the case at a reduced cost as a public service to the child.

You should also contact your local Bar organizations to see if there are any members who will charge a reduced fee to take your case. Some attorneys do this because often these cases get good publicity. Several of the discrimination laws also say that a judge can force the discriminating agency or business to pay the attorney's fee, though only if you win the case. You should discuss this possibility with the attorney when you agree on a fee arrangement.

There are private groups that may agree to provide low- or no-cost legal services or help in other ways. The best known of these is the American Civil Liberties Union, which has a chapter in most larger cities. But there are many other groups and agencies that help people with particular kinds of disabilities. It would be a good idea to identify these groups or agencies and contact them to see what help they may provide.

Central libraries and law libraries have directories with the names of many of these organizations. Ask the librarian to show you the section with books about the Americans with Disabilities Act. One important book is the *Resource Directory for the Americans with Disabilities Act*, which was prepared by the federal government and contains more than 200 pages of information about disability-related organizations, including state-by-state listings, and listings for particular kinds of disabilities.

PART III
THE STATE AND THE CHILD

11
WHEN DOES A CHILD BECOME AN ADULT?

Up to the last century, the law considered children to be "infants" under their father's absolute control until age 21. A woman under the age of 21 was considered to be under her father's absolute control until she married and came under the control of her husband and his family. Anyone under age 21 could not enter into binding contracts or own property, and was obligated to give their earnings to the father. Children were regarded as "property" owned by their father.

However, there have always been exceptions to this broad rule. Judges usually had the authority to give a child the rights of adulthood. Even without a judge's approval, children were able to contract to buy what they needed to live — food, clothing, shelter, etc. Moreover, early American law allowed children to marry at quite a young age by today's standards. The common law age of consent for marriage was 14 for males and 12 for females, though in practice, couples who wished to marry at such a young age needed their parent's consent.

These laws remained in effect in many states until well into this century. The differences in the laws among the states were dramatic. Many people remember a time when young couples eloped to a state that allowed people to marry at a young age without parental consent. This was because some states raised the age of consent for marriage while others lagged behind. Likewise, the states varied widely about the kinds of rights that were given to children.

All of that has changed now. The states are far more uniform today in how they treat children's legal rights. Every state, for example, has substantially modified the earlier rules. No state today would permit a 14-year-old boy to marry a 12-year-old girl without a state judge's permission and an extraordinary reason for the marriage (most often, pregnancy or the birth of a child). A few states will not permit such a marriage under any circumstances.

At the same time, many states now give children the right to decide a number of matters that previously would have been the parents' sole concern.

a. THE GENERAL AGE OF CONSENT

Legal age is often called the "age of majority" or the "age of consent." A person who has not yet reached this age is called a "minor." Lawyers and judges sometimes say that minors are under the "disability of nonage," meaning that they have not yet reached legal age. Legally, a minor child remains under the control of the parent or other lawful guardian to a greater or lesser extent in different states. All major decisions regarding the child's property and well-being are usually left to the parent or guardian, but with an increasing level of supervision by the state.

Until the end of the Vietnam War, the legal age in most states was 21. This rule of law stretched back to ancient English history. However, the Vietnam War led to a protest movement in the United States, and one grievance was that young men could be drafted and sent to war at age 18 but had no rights as adults as a result. As a result, Congress and the state legislatures approved an amendment to the United States Constitution lowering the federal voting age to 18. This prompted many states to review their own laws about legal age.

Today, all states have established the legal age at 18 except for the following:

- Alabama — 19
- Colorado — 21
- Mississippi — 21
- Nebraska — 19
- Pennsylvania — 21
- West Virginia — 21

Puerto Rico recognizes a legal age of 21, although the Virgin Islands has established legal age at 18.

However, states with higher legal ages usually give special rights to persons who are 18 are older. This sometimes includes the right to vote, to marry without parental consent, and to enter into certain kinds of contracts. (Not all of these states grant 18-year-olds these rights, however.) The age of consent is never absolute. In practice, the age of consent is different depending on the state and the situation.

b. MARRIAGE

No state allows a couple to marry without permission if one of the parties is under 18. In most states, parents can give permission so long as the younger party is not under 16. In a few states, a judge can give his or her consent if the parents are not available or if the couple can demonstrate some other reason to justify the marriage (e.g., pregnancy or the birth of a child).

Most states forbid marriage under the age of 16, although some allow it if the parents consent and a judge gives permission. Generally, a very compelling reason for the marriage must be given to the judge before authorization will be granted.

A few states, most notably Mississippi, still require parental consent for marriages under the age of 21. But not all states do, and age of consent laws are changing. There is now a clear trend to allow people who are 18 to marry without parental consent.

Call the marriage license division at your local courthouse for more information.

c. THE DRINKING AGE

Until the 1970s, it was against the law in most states to sell alcohol to anyone under age 21. By the end of the Vietnam War, however, there was a strong movement to lower the drinking age to 18 or 19. A large number of states actually did so.

However, federal transportation officials became alarmed at the rise in the number of alcohol-related automobile injuries among young people after the drinking age was lowered. In the 1980s, Congress passed a law to withhold certain kinds of federal transportation funding from states that had an under-21 drinking age. There was a strong political movement throughout the United States in the 1980s to "get tough" on drunk driving.

This has led to a dramatic reversal of the lower drinking age. Now the drinking age in all states is 21, although a few states allow parents or guardians to give alcoholic beverages to their own children under certain circumstances (typically, as part of a meal). The new age limit is vigorously enforced in some states, and violations can result in serious legal problems. These may include criminal charges or being sued for any injuries or damages caused by the child's intoxication. Some multi-million dollar lawsuits have resulted when adults allowed minors to drink, and the minors then killed someone in an automobile accident.

Store owners and bartenders have a special problem. There is a growing trend to hold store owners and bartenders liable for injuries caused after they sold alcoholic beverages to minors. In some cases, juries have awarded huge verdicts against the store owners and bartenders even though the minors seemed to be adults and did not appear to be drunk. In 1993, for example, a court awarded $7.5 million against a bar in Quincy, Massachusetts, for selling alcoholic drinks to a 19-year-old who later died in a fiery automobile crash. To protect themselves, many store owners and bartenders now have a rule of asking for valid identification from anyone who appears to be less than 30 or 35 years of age.

Special problems arise if young people present false identification in order to buy alcoholic beverages. Evidence of false identification may help reduce the store owner's or bartender's liability. However, if the seller has reason to believe the identification is false, he or she has little protection. In many states, the law places a heavy burden on the seller to make sure the buyer has reached the drinking age. Some parents have successfully sued bartenders or store owners for their children's injuries even when an effort was made to verify identification.

d. MEDICAL CARE

Until well into this century, medical procedures involving children usually required advance permission from their parents or guardians. Failure to get permission was generally regarded as a serious wrong that could lead to a lawsuit for an unauthorized "battery" upon the child.

Today, most states allow doctors to give certain kinds of medical care to a child in an emergency if the parents or guardian cannot be located after a reasonable search. It must be a genuine emergency and some effort must be made to contact the parents or guardian. As a general rule, any major medical procedure performed on the child should be delayed until the parents can be found, unless there is no other way to preserve the child's health or life.

There are some state laws that allow children themselves to consent to emergency medical care, including procedures as serious as surgery. However, these laws are of little help if the minor child is unconscious. Moreover, medical providers as a rule should not rely on the minor's consent if there is any other alternative. Parents or guardians may later claim that the child did not understand the nature of the medical procedure and therefore did not give the legally required "informed consent." If there is any doubt on this question, a lawsuit could result that would be put to a jury.

In the absence of a parent or guardian's consent, most doctors or hospitals should consult with their own attorneys before proceeding, if there is time. Medical providers in the past protected themselves by getting an emergency court order authorizing treatment of the child when the child's parents or guardians could not be located. A skilled attorney can often get an emergency court order quickly. A judge can almost never be sued for an official act, and medical providers are legally required to obey a court order. As a result, lawsuits arising from a court-ordered medical procedure rarely succeed.

e. TESTING AND TREATMENT FOR VENEREAL DISEASE

In recent decades, the number of minors contracting venereal disease has risen dramatically. State legislatures and local elected officials have tried to address the problem, but any method is controversial. Most states now authorize minors to get testing and treatment for some forms of venereal disease, and parental consent is not needed in many cases. A few states require that parents be notified (whether or not they consent) or health care providers have the option of notifying parents if they choose. Some states impose a minimum age (usually in the 12 to 16 range), so that children below the minimum must have parental consent.

For most venereal diseases, state laws that allow testing and treatment of minors have produced very few legal difficulties. The bulk of the states give the minor child near-complete confidentiality, meaning that the parents will never know about the testing or treatment. Parents in these states have no legal means of learning about the test or treatment other than asking the child. Only if the state requires parental consent or notification is there likelihood of a lawsuit or other legal action if parents are not involved in the testing or treatment decision.

The major exception, of course, is AIDS. Only a handful of states have expressly authorized minors to consent to testing and treatment for AIDS-related illnesses, although it seems likely that AIDS would fall under some states' venereal disease testing laws.

Few legal problems arise when children test negative for AIDS, but a far different problem arises when the test is positive. AIDS is generally regarded as fatal, and it involves medical decisions and expenses of a completely different magnitude. The cost of treating a single AIDS patient can be more than $100,000 and involves treatment with novel or experimental therapies.

This places health care providers in a difficult position when a minor child tests positive for AIDS. Many state confidentiality laws apply to AIDS-related test results, and health providers break the law if they disclose test results to a parent or guardian. However, few minors have the emotional or financial resources to deal with a terminal illness alone. Some health providers follow a practice of counseling the child with the hope of getting the child's permission to inform the parents or guardians. If the child still refuses, some medical facilities routinely refer the matter to their attorneys for further guidance. Once again, it may be possible to get a court order authorizing disclosure to the parents or guardians.

Special care must be taken, however, in dealing with any AIDS-related information. Health care providers can be sued for invasion of privacy or other injury if they fail to maintain a strict level of confidentiality. Children infected with AIDS have been a special source of trouble in the past. Throughout the United States, unauthorized disclosures of a child's AIDS infection have caused hysteria among the parents of other children in the community or the child's school. In Florida, three infected boys had their house burned to the ground after such a disclosure, and elsewhere other parents have risen in protest at the idea of AIDS-infected children attending the public schools. If a health care provider was the source of the "leak," an expensive lawsuit may follow.

f. CONTRACEPTIVE SERVICES

About half the states now have laws authorizing minors in some form or another to get contraceptive services without parental consent. Usually, state laws require that:

- the child must be a certain age,
- the child must be referred by another professional, or
- the child must show sufficient maturity.

Some also require parental notification or consent in particular circumstances or for children of certain ages.

On the whole, however, state services give teenagers access to contraceptives with a minimum of parental involvement. A few states or school districts even provide contraceptive services in the high school setting, although all such services have been very controversial.

Many adults believe that all sexual lessons should remain strictly a family matter. Nevertheless, the law allows teenagers greater access to contraceptives, especially condoms in the aftermath of the AIDS epidemic. Even those states that do not expressly authorize such services have shown a tendency to look the other way. Ironically, almost all the states providing these services still have statutory rape laws that make sex with a minor a criminal act. In many cases these laws apply even if both partners are minors.

g. ABORTION

The possibility of minors getting abortions has been an explosive legal issue in the last decade. Abortion is controversial in itself, but a substantial number of Americans feel very strongly that parents must be involved in a minor's decision to abort. Others hold the opposite viewpoint with equal strength. The resulting clash has led to some of the most confusing and contradictory laws in the nation.

Generally, minors still have access to abortions in certain circumstances throughout the United States. However, some states impose severe limitations on minors, but not on adults. For a further discussion of the limitations placed on minors, see chapter 22.

h. WITHHOLDING TREATMENT ON RELIGIOUS GROUNDS

Some parents and guardians do not want their child to receive certain kinds of life-saving medical procedures because of religious beliefs. The most common cases involve refusal of a blood transfusion. While adults usually have the legal authority to refuse these treatments for themselves, the states have been unwilling to allow either the child or the parents to refuse when the child's life is at stake. Judges often say that unusually mature children should be allowed to make such a decision, but in practice few children are deemed sufficiently mature. One New York judge even balked when a request was made by a young man only weeks from his 18th birthday, when he legally would become an adult.

Withholding medical treatment on religious grounds almost always results in lawsuits and considerable attention by the news media. When a parent or the child refuses permission for the treatment, health care providers go to court as soon as possible. This is the only way they can protect themselves from future lawsuits, either for refusing to honor the parent or child's wishes, or for letting the child die without proper treatment. A judge's decision is binding on all concerned, and the judge can seldom be sued for official acts.

i. THE TERMINALLY ILL CHILD

Children with terminal illnesses pose special legal problems. Most often these problems deal with a child on an artificial life support system. In recent years, the courts have shown a willingness to allow adults to choose to die with dignity. However, this rule of law is much more difficult to apply to children who may never have even considered the prospect of dying, much less expressed their wishes.

Nevertheless, judges generally allow parents to make a reasonable decision to terminate artificial life support on behalf of a child once the child is brain dead or there is no hope of recovery. However, a judge's approval is often required before health care providers will honor the parents' wishes. A judge's order can protect health care providers from a lawsuit.

Sometimes children are born with defects that make it impossible for them to live more than a few days. One of the more common defects of this type is called "anencephaly," in which the child is born with most of the brain completely missing and the top of the skull absent. These children may have a heart beat for a few days but always die soon after. As with other terminal children, judges will usually permit parents to have life-support devices removed from the child.

A different problem can arise when parents want to donate organs from a dying child to help save other sick children. Transplants from very young children are usually not medically possible once the child is actually dead, so there has been some sentiment for removing the organs of severely deformed children prior to actual death, if the child will unquestionably die in a short while. However, by late 1993 judges have been unwilling to let parents authorize the removal of the child's organs for transplant purposes until the child is either brain dead or the heart has stopped beating. This is true no matter how serious the child's birth defects may be.

Another problem can arise when a child is born with a serious abnormality that is fatal unless treated with massive and expensive care and technology. In the 1980s, the federal government was hostile to parents' decisions to refuse consent for this kind of "heroic treatment." Officials in President Reagan's administration even issued regulations forbidding most health care providers from complying with the parents' wishes. However, the federal courts later overturned the bulk of these regulations.

Today, legal problems still may arise if a newborn can be kept alive only at great expense and with only a slim chance of a normal life. Many hospitals or health care providers still show reluctance to go along with parents who want to refuse heroic treatment. As a result, it is quite common for health care providers to demand that a judge officially authorize what the parents say they want. This means a court hearing may be inevitable in all such cases. However, once again, a judge's authorization usually eliminates many of the legal problems and paves the way for the parents' wishes to be honored.

j. EMANCIPATION OF CHILDREN

In one form or another, all states allow judges to give minor children all or some of the rights of adulthood. The procedure most often is called emancipation. In most states, this is unusual and authorized only in exceptional circumstances. A common requirement in these states is that the child must either already be successfully living independently or show the maturity to do so. Normally, emancipation can occur only by court order.

However, some parts of the United States have quite liberal procedures. Louisiana and Puerto Rico, whose legal systems rely heavily on European continental law, allow parents to confer a limited form of emancipation on their children with little involvement from the judicial system. A number of states or regions including Illinois and the Virgin Islands also allow an expedited form of emancipation if the parents consent, although this legal procedure is limited to older teenagers.

Emancipation may be a viable alternative in some situations where a child shows sufficient maturity and needs the legal authority to leave an abusive home. Teachers and youth counselors, for example, may be able to assist the child in filing the necessary court papers. Usually, the clerks or registrars of the local courthouse can assist in this procedure. However, the child's parents usually have a right to object to emancipation if they so choose.

Certain events in a child's life may also have the effect of emancipation. In many states, for example, the lawful marriage of a child is recognized as granting a form of emancipation, though the child does not necessarily acquire all the rights of adulthood. Some states also recognize other events, such as enlistment in the military, as a form of emancipation.

12
WHAT HAPPENS IF A CHILD BREAKS THE LAW?

Until the last century, most children who committed crimes were generally treated the same as adults. American law followed English law, which held that children seven years of age or older could be prosecuted for crimes. (Children younger than seven were thought incapable of forming criminal intent. By today's standards, they were subjected to severe punishment.) Children between the ages of seven and 14 could be punished as adults. However, under earlier law, a judge could decide that such a child could not form a criminal intent and thus could not be treated like an adult.

The law made no other distinctions once an older child or adult was convicted of a crime. All were treated the same, even children only 14 years old. Children were subject to the death penalty for serious felonies and, for lesser offenses, could be jailed together with adult offenders. At one time under English law, the death penalty was possible for nearly every felony, including crimes like theft or (using its older English name) "larceny." The law had become considerably more lenient by the time the American colonies were founded. Nevertheless, early American law allowed the death penalty in far more cases than we do today, including for children. More serious forms of rape, for example, sometimes were punishable by death — a legal rule that endured in some states well into this century.

Social scientists began to realize, however, that placing children among hardened criminals or treating them like adult offenders probably caused more harm than good. Children in such an environment generally became even more disposed to commit crimes after leaving a prison or jail. Some scientists noted that this was little better than teaching children how to become better criminals. As early as 1849, the State of Massachusetts created one of the first state-operated reform schools for juvenile offenders in an effort to address this problem. In 1899, Illinois became the first state to create a comprehensive juvenile justice system, though Massachusetts had created a children's tribunal in 1874. By the 20th century, the reform movement had swept throughout the United States.

a. THE JUVENILE JUSTICE SYSTEM

All states now have separate and distinct legal procedures for juvenile offenders, and most also have a separate juvenile court system. The general purpose of these procedures is to rehabilitate young offenders before they can become hardened criminals, although many states clearly have a high failure rate. The juvenile court procedures are supposed to operate more quickly and offer a greater opportunity for juveniles to reform themselves. In most states, these procedures potentially are available for any offender under 17 years of age, though several states set the age at 16 and others at 18.

Most of the trappings of an adult criminal trial are not permitted in a juvenile proceeding. With some exceptions, trials are not conducted before a jury, but before a judge who has experience with juvenile matters. The proceedings are informal, and the judge asks questions of the child, the parents (if present), state social workers, and other participants. The juvenile generally is not called a "defendant" but a "detainee" or some other similar term. A juvenile convicted of an offense is usually not called a convict but a "delinquent," a "juvenile offender," a "child in need of supervision," or something similar.

The entire emphasis is on removing much of the stigma associated with a criminal trial. In many states, most juvenile proceedings do not result in a criminal record for the child. (However, information on the child's arrests usually remains available to police, prosecutors, and judges in the form of police rap sheets.) In many states, first-time juvenile offenders are put in diversion programs designed to help reform them. Some states are experimenting with military-style boot camps for serious or habitual offenders — a reform supported in 1993 by Attorney General Janet Reno. In many states, supervision of detained children is placed in the hands of state social services agencies, though some states leave the matter to their department of corrections or prisons.

Today, most people concede that the juvenile justice system is seriously inadequate. As a rule, juvenile programs in most states are underfunded and understaffed. While diversion programs have some success, the rate of repeat offenders remains high. A number of habitual juvenile offenders go on to an adult career of serious crime.

b. JUVENILE STATUS OFFENSES

The juvenile justice system in most states has another important difference from adult criminal procedures. Juveniles can be detained for what are called *status offenses*. Failing to attend school (truancy), running away from home, or being ungovernable or beyond parental control are juvenile status offenses.

The procedures used in these cases are often the same as for criminal offenses, but the results may be somewhat different. In many instances, a status offense case may take on the character of a child dependency proceeding, especially where the parents have failed to exercise adequate control over the child. Children who have committed status offenses are often taken away from their homes and placed in rehabilitation programs, a state facility, private foster care, or some combination of these for a period of time.

Recent studies show that girls and boys are treated somewhat different by the juvenile justice system. Boys are more likely to be accused of criminal offenses, whereas girls are more likely to be brought before a judge for a status offense. Part of the reason is that boys are more inclined to violence by disposition, but there is also a growing belief that juvenile judges are less willing to tolerate status offenses by females. In other words, there may be a hidden double standard based on some judges' "boys will be boys" attitude.

c. WHAT SHOULD THE PARENT OR ADULT DO?

Most juvenile justice cases deal with relatively minor offenses for which the child is unlikely to receive serious punishment. Many parents and children in that situation choose not to seek legal help from an attorney, but go to court to answer the judge's questions themselves. However, juveniles are sometimes charged with serious offenses that lead to major problems. Some states even have special procedures so that juveniles can be charged and tried as adults. Usually a juvenile will only be tried as an adult for a serious offense (e.g., armed robbery or attempted murder).

Any serious charge against a child is best handled by an attorney. Although children in a juvenile proceeding are not entitled to the same rights as adults, the United States Supreme Court has said that juveniles have a right to:

- receive adequate notice of the charges and proceedings,
- talk to an attorney,
- present witnesses of their own and to question witnesses who testify against them, and
- be free from forced or involuntary self-incrimination.

If the child is being tried as an adult or faces a possible felony conviction or a substantial jail or prison term, the child may have the right to a free court-appointed attorney if the parents cannot afford to hire a lawyer.

In many states, parents or guardians of the child may have a right to see and speak with the child after arrest. This right varies from state to state, and it is not entirely clear exactly when the parents or guardians can exercise the right.

Law enforcement officers have prevented parents from interfering with police questioning of the child. This practice could be challenged as illegal in some situations. On the whole, the parent or guardian should get an attorney's help if there is any problem in getting access to the child after arrest.

Each year the number of murders committed by juveniles rises. In many states, the death penalty is a possible option for the most serious forms of murder. Some states now prohibit the death penalty if the murderer was a minor at the time of the killing, but in other states the law is not entirely clear and is changing rapidly.

Until World War II, minors were regularly executed in the United States; this has been far rarer since. In 1988, the United States Supreme Court issued an opinion on the subject that seems to stop just short of saying that death is improper for a child who was under the age of 16 when committing a murder. However, after the 1988 opinion was released, a number of states prohibited any such penalty for a child 15 and under. Needless to say, any child charged with murder faces a very serious problem that requires a lawyer's help.

Finally, status offenses pose a special problem. Under a law called the Federal Juvenile Justice and Delinquency Prevention Act, children found guilty of a status offense are not supposed to be detained in facilities meant for criminal offenders. Some states, however, don't always follow this law. When this happens, the parent or other adult representative of the child may be able to ask for a court order declaring the detention illegal and get the child removed. Having the child taken out of detention with adults is very important, because some children have been physically and sexually abused in adult facilities.

d. IMPROPER TREATMENT OF DETAINED CHILDREN

In recent years, parents have shown an increasing willingness to sue state and local governments for improper treatment of detained children. The most common lawsuits have involved children placed in adult facilities, such as a county jail, where the children were abused or sexually attacked. Some parents have successfully sued on the grounds that the children's civil rights were violated. Suits of this type, however, can be quite complex and should only be handled by a skilled attorney.

13
WHEN CAN CHILDREN "DIVORCE" THEIR PARENTS?

In 1992, a Florida boy, "Gregory K." made national news when he filed suit against his parents in an effort to end his legal ties to them. Gregory K. said his parents had abandoned or neglected him so severely that they no longer deserved to be his legal parents. The news media quickly labeled the suit a kind of "divorce." Many adults and child care providers were shocked at the idea of children being able to divorce their parents. Religious leaders denounced it as the latest attack on the American family.

What Gregory K. wanted was a good deal more complicated and a lot harder to get than a divorce. Most important, the news media gave very little attention to the fact that a crucial part of Gregory K.'s case was reversed on appeal. The Florida appeals court especially disagreed with the idea that the child, Gregory K., could sue his own parents. As a result, the Gregory K. case is not nearly as troublesome as it sounds.

In broad terms, children do not presently have a right to divorce their parents in any American state, district, or territory. But the *Gregory K.* case does indicate that the parents' rights could be terminated in other ways if the parents clearly are unfit. However, this is nothing at all like a divorce.

a. "DIVORCE" VERSUS TERMINATION OF PARENTAL RIGHTS

The news media's use of the word divorce was misleading in the *Gregory K.* case because most people know that a divorce is easy to obtain. Every state has some form of "no-fault" divorce, which means the parties agree to "call it quits" and sign the necessary papers. As a result, saying that Gregory K. divorced his parents conjures up the idea of a child getting mad, deciding he wants new parents, and filing a hasty lawsuit. That is not what actually happened.

Gregory K. had endured a long history of parental neglect and abandonment. His biological father showed little interest in the boy, and his mother allowed Gregory K. to be placed in foster homes, partly because she was unable to provide necessary care. Gregory K. spent most of his childhood being shifted from home to home until he was placed with a couple who came to love him. His new foster father was an attorney well versed in children's legal issues, who encouraged Gregory K. to learn about the new children's rights movement. (In fact, Gregory K.'s father later served as an attorney to Kimberly Mays, the young Florida girl who had been "switched at birth." The Mays case is discussed below.)

In 1992, Gregory K. filed a lawsuit to terminate the parental rights of his biological parents so that his foster parents could legally adopt him. The subject of the lawsuit itself was not very unusual. Under long-established law, the state has the authority to terminate the parental rights of parents who are unfit. However, this case was unusual because it was the child — not the state — that filed the lawsuit. That fact alone explained the massive amount of press coverage for Gregory K.'s case. The story was dramatized in a made-for-TV movie.

However, terminating parental rights is not a no-fault divorce, contrary to the impression the news media gave many Americans. Under the United States Constitution, parents have a very strong right to maintain their legal relationship with their own minor children. This right is so strong that the courts require the state to prove by clear and convincing evidence that the parents are unfit before those rights can be terminated. Usually, this means the parents must be given a chance to "mend their ways," undergo counseling, or take other measures to better prepare them for parenthood. On the whole, termination is granted in only the most serious cases and usually is the end product of a state "dependency" proceeding.

However, Gregory K. and his attorneys noticed that the Florida law on terminating parental rights did not say that only the state could start the lawsuit. Instead, the law said that any interested person could file the suit. (The same is true in many other states, though not always so.) As a result, Gregory K. and his foster parents took several precautions. Not only did Gregory K. file suit, but so did his foster parents, the state child welfare agency, and another adult who had been appointed as his guardian ad litem. (The role of the guardian ad litem is discussed in chapters 2 and 3). If necessary, any one of these suits could stand on its own. This precaution proved very wise.

The trial court later granted the request to terminate parental rights and then, on the same day, allowed the foster parents to adopt Gregory K. However, the biological mother appealed to a higher court. She argued that she had been denied her constitutional rights and that the methods used in the trial had been improper.

b. THE OUTCOME OF THE GREGORY K. CASE

The Florida appeals court found two major problems with the *Gregory K.* case. Foremost, the appeals court believed that the child did not have the legal ability to sue his own parents. Judges on the court believed that such lawsuits could be misused by children who had become angry at their parents over some problem or by unscrupulous adults. However, the appeals court agreed that the state child welfare agency and the other adults who had filed suit were "interested parties" who had a right to sue to terminate the parental rights. As a result, these other lawsuits were proper. Only the child's suit was improper.

This ruling means that children will not be able to file suit to divorce their parents, at least in Florida. Instead, they must be able to convince state child welfare officials or some independent adult to file suit against the parents. It is not enough that the child dislikes the parents or is angry with them. The lawsuit must prove clearly and convincingly that the parents are seriously unfit to care for the child. In this regard, the lawsuit cannot be granted just because some other parents might be "better," have more money, or could provide a happier life for the child. The only question is whether the present parents are clearly unfit.

The second conclusion the appeals court reached was that the trial judge should not have granted the foster parents' request to adopt Gregory K. on the same day parental rights were terminated. By combining these two separate issues, the trial judge might have been influenced by the obvious fact that the foster parents could provide Gregory K. a better home than his biological mother could. This was wrong, the appeals court said. However, the foster parents still would be able to file a completely new request to adopt Gregory K. at a later date. In other words, the adoption was still possible but had not been done properly.

c. WHAT DOES THE GREGORY K. CASE MEAN?

Obviously, the *Gregory K.* case does not stand for the proposition that children can divorce their parents, but only that interested adults can sue to terminate the rights of an unfit parent. An interested adult could include a foster parent or a guardian ad litem.

Even with this limitation, however, the case has been criticized. Some people believe that it was wrong to allow the foster parents (who hoped to adopt Gregory K.) to be active participants in the lawsuit. Critics felt that this risked turning the suit into a competition over who would make the best parent. Some have said that these kinds of lawsuits should never be used as a means of "shopping" for the better set of parents.

The criticism has some merit — and points to a legal problem that can be avoided. There are cases where the biological parents are unfit and the interests of everyone would be better served if the parental rights were terminated. However, the suit probably should be filed by the state child welfare agency or a guardian ad litem appointed to represent the child's interests.

To avoid legal troubles, prospective adoptive parents should not file their own suit unless absolutely necessary because that might lead some judges to be suspicious. Many judges believe biological parents' rights are nearly absolute. Such judges may frown upon other adults who seem to be "shopping" for a child or a child who seems to be "divorcing" the biological parents.

Cases like Gregory K.'s are novel, although several had been filed in other states by late 1993. However, it is too early to say whether other states will follow Florida's lead. Some states may permit children to file suit to terminate parental rights; others may not. In addition, some states may be inclined to say that all lawsuits to terminate parental rights must be filed by the state's child welfare agency. There are states with statutes that already seem to say so.

Because the issues are complicated, always get an attorney to handle the case. An adult such as a teacher or social worker may be able to contact local groups or Bar associations that can find an attorney to help out. Sometimes attorneys will agree to take cases of this type as a matter of public interest. Certain private civil-liberties organizations may also be willing to assist, such as the American Civil Liberties Union and child welfare foundations.

If you are a parent who is sued to terminate parental rights, you must get an attorney's help if at all possible. Consult Appendix 1 for further ideas on how to find a lawyer. Cases involving parental rights can be highly emotional affairs, and a trained attorney's assistance is absolutely vital. Keep in mind that it is very difficult to terminate a parent's rights, but termination is possible if the proper legal arguments are not made at the right time.

d. CHILDREN SWITCHED AT BIRTH

Another dramatic case erupted in Florida in 1993 involving a girl who had been switched at birth. Scientific tests conclusively showed that the girl, named Kimberly Mays, was the biological child of parents she had never seen. The girl had been reared from birth by parents who had mistakenly received her at a hospital nursery many years earlier. For reasons that still are a mystery, Kimberly had been switched with another child born at roughly the same time, who later died. A decade later her biological parents discovered the truth and tried to regain some rights over their biological daughter.

When this happened, Kimberly Mays followed the lead of the *Gregory K.* case and sued to terminate all rights her biological parents might have. In 1993, a Florida judge granted her request and ruled that the biological parents had no legal ties to Kimberly. Once again, the news media gave prominent attention to another instance of a child divorcing parents.

The *Kimberly Mays'* case presented a very unusual and rare legal question completely different from the problem in the *Gregory K.* case. The law in every state has recognized for a very long time that a child's biological parents and legal parents are not necessarily the same. Even under early American law, for example, a man usually was regarded as the "legal" father of all children born during his marriage to a woman, whether or not the children were his biological offspring. In much the same way, Kimberly Mays had been reared by a man who was not her biological father but who the legal system had recognized as her "legal" father for more than 14 years by the time her case came to trial.

In that sense, Kimberly Mays was not actually "divorcing" her parents, nor was she "terminating" parental rights. She was only asking the legal system to verify that her legal father would remain her legal father, no matter who her biological parents happened to be. This is quite a different matter than what happened in the *Gregory K.* case.

Obviously, a crucial fact in the *Kimberly Mays'* case was the long delay before anyone discovered that the two children had been switched at birth. It is unlikely a similar result would have been reached if the mistake had been discovered quickly. Biological parents do have very substantial rights over their children and would be able to reclaim a child mistakenly taken from them a few months earlier. However, the legal system may place more importance on the fact that years have passed. Some judges have said that the law does not always require that children be cruelly taken from the people who have reared them and who are regarded as the legal parents.

Nevertheless, the *Kimberly Mays* case was unique. Florida has led the way in reforming the laws about children and their rights. The conclusion reached by the judge rested heavily on the odd facts of the case and the peculiarities of the law in Florida. There is no guarantee that judges in other states would follow Florida's lead even if the facts were the same. If a state's law differs substantially from Florida's or gives special legal rights to biological parents, it is unlikely that a court would terminate the biological parents' rights.

14
ADOPTION

Adoption is a legal concept with roots far back in Western history. The earliest legal codes make reference to the practice. Ancient Roman law recognized a liberal form of adoption, and politically powerful Roman families even used adoption (along with marriage) as a means of allying themselves with other powerful families. However, ancient English common law never recognized adoption, partly because of the unusual Anglo-Saxon preoccupation with blood relationships. In fact, England did not formally recognize a legal form of adoption until 1926, although foster parentage was commonly practiced in Britain from the earliest times.

The United States, however, acted much earlier — at least partly because several American states derived some of their traditions from nations with legal systems based on the Roman model. Texas with its Spanish heritage and Louisiana with its French origins have recognized a more-or-less Roman style of adoption from the very beginning. Other states were influenced by the idea. Mississippi also had early ties to France, and in 1846 it was the first state to pass adoption laws. In 1851, Massachusetts became the first state to have a comprehensive adoption code.

Today, adoption is recognized in every state, though the modern method of adoption has departed considerably from what existed in ancient Rome. Under Roman law, children's needs were not considered, and often Roman adoptions involved one adult "adopting" another adult purely for political or financial reasons. In the United States today, there are 50,000 adoptions each year. Almost all involve children, and the courts as a general rule say that the best interest of the child is the paramount concern during the proceedings.

a. ADOPTION PROCEDURES

A child's best interest, however, means different things to different people and may be gauged differently from state to state. In all states, there are rules that specify what requirements must be met. Apart from that, the laws vary a good deal.

Most states specify some minimum age for the adoptive parent (often 21) before an adoption will be approved, although some states say that married couples of any age can adopt. (Married couples are sometimes given preference over others.) A few states also require that the adoptive parent must be a certain number of years older than the adopted child — often 10 or 15 years older.

All states require a background investigation of an adopted parent or parents. This can include a check into a person's fitness to be a parent. Evidence of alcoholism, drug abuse, a criminal background, violent acts, sexual indiscretions, or similar problems may be sufficient for the state adoption agency to refuse permission. Some states forbid adoption by homosexual parents, although these laws have been successfully challenged in court. Many states make an effort to see that children are adopted by adults with similar ethnic or racial backgrounds, an idea encouraged by pressure from ethnic communities today. However, children of color continue to have trouble finding suitable homes for adoption.

If you are interested in adopting a child, contact the child welfare agency responsible for adoptions in your state. A good deal of paperwork is involved, and the process of adoption can take many months or even years. The process can be speeded up if you are willing to adopt a "special needs" child, (e.g., a child that is older, a member of a minority, or has a disability or a behavioral disorder). There are international agencies that help parents adopt children from other countries such as China, India, Romania, and Brazil.

International adoptions are expensive and you must comply with foreign adoption laws, but you may find that there are fewer complications after the adoption is finalized. However, babies not born to U.S. citizens or not born within United States territory have to undergo naturalization procedures before they can become citizens. Some states also impose restrictions on the "importation" of children for adoption, meaning that you have to get permission in advance from the state authority. Any couple planning to adopt a child from out-of-state should contact a qualified attorney to make sure all legal requirements are met before any attempt is made to accept custody of a child.

State adoption agencies often help adults through the necessary procedures. Private organizations also help with child placements, and they will assist with paperwork. However, adoptive parents cannot count on a state agency or private placement organization to make sure that all legal problems are resolved. These agencies and organizations can and do make serious mistakes — some that have proven costly for the adoptive parents. For that reason, adoptive parents should invest the time and money to get sound legal advice to make sure the adoption is legally correct. This can save considerable trouble and heartache later on.

There is growing pressure for some parents to become involved in "black market" or "gray market" adoptions. These typically involve individuals or agencies that charge a substantial fee, and in return promise that a suitable child will be found for adoption. Sometimes these individuals or agencies cut corners or engage in questionable tactics to get children or speed up the adoption process.

Anyone who wants to adopt in this situation should be very careful. It is illegal in all states to "buy" a baby. If the agency does not ensure that the biological parents have properly consented to the adoption, the adoptive parents may go through the heartache of having the baby seized and returned to its biological parents.

Before using any agency for adoption, make sure the agency is properly licensed, has no previous legal violations, and has a good track record. Contact government regulatory agencies to see if any complaints have been filed. Try to learn the names of people who have used the agency in the past, and ask these people if they encountered any problems.

It is always a good idea to contact a qualified, independent attorney for a legal evaluation of an agency's adoption procedures before any money changes hands. Do not rely on advice from the agency's attorney, even if the adoption agency is run by a licensed attorney. In that situation, get a second opinion. It is always better to pay for an evaluation than deal with the serious legal problems of a botched adoption.

For more information about adoption in North America, see *Adopting Your Child*, another title in the Self-Counsel Series.

b. PROBLEMS IN ADOPTION

Problems can arise during an adoption if you don't follow all the rules. For example, if you fail to tell the truth on adoption forms, you could be investigated by the state, face criminal charges, or have the adoption canceled. You should avoid anything that might be considered fraudulent at all cost. Similarly, if the biological parents of the child were pressured into giving the child up for adoption, you will have problems. The parents can later claim that they gave up their child under coercion or duress. In that case, the adoption would be canceled.

In 1993, the adoption of "Baby Jessica" posed a far more serious problem. A Michigan couple wanted to adopt a young girl popularly known as Baby Jessica, but before the adoption was finalized, Baby Jessica's biological father tried to reclaim her. The child's biological mother and father lived in Iowa, and were not married at the time the child was born, and the mother had already consented to the adoption.

However, the mother had not told the biological father about the child, and she had even told authorities that another man was the father. Biological tests proved, however, that Baby Jessica was the child of the man who claimed to be her father. Eventually, the courts ordered Baby Jessica returned to her biological parents even though the child had lived her entire two-and-a-half-year life with her foster parents, whom she regarded as mommy and daddy.

The *Baby Jessica* case alarmed adoptive parents. There have been other cases since where a biological father's rights over the child resulted in an adoption being canceled. This "father's rights movement" is a major new worry in adoption, and one that potential adoptive parents *must* pay very special attention to.

The reason is obvious. A considerable number of adopted children are born out of wedlock, and mothers often do name the wrong man as the father or aren't sure who the father is. In the past, adoptive parents assumed that the biological father had abandoned all claim to the child. In today's legal climate, this is a *very* dangerous assumption to make.

It is more common now for biological fathers to file lawsuits claiming that they never consented to the adoption. Courts in many states (including California, Iowa, Michigan, and Tennessee) have supported the father's claims and are making changes to the law to give biological fathers far more rights than they once had. As a result, many attorneys now feel it is absolutely essential to get the true biological father's consent for every adoption.

The *Baby Jessica* case highlighted the problem, although it did involve special facts. In that case, the biological father tried to reclaim his daughter *within days* after the child was placed for eventual adoption and *before* the adoption could be finalized. However, in some cases finalized adoptions are being challenged by biological fathers. A lawsuit to challenge the adoption is less likely to succeed if it is filed many months after the adoption is final. But if it is filed soon after the adoption, the case can drag on for many years before the child's custody is resolved.

Baby Jessica and similar cases are heart-rending examples of a very real pitfall some adoptive parents face — and another reason an attorney's help can be crucial. Adoptive parents should make absolutely sure that *every* potential biological father (however many there may be) is identified and signs legal papers waiving any right over the child.

Reputable adoption agencies today follow a practice of contacting each potential father personally. If any one of the men says he will challenge the adoption, a reputable agency will not place that particular child for adoption. This is a sound legal strategy designed to avoid much cost and heartache for the adoptive parents. Potential adoptive parents are wise to use only those adoption agencies that follow this legal tactic.

Sometimes it may not be possible to contact all of the potential biological fathers. In that situation, the adoptive parents, their attorney, or the adoption agency should order genetic testing of both the child and potential fathers who are available. Once a genetic test establishes that one man is the father, the adoptive parents generally are safer in adopting the child if that particular man waives all rights over the child.

Note: Adoptive parents cannot always rely on what the biological mother says, as the *Baby Jessica* case showed. Many mothers conceal the identity of the true father.

The adoption should be finalized as soon as possible. A biological father will have a far more difficult time overturning a final adoption, although sometimes an adoption can be canceled. Adoptive parents also have no guarantee that one or both biological parents will not change their minds and try to revoke the adoption they previously agreed to. An attorney's help can be crucial in making sure that the adoption is ironclad.

Adoptive parents should also look closely at adoption agencies that work closely with crisis centers that assist women — particularly teens — in dealing with unplanned pregnancies. On occasion, these groups have been accused of pressuring younger women into giving up children for adoption. Some of these agencies assume that teens cannot provide adequate care for a child and should give the child up for adoption.

A few agencies have engaged in the legally questionable practice of telling these young women that it is best to give the child away. At least one agency was even accused of refusing to take a young woman in mid-labor to the hospital until she signed away her rights to the child.

More and more women in this position and the fathers of their children have filed suit to revoke adoptions. Any pressure to force the biological parents to place a child for adoption is a prescription for legal trouble, especially if the pressure might be construed as a threat or extortion.

Legally, adoptions can be overturned if the biological parents of the child surrendered the child because of pressure, sometimes called by the legal terms "coercion," "duress," or "overreaching." Occasionally, biological parents have even claimed fraud by the adoption agencies and the adoptive parents. As a rule, the biological parents are successful only a fraction of the time provided it is clear that both biological parents knowingly and freely signed legal papers surrendering their rights to the child. Nevertheless, suits of this type can be a serious worry, an embarrassment, and a costly legal expense for adoptive parents.

Potential adoptive parents should take the time to investigate the practices of any adoption agency they plan to use. Check to see if the agency has ever been accused of pressuring biological mothers to surrender their children. Ask the agency what kind of counseling they give to the biological mothers. Be especially wary of agencies that appear to have a political agenda, especially on the question of teen pregnancy. For an adoption to be irrevocable, the biological parents must knowingly and freely give the child up and must sign valid legal papers saying so.

A few other adoption-related problems deserve mention. In some states, children who have reached a certain age (usually in the teens) cannot be adopted without their consent. The justification for these laws is that older children should not be placed in homes against their wishes. These laws usually do not apply to younger children.

On occasion people have been unable to cope with the problems of some adopted children, especially those who are disabled or have emotional disorders. These parents have tried to give the child back to the placement agency.

As a general rule, few states allow this. The law usually treats adopted parents as though they were the natural mother or father of the child — meaning that a sick or disturbed child is the adopted parent's legal responsibility and no one else's. A few states permit an adoption to be annulled, but this is rare. Sometimes the adoptive parents give the child away to another adult who volunteers to readopt the child, but again this is rare.

If you are to adopt a child, make absolutely sure that you can meet the child's needs. If you have any doubts, have a pediatrician or child expert examine the child. Pay special attention to hidden illnesses or other conditions. Prenatal exposure to narcotic drugs such as cocaine and "fetal alcohol syndrome" are serious problems. Children with these conditions typically have a low birth weight, reduced intelligence or mental retardation, and a variety of other problems such as attention disorders.

c. RIGHTS OF ADOPTIVE CHILDREN AND BIOLOGICAL PARENTS

For many years now the law in most states has assumed that adopted children are better off if they know little or nothing about their biological parents. However, today this has changed. Many adopted children and their biological parents are demanding greater access to information about their blood relatives. In many states, government agencies are now far more willing to open up adoption records, at least after the adopted children have reached adulthood.

Nevertheless, tracking down biological parents or biological children can be difficult. Records are often lost or misplaced, and sometimes records simply may never have been created in the first place. A large number of adopted children and biological parents find themselves unable to track down their lost relatives.

Several national detective organizations now exist that specialize in tracking down information on adopted children and their biological parents. Most charge a fee, and a few have been very successful, although their success has often come by cutting legal corners, bribing record keepers, and engaging in other questionable acts. Anyone hiring one of these agencies should make sure nothing is done that could cause a legal problem.

There are a number of private support organizations that assist adult adoptees who want to find their biological parents and biological parents who want to find the children they gave up for adoption. Adoptees in Search is one such organization. You can write to them at this address:

Adoptees in Search
P.O. Box 41016
Bethesda MD   20824
(301) 656-8555

d. INHERITANCE BY ADOPTED CHILDREN

As a general rule, adopted children are treated exactly like biological children when inheriting property from the adoptive parents. By the same token, the adopted child usually — but not always — loses the ability to inherit anything from the biological parents unless a valid written will says something to the contrary. (Biological parents and the children they placed for adoption are free to sign wills leaving each other property, if they so choose.)

However, states will sometimes allow the biological child to inherit as though the adoption never occurred. Usually there are special circumstances in these cases, such as the biological parent has died without any other close relatives. This also applies to biological brothers, sisters, or other blood relatives of the adopted child. Biological parents can inherit from the children they placed for adoption, though this is rare.

The law on this subject can be very complex. However, there is an obvious incentive to pursue a claim when a large fortune is at stake. An attorney's help is always wise in these cases, and especially where the issues spill across state lines. All lawsuits over inheritance can be complex, and are only more so when the legal relationship of the parties has been called into question because of an adoption.

e. STEPPARENT ADOPTIONS

One of the most common forms of adoption today occurs when a stepparent formally adopts a spouse's child by an earlier marriage. This kind of adoption can be one of the easiest if it is uncontested. An uncontested adoption usually means that the other biological parent of the child is either dead, has abandoned the child, or is willing to consent to the adoption. All the stepparent has to do is fill out and file the necessary parers.

In most states, there are simple pre-printed forms for stepparent adoptions. You can get these forms from your state Bar association, a legal stationery store, an office supply company, or your local library. To adopt a stepchild, you must complete the necessary forms and show proof that the other parent is dead, has abandoned the child, or consents to the adoption. For a small fee, an attorney can review these documents before you file them in court.

Contested stepparent adoptions can be complicated. As a general rule, the law will not strip the other biological parent of rights over the child unless there is a very good reason to do so. That means the other parent has a good deal of power to prevent a stepparent adoption. Always get an attorney's help if the child's other parent disagrees. Adoption may be possible in that situation, but it will be more difficult.

f. BIOLOGICAL GRANDPARENTS' RIGHTS OVER ADOPTIVE CHILDREN

In the old days, once a child was adopted, his or her biological grandparents had no rights. However, in recent years, the grandparents' rights movement has begun to change these earlier laws. In a few states, it is possible — though difficult — for grandparents to get visitation rights with their biological grandchildren even after the grandchildren have been adopted by someone else. Sometimes this is done informally, but grandparents have hired their own attorneys to get continuing legal visitation rights.

Also, several states now give biological grandparents a very important right when their grandchildren are to be placed for adoption: the grandparents are given the option of adopting their own grandchildren. In a few states, grandparents are even given first option to adopt the grandchildren, meaning that no one else can adopt the grandchildren if the grandparents choose to adopt them. In other states, grandparents may have to compete with other potential adoptive parents. However, courts are often swayed to the grandparents' side if there is evidence of a longstanding, loving relationship.

This aspect of the grandparents' rights movement is still very new. If you want to adopt your grandchildren, get a lawyer's help. Many complex legal issues may be involved. The help of a skilled attorney could mean the difference between a successful adoption or losing the grandchildren to some other adoptive parent.

g. RIGHTS OF OTHER BIOLOGICAL RELATIVES

A few states are beginning to recognize that an adopted child can benefit from continuing contact with other blood relatives. Usually this involves the child's other brothers and sisters, especially if a child has spent substantial time with them. Visitation with brothers and sisters may be important emotionally, and sometimes can be made a legal requirement of the adoption. The law in this area is still somewhat new and will continue to develop in the years ahead.

h. ADOPTION OF OLDER CHILDREN AND ADULTS

Most couples want to adopt children who are very young, usually less than a year old. However, there are more older children available for adoption throughout the United States. These children often have a hard time finding an adoptive home. As a result, couples may find it legally much easier and often less expensive to adopt an older child.

There are special problems involved in adopting older children. Many of these children have vivid memories of being abandoned by their natural parents or of being moved from foster home to foster home over many years. It is very common for older adoptive children to suffer a strong emotional reaction to the problems they have faced in their short lives. Even two-year-olds who have been abandoned or neglected have feelings of being unwanted, even though they may not be able to put these feelings into words.

Many children's counselors have observed that older children go through a "honeymoon" period after their adoption. The honeymoon often lasts several months, and during this period the child may be a model child, seemingly quite happy, and the picture of perfect manners. However, the honeymoon period comes to an end after the child begins to understand that the new home is permanent and misbehavior will not likely result in removal. When the honeymoon ends, some adoptive parents are quite surprised to see the child suddenly change into a sullen, unhappy, angry youngster.

If you adopt an older child, you've got to be prepared for the end of the honeymoon and be ready to deal with your child's changing moods. Older adoptive children need to grieve over the loss of their natural families and their feelings of being unwanted or abandoned. If the child is not allowed to grieve, he or she may misbehave or act aggressively. Don't blame yourself for your child's anger; it is a common reaction.

You and your adopted child should go to a trained family counselor for family therapy sessions. A counselor can help the child grieve and help you understand what is happening to your child. Some states provide resources to help parents deal with the emotional problems of a newly adopted older child. Often, such services are made available to any adult who adopts a special needs child.

In some states, one adult can adopt another adult. This happens rarely, and usually involves an adult who wants to be adopted by an older mentor or stepparent. Some states do not allow adult adoptions, or require that the adopted adult must be a certain number of years younger than the adult who is adopting. Anyone interested in an adult adoption should seek help from an attorney to avoid legal problems.

15
CHILDREN BORN OUTSIDE OF MARRIAGE

During the 1992 presidential election, Vice President Dan Quayle made headlines when he criticized a fictional television character for glamorizing having a child out of wedlock. The intensity of the debate that followed highlighted a fact of modern American life: it is no longer rare for children to be born outside the traditional family setting. This is a dramatic change from earlier in this century, when a nontraditional pregnancy was a source of outrage and scandal.

Until the 1960s, most states followed an ancient legal tradition of regarding children born outside of marriage or because of adultery as legally inferior. "Illegitimate" children in particular suffered serious limitations. Legally, illegitimate children were not entitled to inherit from their fathers and sometimes even had diminished legal rights with respect to their mothers. In many states, lawyers and judges often said that the illegitimate were "children of no one."

a. THE SITUATION TODAY

That situation has changed dramatically because of changes to federal laws. In the late 1960s, the United States Supreme Court struck down state laws dealing with illegitimacy. With a few exceptions, almost all state laws dealing with such children were declared invalid. On the whole, any law or regulation that treats illegitimate children differently from others is unconstitutional.

Under federal law, all state laws and regulations on illegitimacy must substantially promote a permissible state purpose. The federal courts have found that a large number of state "purposes" are not permissible. For example, if a parent dies without signing a will, inheritance must be roughly the same for both legitimate and illegitimate children. Likewise, the government cannot deny benefits to illegitimate children that would be available to legitimate ones, including benefits such as welfare, survivor's benefits, social security, or parental child support payments.

The only laws and regulations that have been declared valid usually deal with the problem of proving who the actual father of the child is. For example, some state laws have been upheld where they required sufficient proof that a child was the biological offspring of a man before the child could collect certain benefits. Occasionally, regulations have been upheld if they prohibited benefits being paid to a child who was not a dependent of the man in question. However, laws and regulations that limit benefits to dependent children are relatively rare.

Today, most states are fully aware of the court decisions dealing with children born out of wedlock. As a result, discrimination against illegitimate children is unlikely. Nevertheless, sometimes parents of children born outside marriage do encounter problems. As a broad rule, any discrimination based on the child's status should be assumed to be illegal. If you are a parent or caretaker whose child is discriminated against in this way, you may be able to stop the discrimination by making a phone call to elected officials who oversee the agency or business. Many elected officials are happy to help out local constituents.

If making elected officials aware of the discrimination does not solve the problem, you should contact a local attorney or a civil rights group. Groups such as the American Civil Liberties Union have been very active in supporting the rights of children. Some child welfare organizations may help out, as well as local attorneys willing to volunteer their time to assist a child. You may be able to legal help at minimal expense by contacting one of these groups.

b. PATERNITY PROBLEMS

In every state, a woman who has given birth to a child can usually file a "paternity suit" against the man she says is the biological father. This may be true even if the woman is married at the time the child is born, provided she claims someone other than her husband is the biological father. If the paternity suit succeeds, the court will order the man and the child to undergo blood tests. Today, scientific tests can tell whether a man has fathered a particular child with a high degree of accuracy.

State child welfare agencies may also be able to sue over paternity. Usually this is done because the child is being supported in part by public welfare assistance and the alleged father has not been helping to support the child. The state, in other words, wants to identify the "deadbeat dad."

Once a child's paternity is verified, the biological father is liable for paying a fair share of the child's expenses until the child reaches adulthood. In other words, the father may have to pay child support. If the father has substantial property, a paternity suit may be necessary to establish the child's right to inherit property on the father's death.

Paternity suits are most common when the child's mother is unmarried. However, special problems arise if the mother was married but claims that some other man was the father. In every state, the law creates a strong presumption that a child born during a marriage is the child of the husband. If the husband has claimed the child as his own or if the mother has told people that the husband was the father, it may be a waste of time to file a paternity suit against some other man. This is because the law will forbid the husband and wife from denying their own earlier claims about the child's paternity.

Paternity suits are fairly routine matters in most cases. Many state child welfare agencies have preprinted forms they use when filing a paternity suit, and a number of legal organizations do the same. Women wishing to sue a man for paternity can find help from public interest groups such as legal aid clinics or the civil clinics located at many law schools throughout the country. Often these organizations charge little or nothing if the woman truly cannot afford to pay for an attorney.

A far different problem may arise, however, if the biological father of the child is a wealthy or powerful person. In that situation, a paternity suit can attract huge publicity and could be difficult to resolve. Any woman who believes her child was fathered by an influential or wealthy man should obtain the help of an attorney skilled in family law. A paternity lawsuit that is not handled properly could result in other serious legal problems, such as a suit for defamation, libel, or other damage to the "father's" reputation.

16
WHAT IS THE LAW DOING ABOUT MISSING, KIDNAPPED, AND EXPLOITED CHILDREN?

The problem of missing, kidnapped, and exploited children first began to receive organized national attention in the 1970s. But it was not until the 1980s that national and state governments began establishing significant new programs to address the problem. Today, state and federal law enforcement now has a well-organized set of agencies and programs designed to assist in locating and helping missing, kidnapped, and exploited children. There are a number of private agencies involved in the movement, some supported with federal grant money. Among the more prominent of these is the National Center for Missing and Exploited Children, which operates a toll-free national hotline at 1-800-843-5678.

The number of missing and exploited children has grown steadily in recent decades. In 1988, for example, the federal government estimated there were more than 438,000 lost, injured, and otherwise missing children in the United States. That same year, there were an estimated 354,100 children abducted by family members (often by a parent), and another 3,200 to 4,600 abducted or kidnapped by nonfamily members. About 450,000 runaways were reported in 1988, and another 127,100 children were reported as "thrown away" — abandoned by the parents or "kicked out" of their homes.

a. PARENTAL KIDNAPPING

As the statistics above show, one of the most serious problems is parental kidnapping of children. Most abducted children fall into this category. In a real sense, parents — and especially divorced parents — have far more to worry about from each other than from total strangers.

Parental kidnapping usually occurs during or after a divorce when two parents begin squabbling over child custody issues, and one parent then violates the judge's child custody order by taking the child and vanishing. As a general rule, any serious violation of a divorce court's child custody order can result in criminal charges. In most states, parental kidnapping is a felony. If the abducting parent then takes the child across state lines, any felony case of parental kidnapping can be referred to the FBI.

Some cases of parental kidnapping have gotten a lot of attention from the press. These often involve allegations that one parent is abusing the child, so the other parent then abducts the child supposedly to stop the abuse. As touching as these cases may seem, the fact remains that parental kidnapping is a serious criminal offense that is unlikely to solve the legal problems at stake. If a parent illegally abducts a child, that parent commits a crime and may lose all future custody rights.

Any parent who genuinely believes the other parent is abusing a child should not flee, but should get qualified legal help and fight the other parent in court. That is the best way to enforce the legal rights of both parent and child. Two wrongs do not make a right, and two crimes will only get both parents in legal trouble without necessarily solving the real problem.

In recent years, there have been many reports of underground networks of safe houses that help parents hide the children they have abducted. These networks have arisen because of a perception that some state legal systems have not done anything to stop child abuse by the other spouse. Some have compared the networks to the underground railroad that helped smuggle slaves out of the South prior to and during the Civil War. However, the fact remains that anyone helping to kidnap a child is guilty of a crime, including conspiracy.

If your child is the victim of parental kidnapping, your divorce lawyer should make a report to the judge and local law enforcement officials. If your lawyer is not available, you should make the report directly.

The divorce judge may issue a contempt citation against the kidnapping parent or may be inclined to modify the custody arrangement so that the kidnapping parent is stripped of all custody rights. Law enforcement officers refer parental kidnapping cases to a prosecutor so that state criminal charges may be brought.

Once the kidnapping parent is charged with a state felony offense, the state prosecutor can ask the FBI to become involved in the case. FBI involvement is very important if the child has been taken across state lines. On the prosecutor's request, the U.S. Attorney can issue a Federal Unlawful Flight to Avoid Prosecution warrant authorizing FBI agents in all states to arrest the kidnapper and take the child into custody for eventual return. The FBI will also coordinate an investigation with international authorities if the child has been taken out of the country.

If the kidnapping parent is a member of the United States' armed forces, the U.S. Department of Defense (DOD) may be able to offer special help. DOD's Office of Family Policy, Support and Services in Arlington, Virginia, will help track down the service member and resolve any dispute over custody. If necessary, DOD will return that person to the proper state for prosecution and will help locate the missing child.

b. OTHER MISSING CHILDREN

A large number of children vanish each year for reasons other than parental kidnapping. Some are abducted by strangers, and some are later found to be runaways. Unfortunately, many abducted or runaway children are later found to have been murdered, abused, or sexually assaulted. Many parents and caretakers today feel they cannot safely leave children alone even for a minute, for fear that some psychopath may kidnap them.

The disappearance of children (when parental kidnapping is not suspected) immediately should be reported to local law enforcement officials. Parents and other caretakers should not hesitate to make the contact, even if there is a possibility the child simply has forgotten to call home or return home by a curfew. It is better to report a possible missing child and be mistaken than to lose precious time that could save an abducted child's life. If there is any clue what happened to the child, law enforcement may be able to locate the abductor before the child can be removed from the local area.

A large number of organizations are involved in helping locate missing, kidnapped, or runaway children (see Appendix 7). If your child has been abducted by a stranger, you should contact these organizations for help. Also make sure that the local prosecuting attorney is actively involved in the case. Prosecuting attorneys can get help from federal law enforcement officials.

c. EXPLOITED CHILDREN

Another growing problem in the United States involves exploited children. This includes children who are illegally employed in hazardous occupations, as prostitutes, or in making child pornography. Sometimes, abducted children are kept in a form of slavery and abused by adults. Occasionally, child runaways are exploited by others, especially young girls who have already fled an abusive home environment. Studies throughout the United States show an alarming number of girl runaways end up selling their bodies to make a living.

State and federal laws have severe penalties for child exploitation. Generally, it is against the law to employ children in hazardous occupations of any description, and adults who use children in this manner could be charged with engaging in slavery or "peonage." Every state has especially strict laws dealing with child prostitution and pornography. In some states, offenses of this type are life felonies when very young children are involved. Likewise, the federal government now has severe criminal penalties for child prostitution. Even purchasing child pornography is a potential federal crime.

There are several agencies who actively investigate charges of illegal child exploitation (see Appendix 7). Any person who has witnessed a child-exploitation offense should report the incident to local or federal law enforcement officers. This can include the U.S. Department of Justice's Child Exploitation and Obscenity Section in Washington.

The trade in foreign child pornography flourishes in the United States. All such shipments are illegal under federal law, and purchasers can be arrested. Anyone who wants to report international shipments of child pornography should contact the postmaster of the local post office, or call the Pornography Tipline of the U.S. Customs office. The address and phone number of the Tipline is included in Appendix 7.

17
WHO CONTROLS A CHILD'S EDUCATION AND RELIGIOUS TRAINING?

Throughout most of American history, each state was responsible for the education of young people. However, since the 1950s, the federal government has regulated education through a variety of means. The federal courts have been the most obvious instrument of regulation, especially through lawsuits that ended racial segregation of public school systems and prohibited other forms of discrimination. Federal funding has been another important means of regulation, because Congress and the federal bureaucracy have attached conditions to federal dollars sent to local schools.

This "federalization" of education has eliminated old practices that were unfair and deprived certain groups of an equal education. However, there have been drawbacks as well. One of the most serious is that schools now worry about being sued over matters that would not have been a concern in the past. Public schools in particular shy away from anything controversial for fear of a possible lawsuit. For example, a large number of school systems now prohibit corporal punishment even though it often is not illegal in milder forms. (The law on corporal punishment is discussed in chapter 7.)

The religious training of children is also a prominent legal issue. Until the 1960s, most schools had some form of religious ceremony or training. However, a series of lawsuits starting in the sixties resulted in court decisions barring the use of public school facilities for many forms of religious practice. These rulings have been controversial, and some schools have defied the federal courts on this question. Nevertheless, a large number of public school systems now avoid religious material of any description for fear of a lawsuit.

a. PUBLIC VERSUS PRIVATE SCHOOLS

Obviously, the public schools are most closely regulated by government because they are funded through public tax money. Every state, district, and territory provides a system of tax-paid public education. Federal courts have said that once such a system is provided, a public education must be equally available to all children who wish to attend. This has been the basis for court decisions outlawing racially segregated schools, discrimination against disabled children, and similar matters. (See chapter 10 for a full discussion on discrimination against children with disabilities.)

All states now have laws that require children of a certain age to attend a school, whether public or private. Attendance is compulsory until age 16, though some states set the age at 17 or 18, and a few allow some students to drop out if they meet certain conditions, such as having a job. However, under the Constitution, students have the option of attending private schools if they or their parents wish it. Compulsory attendance does not mean that a student must attend a public school.

Public education throughout the United States is financed through a combination of local property taxes and revenues shared with school systems by state and federal agencies. As a result, every taxpayer helps pay the cost. This has led to criticisms that students who attend private schools should be allowed at least some benefit of the tax dollars paid to educate them. Prior to 1992, President George Bush was a prominent advocate of a "voucher" system that would have allowed students to use a certain amount of tax dollars to pay for a private education. This voucher proposal, however, has not been made law and almost certainly would result in a new round of lawsuits if it were ever approved.

Private schools are subject to far less government regulation, but even they are not entirely exempt. For example, private schools must obey nondiscrimination laws. Any private school that receives public grant money in any form must follow federal guidelines. Many private universities, for example, receive millions of dollars in government grants and are legally bound to follow federal and state nondiscrimination laws.

However, private religious schools usually have the legal authority to refuse admission to students who do not share a particular religious faith or creed. This is true even if most people who share that faith or creed are members of only one race or group. In some parts of the United States, the religious-faith exception has resulted in private schools that are racially segregated. However, the courts have done nothing about this situation if the private school is consistent in imposing the religious-faith requirement on all applicants. Public schools, on the other hand, could never impose a similar requirement under present law.

Any form of group-based discrimination in a public school may give rise to a lawsuit. Suits are less likely to be successful against private schools that do not receive public grant money. Lawsuits involving discrimination in educational settings can be quite complicated and almost always involve questions of federal law.

Anyone who wants to sue a school for discrimination must get the help of a qualified civil rights attorney. Help is available from private organizations, such as the American Civil Liberties Union and the National Association for the Advancement of Colored People. These organizations have been involved in many major education discrimination cases over the past 30 years.

b. HOME SCHOOLING

Some states now permit "home schooling" as an alternative to public or private school education. Home schooling usually means the parents either provide or hire someone to give educational instruction in the home. Instruction of this type must meet certain minimum requirements. However, minimum requirements differ among the states that allow home schooling.

Some states, for example, prohibit home schooling unless the instruction is provided by a licensed teacher or tutor. Licensing requirements are so severe in some states that, in effect, home schooling is seldom permitted. Courts are unwilling to find fault with these strict laws, and many judges conclude that there is no absolute right to have a home schooling program.

Other states permit parents who hold no teaching licenses to provide education only to younger children. A few states are quite liberal in the authority they give to parents who wish to home school their own children. However, these states usually impose other requirements. For example, some states require that the parent who will home school children must have a college degree or some other advanced training.

As a general rule, home schooling is not permitted unless the parents get advance permission from the local public school system or some other public authority. This usually means that the parent must fill out an application and must submit some sort of plan for the children's education. The plan must meet minimum requirements imposed by the state. Usually, parents must agree to have their home schooling arrangement inspected from time to time.

Home schooling has become increasingly popular among parents who disagree with the secular nature of public education in many parts of the United States. These parents often want the children's education to include a particular moral or religious viewpoint that is not available in the public schools. There are companies that sell prepackaged lesson programs that parents can use. However, parents should never assume that a prepackaged educational program will always meet local home schooling laws. Check to make sure before buying the program.

In recent years, home schooling has been a fertile source of legal disagreements. Many parents involved in home schooling resent the intrusion of school officials into the home, and have sued when local officials were unreasonable. School authorities, meanwhile, have taken parents to court on the grounds that particular home schooling programs are legally inadequate. If you want to set up a home schooling program for your child, make sure all legal requirements are met. An attorney's help in fulfilling legal requirements could be useful.

Another aspect of home schooling deserves some thought. Many parents are unable to provide advanced educational courses to students in upper grades. Few parents, for example, are qualified to teach organic chemistry, calculus, or literary criticism at the level that is needed to prepare students for college. For that reason, some parents interested in home school either place upper-level students in private schools or hire qualified teachers to assist in home schooling.

Also, parents should give some thought to the impact home schooling may have on a student's ability to win acceptance to particular colleges or universities. As a general rule, students who can prove academic achievement through competitive test scores may suffer few drawbacks as a result of being home schooled. Some internationally known universities have a policy of encouraging great diversity on the campus, and may be excited about accepting a home schooled student who has high test scores. However, students who cannot prove academic achievement may suffer a disadvantage in college applications. Some colleges and universities are unwilling to accept a student who has few of the traditional measures of academic achievement, such as good grades achieved in a competitive educational environment.

c. GENDER-BASED DISCRIMINATION IN THE SCHOOLS

Private schools have considerable leeway in establishing special programs based on gender, or even in admitting only male or only female students. However, gender-based discrimination in public schools is on far less firm legal footing in today's world.

South Carolina's famous military academy, the Citadel, provided a striking example of the problems publicly funded schools face today. In 1993, the Citadel faced a serious lawsuit filed by a female applicant denied admission because of her gender. Some people felt the Citadel faced the prospect either of admitting women or converting to a wholly private school (receiving no state funding). Without doubt, gender-based discrimination is one of the more serious legal problems American schools will face in the decades ahead.

1. Gender-based discrimination in general

Gender-based discrimination has been a special problem because the traditional

English and American view of education holds that boys and girls should be educated differently. Until well into this century, "male" schools focused on military skills, science, professional careers, sports, and achievement-oriented pastimes. "Female" schools concentrated on housekeeping, the fine arts, social skills, preparing for motherhood, and becoming a suitable hostess for the husband's household. All of this has changed radically.

Today, the old view of separate education for boys and girls is under legal attack. The civil rights movement in the 1950s and 1960s made successful gains for racial minorities, and inspired a similar women's movement against gender-biased traditions. Beginning in the late sixties, lawsuits have been brought by women who believed they were legally disadvantaged solely because of their gender. Congress approved Title IX of the Education Act Amendments of 1972, which outlawed gender-based discrimination in many educational programs.

Gender-based discrimination has been an especially difficult problem for the courts. Most judges agree that males and females must be treated differently at least some of the time, if only because of their different roles in human reproduction. However, the courts have had a very hard time saying exactly what kinds of "discrimination" are proper and what kinds are not. As a broad rule, federal law now requires that males and females have equal educational opportunities. In practice, cases of alleged discrimination can be very hard to resolve.

2. Sports opportunities

No topic has demonstrated the complexity of this problem like sports in the schools. Sports-related gender discrimination suits have become almost trendy throughout the United States, and many public schools and schools that receive public grants are trying to overhaul their sports programs as a result. Female students are suing schools to get an equal chance at sports activities.

For many years now, the courts have struggled to find a way to give females equal opportunity to engage in competitive sports while recognizing the different physical abilities of males and females. The results are inconsistent and unsatisfactory.

The first question courts usually ask in these cases is whether the female is asking to engage in a "contact sport." There seems to be broad agreement that contact sports include boxing, rugby, wrestling, ice hockey, and football. However, some courts have included basketball, baseball, and soccer, while other courts have not. Subject to some notable exceptions, the courts frequently have held that schools are entitled to treat male students differently with respect to contact sports, usually because more physical danger is involved.

However, the courts have not been completely consistent. In 1974, a 12-year-old girl who was 5'9" tall and weighed more than 200 pounds was refused permission to try out for interscholastic football. The Ohio school system refused permission on grounds that all girls had a lighter bone structure and were more susceptible to injury. A federal judge found this argument unpersuasive because the school had made no effort to "weed out" boys who had lighter bone structures and who also might be more easily injured. In 1983, a Missouri court reached a similar conclusion.

Lawsuits involving access to noncontact sports are more successful. Noncontact sports may include everything from tennis to ultimate Frisbee competitions. A typical lawsuit in this area involves a school that has a fully funded team for a particular sport but denies admission to females and has no similar team for females. In this situation, a lawsuit is far more likely to succeed.

However, judges generally try to avoid requiring that males and females must always be integrated into the same teams. Schools have been able to escape legal trouble by seeing that there are roughly equal sports programs for males and females. Court-ordered integration of a previously all-male team has occurred only where a school completely failed to provide a similar team or opportunity for females. In other words, the courts are willing to use a "separate-but-equal" analysis here, even though this would be unthinkable in a racial discrimination case. The courts justify this on the grounds that males and females have different physical abilities.

Cases involving gender discrimination in sports involve complex civil rights issues that still are changing at a rapid pace. As a result, these cases always should be handled by lawyers. Any student or parent who wants to pursue such a lawsuit should find an attorney to handle the case. Certain civil rights-oriented groups may be willing to provide an attorney in noteworthy cases.

d. STUDENTS WHO ARE ALSO PARENTS

Statistics show that the rate of pregnancy among school-aged females has risen steadily over the last few years. In earlier times, pregnancy of a student was grounds for expulsion. Schools justified this policy because a student's pregnancy created a bad example and was a disruptive influence.

However, federal law now prohibits public and publicly funded schools from engaging in most forms of discrimination against students who are pregnant or have become parents. Some courts have even forbidden schools from forcing pregnant females or young mothers into special programs designed to segregate them from other students. However, females can voluntarily agree to participate in such programs, provided the educational opportunities are at least equal to what other students receive.

Larger school systems throughout the country have created strong incentives for young mothers to enroll in these programs. Students may get special transportation for themselves and their babies, access to free day care, special nutritional meals, and child care training. These benefits are far better than what the student would receive in a standard school setting.

Students who are pregnant or who have become parents are entitled to take time off from school whenever necessary to give birth or provide necessary child care. Schools usually cannot penalize the student, other than requiring that the lost time be made up.

Discrimination can still happen to students who are pregnant or who have become parents. Usually, most elected school officials are well aware of the federal laws on this subject. If not, a complaint filed with an elected official may be enough to end the discrimination. Otherwise, the student or her parents should seek the help of a qualified civil rights lawyer or a civil rights organization.

e. SEXUAL HARASSMENT IN SCHOOLS

Many people remember teachers who liked to touch students or talk to them in sexually suggestive ways. Until the 1970s, no effort was made to recognize this type of behavior as a special problem. Some unusually bold teachers were disciplined, but many people ignored the problem. Today, the law is far less tolerant of this type of behavior.

In the 1970s, tough new laws and regulations were made to deal with sexual harassment. As a general rule, teachers and other school personnel are strictly required to avoid any suggestive behavior toward a student. This can include everything from telling off-color jokes, referring to sexual matters, or unnecessary and suggestive touching. Teachers and other school personnel should avoid any behavior that might be construed as sexual in nature, no matter how innocent or "fun" it might seem. School workers' careers have been ruined because of very serious lawsuits.

Many schools now have written policies dealing with sexual harassment. Teachers and other school workers should read these policies carefully. Students who have suffered harassment or their parents have a right to file a written complaint, usually with the head of the school or the elected body that governs the school system. Federal and state regulations require that these complaints be taken very seriously. In severe cases, a state or federal lawsuit may be possible, and students have sued for a large amount of money as damages for pain and suffering.

If a complaint of sexual harassment is made against you, consult a lawyer immediately. Alleged sexual harassment in a school setting arouses strong feelings in a community. Any publicity can jeopardize careers and cause serious disruption, even if the complaint later proves to be false. In that environment, a teacher or other school worker may be unable to get a fair hearing of the complaint.

f. SEX EDUCATION

Traditionally, many Americans viewed sex education as a private family matter that should be handled according to the family's religious and moral beliefs. Today, the traditional view is under increasing challenge. Rising rates of teen pregnancy and venereal disease have spurred a number of states and school districts to institute sex education programs in the schools. Many states now require some type of instruction, often including lessons on the benefits of sexual abstinence and the risk of contracting venereal diseases or AIDS. The Secretary of Health and Human Services has even advocated some type of sex education in elementary school.

There is little agreement throughout the country on exactly what should be taught. Some states or school systems refuse to permit any instruction whatsoever, while other schools or districts give free contraceptives at school clinics. The controversy surrounding sex education in the schools means that widely different policies will be followed in different parts of the country for some time to come.

g. PRAYER IN THE SCHOOLS

Another highly controversial topic has been prayer in the schools. Beginning in the 1960s, cases were brought challenging mandatory prayer policies. Most suits were brought by students who were non-Christians, including some atheists, on grounds that mandatory prayer subjected them to religious indoctrination contrary to their beliefs. On the whole, the suits have been successful in the public schools, though private religious schools can enforce a mandatory prayer policy.

Many public schools prohibit any type of religious activity because they are afraid of possible lawsuits. In 1993, for example, a school principal in Jackson, Mississippi, was disciplined for allowing a nonsectarian prayer each day in the school after an overwhelming majority of students voted in favor of the idea. As this example showed, the legal issue does not involve a simple question of "majority rule." It only takes one person to file a lawsuit, and many school districts have spent enormous amounts of money on cases they later won. For this reason, many public school systems do not permit any type of religious activity whatsoever.

The United States Supreme Court has shown some willingness in recent years to retreat from its earlier hard-line stand against school prayer. A school may conduct certain kinds of nondenominational activities without violating federal law. However, many schools are unwilling even to try. They have decided the wiser policy is to avoid any possibility of a lawsuit because even winning lawsuits can be very expensive.

As a general rule, teachers and other school personnel should become familiar with their school's policy on prayer. Private religious schools can permit or require mandatory prayers, but public schools are on far shakier ground. No school worker, however, should ever engage in any religious activity on school time that is contrary to the school's policy.

h. RELIGIOUS TRAINING OF CHILDREN

Outside the public schools, the government and the courts generally will not interfere in the religious training of children. Public schools must maintain a secular approach to education, but this does not apply to parents and other adult caretakers. The First Amendment of the U.S. Constitution guarantees a right to religious liberty, and the courts consistently have held that the government cannot interfere in the private religious affairs of the family.

However, there are times when private religious training can become a concern of the courts. For example, when parents of different religions divorce, they may disagree over their children's religious training. The divorce judge can make a reasonable order specifying which parent controls religious training. Often, the judge chooses the parent who has primary responsibility for the child's care or uses some other neutral method of deciding the issue. Orders of this type have been upheld in the past, provided the court does not try to impose its own particular religious beliefs on parents of a different faith.

Religious training also concerns children who are in the state's custody, including foster care arrangements. Many state-owned institutions try to maintain a more-or-less secular approach to child-rearing. However, state facilities will often give the child access to religious teachers from the faith to which the child previously belonged or that the child prefers. Likewise, the state may place the child in a private facility or foster care family appropriate to the child's religious faith. For example, a child born a Catholic may be placed in a Catholic foster facility. Some religious groups have insisted that the states allow children to continue being trained in the faith of their birth, wherever possible.

18
BENEFITS AVAILABLE TO CHILDREN AND THEIR FAMILIES

The American government is generous in the benefits it gives to children and their families, though there are other industrial nations that give more. On the whole, American policy encourages families to have children by offering tax breaks and credits, public assistance, and parental leave from work when a child is born or when a family member has a serious health problem.

a. FAMILY LEAVE

In 1993, the United States Congress approved the landmark Family and Medical Leave Act, which President Clinton signed into law. The new federal law took effect August 5, 1993, and provides a significant new benefit to families. Now a parent or family member can take time off from work to deal with family medical problems, with no risk of being penalized by an employer. Employers do not have to pay employees on family leave, but they cannot fire the employee or diminish job rights or privileges because of the time off.

Not all employers are covered by the federal law. To be covered, the employer must have had at least 50 workers within a 75-mile radius of the work site. The 50-worker requirement can be met if at least 50 workers were employed for each workday of any 20 or more calendar work weeks in the current or preceding calendar year. (Any 20 weeks are sufficient, even if they are not consecutive.) In practice, this means that the law only applies to larger employers. However, state and local governments can be included, as well as larger private businesses.

Employees are not eligible for the family leave benefits unless they have been employed for at least 12 months and have worked at least 1,250 paid hours of service during the previous 12 months. In other words, many part-time workers will not be able to claim the benefits.

Under the Family and Medical Leave Act, each eligible employee can take up to 12 work weeks of leave in any 12-month period for the birth of a child. The same amount of leave can be taken if a child is placed with the employee as part of an adoption or foster care arrangement, provided the child is under 18 years of age or is incapable of self-care because of a disability. However, the leave must be taken within a year after the date of birth or placement of the child. The employee can begin the leave period before the birth or placement of the child if necessary for medical reasons or to complete the adoption or foster care arrangement.

Both fathers and mothers are entitled to the same amount of leave after a birth, adoption, or foster care placement. However, if both the father and mother work for the same employer, then the employer is authorized to limit them both to no more than 12 weeks of leave during any 12-month period. This restriction may seem unfair, but it was designed to prevent employers from temporarily losing two workers just because they have hired both spouses.

Sometimes employees may have accumulated substantial amounts of paid vacation time, paid personal leave, or paid family leave. If so, the employee can choose to substitute this paid leave for any portion of the 12-weeks of unpaid leave. Employers can require this substitution if they wish. In effect, this means that bosses can force their workers to use up accumulated paid leave time during the 12-week family leave period.

The same general requirements govern taking time off to nurse a sick child. Workers can receive up to 12 weeks of leave penalty-free if necessary to care for a child or other family member who has a serious health condition requiring hospitalization, residential care, or continuing treatment by a health care provider. However, there is one important exception. If both parents work for the same employer, *each* parent will be entitled to a full 12 weeks during any 12-month period. This is based on the belief that a serious illness may require more attention from both parents than a newborn or adopted child.

To take advantage of family leave, a worker must give advance notice to the employer. In addition, the employer can ask for verification proving that the leave really is being taken because a child or family member has a serious medical condition.

Special conditions apply to teachers and other instructional personnel in public and private schools. Employers of these teachers may impose some special conditions about leave that will be taken near the end of an academic term. These conditions are somewhat complicated. Most school systems should have written policies explaining the conditions to their employees. Teachers and other instructional personnel should request information about the special conditions before giving notice of their intent to take family leave.

Other special conditions apply to federal civil service workers and employees of the United States Congress. Again, these workers should request copies of their employer's policies in advance.

Violations of the Family and Medical Leave Act can result in two possible actions:

(a) Any employee who has been denied family leave may file a complaint with the Wage and Hour Division of the U.S. Department of Labor. Offices of the Division are located in major cities throughout the United States. Check the government pages of your phone book for the address and phone number.

(b) An employee denied family leave benefits can also file suit against his or her employer. In a successful suit, the employer can be forced to pay lost wages (if any), a sum equal to as much as 12 weeks pay, interest, restoration of employment or benefits, or the costs of the suit (including attorney's fees).

If your employer denies family leave, you should file a complaint with the federal Wage and Hour Division first. This agency can force your employer to comply with the law and save you the cost and trouble of a lawsuit. However, if the Wage and Hour Division does not take action to your satisfaction, you should consult an attorney with experience in federal labor law issues. Call your state bar association to get the name of a qualified attorney (see Appendix 1).

Many states and local governments have their own family leave laws. Most duplicate the federal law, but some are more generous. Hawaii, for example, gives some employees a right to family leave after working only six months on the job. Florida gives some state workers up to six months of leave for family reasons, and Kansas allows some of its state workers up to a year. North Carolina, meanwhile, has a special family leave law authorizing parents to take up to four hours leave a year to visit their children in the schools. The idea behind the North Carolina law is to involve parents more in school-related activities.

Anyone considering taking family leave should investigate whether state or local laws give greater benefits. You can ask your company's personnel officer or your local labor department or state elected official.

b. SOCIAL SECURITY

Unmarried dependent children and some grandchildren may be able to receive Social Security benefits from their parent or grandparent's account. Benefits may be available if the parent or grandparent was fully or currently insured under the Social Security program and has retired, has become disabled, or has died.

In the case of children (but not grandchildren), benefits are potentially available in three situations:

(a) for unmarried dependent children under the age of 18, if not in school.

(b) for unmarried dependent children under the age of 19, if enrolled as a full-time student in a secondary school, and

(c) for unmarried dependent children of any age who became disabled before reaching age 22.

Children who meet these qualifications must file an application with the Social Security Administration and prove that they met one of the three requirements either on the day the application was filed or on the day the parent died.

Benefits may be available even for some grandchildren, and for children born out of wedlock or who are not biological children of the parent. Under Social Security rules, benefits can be paid to —

- a natural legitimate child,

- an illegitimate child who can inherit from the parent if parenthood is acknowledged in writing, by court order, or if the child was born of an invalid marriage or was living with and supported by the parent,

- a child adopted prior to retirement or death who can prove dependency on the parent,

- a child who has been a stepchild of the parent for at least a year prior to the parent's retirement, or at least nine months prior to the parent's death, and who was living with the parent and was receiving at least half of his or her support from the parent, and

- a grandchild if both parents are dead or disabled and the grandchild was both living with and being supported by the grandparent for at least a year before the grandparent's retirement, death, or disability.

Children do not receive the full amount of Social Security benefits that would be available to the insured parent or grandparent. The child or grandchild will only receive half of an adult's benefit if the parent or grandparent is still alive, or 75% if the parent or grandparent is dead. Permanently disabled children are eligible for benefits until death. The benefits of other children terminate when they reach the maximum age of eligibility.

The child or a supervising adult must file an application before benefits will be received. All applications must be in writing, but the best way to apply is to visit the nearest office of the Social Security Administration. Offices exist in most larger cities. Clerks at the office will help you prepare the necessary forms. The following information is needed:

- Social security numbers of the child, the parent or grandparent, and the spouse of the parent or grandparent

- Dates when the parent or grandparent worked, resumed work, became ill, became disabled, or died
- Descriptions of illnesses or disabilities of the child and the parent or grandparent (if applicable), and the names and addresses of doctors or hospitals that have provided treatment
- If the parent or grandparent was a veteran treated in a VA hospital, that person's service serial number and VA claim number
- Information on the kinds of jobs the parent or grandparent held for the last ten years of work

It is a good idea to bring this information when you visit your local Social Security Administration office.

c. PUBLIC ASSISTANCE

Throughout the United States, a network of public assistance programs exist to help children and families living below the poverty level. These programs vary somewhat from state to state, but all include several features. Any family with dependent children and low incomes can often qualify for food stamps, free distribution of food, Medicaid, subsidized school lunches, special programs for preschool children, and in some cases subsidized day care.

Another important form of public assistance is called Aid to Families with Dependent Children (AFDC). This program is created by federal law but administered by the states under their own regulations. As a result, the rules on AFDC vary considerably from state to state. However, certain features are the same in all states.

Foremost, AFDC is meant to provide a minimum level of financial security to families whose incomes fall below certain levels. This varies depending on the family's particular situation. AFDC is available to families with absent fathers and impoverished mothers, but may sometimes be available in other situations as well. Financial support under AFDC is linked to the number of children under the age of 18 or, in some cases, to children under the age of 21 who are still in school.

Originally, AFDC was established as a means of encouraging such families to become more self-sufficient by giving them some support during periods of relative poverty. In recent years, however, AFDC has been criticized for discouraging self-sufficiency and encouraging unmarried women to have more children as a way of increasing their AFDC payments. The most prominent critic of the program today is President Bill Clinton, who has openly argued that AFDC and many other welfare programs encourage people to become completely dependent on government handouts.

Nevertheless, AFDC cannot be modified unless the U.S. Congress agrees with any changes the President may propose. As a result, many people believe that truly sweeping reforms may be many years in the future. The AFDC program has created a massive governmental bureaucracy both at the federal and state level. Many states receive large amounts of federal funding as a result of AFDC. Efforts to change AFDC may run up against stiff opposition from the states and the governmental bureaucracies that operate the program.

For information on public assistance programs available in your state, call the state agency that supervises services to children. Phone numbers for public assistance or children's support services are usually listed in the government section of the phone book.

d. TAX BREAKS

The federal government and some states also give significant tax breaks to parents. These breaks include a tax deduction for each dependent child, an earned income credit for families falling below certain income levels, and special programs for deducting child care and medical costs from a parent's income before taxes.

Your local Internal Revenue Service office or any personnel office will have information about tax benefits for families. Parents may find it worthwhile to hire a professional tax accountant to prepare tax forms. Professionals can save you enough money in taxes to more than offset any fee you pay.

19
OTHER LEGAL PROBLEMS INVOLVING CHILDREN

There are other laws that apply to children's safety and well-being that can't be easily categorized. However, adults who care for children should know about these laws because they can present significant legal problems. Several of the major issues are discussed below.

a. SEAT BELT LAWS

Many states now require parents to use proper seat belt procedures when transporting children by motor vehicle. For very young children, this usually means placing the child in a properly designed child safety carrier. Carriers may either be built into the car or may be strapped in place by seat belts as required by law or, where there is no law, as recommended by the manufacturer. (**Note:** Some states require that a carrier always be placed in the back seat of a car.) For older children, parents may be required to see that each child is properly strapped inside a seat belt before the car is started.

Some states, including Florida, now absolutely require child safety carriers for younger children, and that all passengers in the front seat of a vehicle (regardless of age) must be in a seat belt. This is a growing trend across the country. Nevertheless, parents can still have legal problems even in states that have no laws on the subject. A parent could be accused of child neglect for failing to use accepted seat belt procedures if a child is later injured in an automobile accident. In serious cases, the parent could be investigated or charged with criminal neglect.

There is another legal problem associated with the failure to use seat belts. In some states the failure to use proper seat belt procedures may interfere with the parent's ability to sue other vehicle drivers who caused the accident or to collect full damages from insurance companies. Attorneys for the other drivers have claimed that some of the injuries caused in the accident resulted from the failure to properly use seat belts. A parent can be held partly responsible for the child's injuries. Likewise, some insurance companies may try to reduce insurance payments based on evidence that a child was not properly seat belted.

Seat belts have not always been widely available in school buses in the United States. However, there is some evidence that certain school bus injuries could be prevented by seat belts. In the years ahead, more lawsuits probably will be filed by parents against school boards who fail to equip buses with seat belts. Eventually, school buses across the country will have to have seat belts. As noted earlier, schools and school systems show a marked desire to avoid the expense of lawsuits.

b. INJURIES TO VISITORS

In many cases, but not always, property owners owe no greater duty to children than to anyone else who enters their property. Most states say that property owners have a general legal duty to take reasonable steps to see that people visiting the property are not injured. This obligation may include clearly marking hazardous conditions or other threats, warning visitors of dangers, or seeing that visitors do not go into a dangerous area. Property owners can be legally liable, for example, if a visitor slips and falls on an icy walkway or a slippery pavement, if a dog bites the visitor, or if the visitor falls into a hole that was hard to see. Many property owners maintain casualty insurance to help pay for any such injuries.

Many states say that the property owner's duty is less serious if people trespass. Even then, the duty may be significant. If the owner knows that trespassing is occurring, the law still requires the owner to take reasonable steps to eliminate or warn about known hazards. This can include posting signs, erecting strong fences, and so forth. Property owners can get into very serious legal trouble if they make a trap designed to injure trespassers. A number of successful lawsuits have been filed, for example, when property owners placed spring traps or blasting devices designed to go off when a trespasser entered the property. Criminal charges are possible in this situation.

Even for less serious dangers, a property owner may be liable if the injured trespassers are children, especially if the property is an "attractive nuisance." The word "nuisance" seems misleading because we usually don't think of a nuisance as attractive.

Under the law, an "attractive nuisance" can be any thing or condition that might be expected to attract young children for play, but that an adult should know poses a threat of danger to children. Examples might be as dangerous as scalding water leaking from a water heating vent or as commonplace as an unfenced swimming pool.

If your property is attractive to children, you cannot protect yourself from liability by posting signs warning of danger. Many small children may be unable to read or may not appreciate what the signs say. The only way property owners can protect themselves is to take steps to see that children do not enter the property at all.

Many construction sites, for example, are enclosed by tall fences partly as a means of keeping out children. Owners often build strong fences around swimming pools for the same reason. In some cases, the owner of the property may even need to contact and warn the parents that children may trespass. The warning should be in writing and a copy of it kept in a safe place. Even then, an injury to a child attracted onto the property by an attractive nuisance may still result in a lawsuit and legal liability, no matter what precautions were taken.

As a general rule, owners should carefully inspect their property to see if anything exists that might be attractive to children. If children often come to play at some location, this should serve as a warning that any injuries to the children could result in a lawsuit. Proper steps should be taken to fence off the area, prevent children from entering, and warn parents or caretakers. If children like to play on your property, you should get insurance, because it may not be possible to completely eliminate the possibility of injuries to children.

If your child is injured on someone else's property, you should consult an attorney. If the property owner took few steps to protect children, you may be able to sue.

If a child is horribly maimed in such an accident, the parent or caretaker may have little hope of providing for the child's future needs except by suing the property owner. This is easier if the property owner has an insurance policy capable of paying for the child's injury and care. A parent should always get the help of an attorney who specializes in personal injury law before filing a suit.

c. **GUN LAWS**

Guns are an increasing problem among young people in the United States. On any given day, a significant number of children bring guns to school. Some school districts now forbid children to bring back packs or other containers that might conceal a weapon unless the container is made of see-through material. Other schools require schoolchildren to pass through metal detectors before going to class each day.

Many parents, teachers, and other adults are worried. One estimate in 1993 indicated that about 14 children are killed with guns every day in the United States. This and other statistics show that minors today view guns as necessary for self-protection, not just as a badge of adulthood or a tool for recreational game hunting. Many children know how to get hold of their parents' guns or weapons owned by other adults. All adults should be especially cautious in that situation.

Today, adults are often liable if they have failed to prevent children from gaining access to firearms or other dangerous weapons. Children have injured other children and passersby with their parent's guns. Children have used other adult's guns in attempted robberies and other crimes. In a few states such as Florida, negligently giving a child access to a gun can constitute a crime. These children's victims and their families can sue on grounds that the gun owner negligently failed to secure the gun. Liability can be substantial, especially if someone was killed.

If you own a gun, keep it in a secure place out of reach of children. This usually means locking it in a secure cabinet or closet and making sure children do not have access to the key. Adults cannot count on protecting themselves from legal problems merely by placing the gun in a hard-to-reach place. Steps should be taken to make sure that children cannot gain access to the gun under any circumstances. Children are more ingenious than many adults think when it comes to finding forbidden objects.

d. DANGEROUS INSTRUMENTALITIES

Guns are only one type of dangerous object children may gain access to. The law in many states recognizes a number of other things as "dangerous instrumentalities" — objects or materials that are dangerous if not used properly. Some states, for example, recognize that cars and other motor vehicles are dangerous instrumentalities. Farm equipment, explosives, poisons, and other hazardous material also qualify. In many cases, parents and other adults can be held liable if they give children access to dangerous instrumentalities and the children then cause an injury.

As a broad rule, adults should treat all potentially dangerous objects and materials the same as they would treat guns. This means that children should never have ready access to them. Adults may wish to inspect their homes and property to identify objects and materials that might qualify as dangerous. Preferably, all should be kept under lock and key so that children have no possible access.

e. CHILD LABOR LAWS

At one time in the United States, child labor was a very serious problem for society. In the early part of this century, many very young children still toiled in factories and fields doing grueling labor for up to 10 to 12 hours a day, sometimes seven days a week. This was common in the last century. Many American industries got their start primarily with a workforce consisting of children and unmarried women. The very first textile mill built during New England's industrial revolution, for example, had a workforce of young boys and girls under the age of 12.

By the beginning of the 20th century, many Americans began to realize how detrimental child labor could be, at least as it was practiced at the time. Major laws were passed by the states and the federal government. Today, these laws prohibit many forms of child labor, except for a few types of work that are traditionally regarded as acceptable for young people. For example, in most parts of the United States children of certain ages can have a newspaper route, help with chores on a family farm or at the family's house, or babysit.

Child labor laws apply most vigorously to children under the age of 14 to 16, although there are exceptions. Some states prohibit all minors from engaging in certain occupations, especially hazardous ones. On occasion, states or federal agencies may require that children be licensed before they can engage in other kinds of occupations. This has been true, for example, in the entertainment industry, where child performers frequently must prove that they are not engaging in hazardous work and are continuing to receive an education.

See Appendix 4 for a list of child labor agencies. Anyone interested in employing a child in any capacity should check with the proper agency first. If the child must be licensed, the employer should see that the license is issued before the child engages in any work. Employers who violate child labor laws can be found guilty of criminal violations. If children are injured in the workplace, employers can face very expensive lawsuits.

f. LEGAL LIABILITY FOR CHILDREN WITH SERIOUS DISABILITIES

Adults who care for children with serious disabilities may run into other kinds of legal problems. An adult has a duty to restrain a child whose disability results in violence or predictable carelessness. The child's parent or caretaker can be responsible for any harm caused by the child, especially if the child harms someone who is unable to stop the child (e.g., another child or another person with disabilities).

Parents of children with serious disabilities may have a legal obligation to care for the children as long as the disability continues. Many states recognize such a duty even after the children grow to adulthood. In some cases, the duty may continue until the parents' death. If parents do not have the means to give this kind of continuing support to a child with disabilities, the state will step in. But other parents may have substantial resources. Parents with enough assets who fail to provide for children with serious disabilities may be held legally responsible for any money spent by the state to care for the children. Such cases are rare, but they do sometimes occur.

PART IV
MEDICAL ISSUES INVOLVING CHILDREN AND THE LAW

20
SURROGATE PARENTING AND REPRODUCTIVE TECHNOLOGY

Modern medical science has made it possible for couples who previously couldn't have children to become parents. Yet, in the process, incredibly complicated new legal issues have been created. Many cases involving the new reproductive technology have prompted troubling headlines that have stunned many Americans. Some of the most personal aspects of family life have been paraded in media reports.

For example, newspapers have reported stories of couples "contracting" other women to bear their infants. Embryos have been removed from their natural mothers and transplanted into other women, who have agreed to give birth to the child. Still other embryos have been fertilized in test tubes and transplanted either into the mother or another "surrogate" for eventual birth. On some occasions, the eggs or semen may even be donated by yet another person unrelated either to the married couple or the surrogate mother.

In another dramatic case, a divorced couple became engaged in a bitter legal dispute over ownership of several frozen human embryos previously fertilized and stored for possible future use. Another lawsuit involved the question of who "owned" the frozen semen of a man who had died. In still other cases, men who donated semen for artificial insemination later tried to claim paternal rights over the children born through this method.

The law on reproductive technology is changing rapidly and dramatically. For that reason, it is not possible for this or any other book to predict exactly how the law will change in years ahead. Even lawyers and judges have been surprised at how quickly the law has evolved. This chapter outlines some of the more important legal issues surrounding the new reproductive technology. It is important to understand the kinds of legal issues that people face when they use these new reproductive methods.

a. SURROGATE PARENTING

Surrogate parenting is a very old concept. The Bible, for instance, tells how Sarah, Rachel, and Leah (who were infertile) allowed their fertile women servants Hagar, Bilha, and Zilpah to be impregnated by their husbands. Throughout history, women have agreed to become pregnant and bear children that are later handed over to a sister or a friend who could not have children of her own. In earlier times these types of arrangements were not viewed as a legal problem. They were done as a matter of unwritten custom or out of kindness, without any involvement by the legal system.

Today, all of that has changed. Women who agree to become pregnant with a child fathered by the husbands of other infertile women present one of the most explosive legal issues on the American agenda. Medical science has clashed with traditional moral attitudes deeply ingrained in the American mind.

The national debate on the subject came to full flower in 1987 and 1988 when the news media began issuing extensive reports on the "Baby M" case in New Jersey. The father of Baby M was married to a woman who suffered from a serious illness that could have made pregnancy dangerous. The couple wanted a baby, however, in part because most of the father's own family were Jews killed during the Holocaust in World War II. The father hoped to continue his family's blood line. They answered an advertisement from a clinic specializing in surrogate parenting arrangements.

The couple entered into a contract with another married woman who agreed to become pregnant through semen donated by the father. This surrogate mother's husband also consented to the arrangement. Under the contract, the infertile couple agreed to pay the surrogate mother $10,000 plus a variety of other expenses, including medical bills. Later, however, the surrogate mother said she developed a strong bond to the child, Baby M, even before the girl was born. After the birth, the surrogate mother became convinced she had to keep the child, and she and her husband secretly took the child to Florida where they remained in hiding.

The child's biological father later located Baby M and filed suit to enforce the terms of the contract. However, the New Jersey Supreme Court ultimately ruled that the contract was unenforceable partly because it was an attempt to "sell" a baby, which is illegal in all states. However, the father still won part of his claim. The court ruled that the biological father and biological mother both should have parental visitation rights, but that the child would be placed in the custody of the biological father and his infertile wife. Like many other news-grabbing cases involving children, this case was made into a television movie broadcast across the country.

The *Baby M* case has sparked an intense national debate. Many states have now outlawed surrogate parenting agreements or placed restrictions on them. The law is still changing rapidly and unpredictably throughout the United States, although most states addressing the issue tend to disfavor surrogate parenting.

By late 1993, Arizona, the District of Columbia, Indiana, Kentucky, Louisiana, Michigan, Nebraska, New York, North Dakota, and Utah had outlawed surrogate parenting contracts in one form or another. New Hampshire and Virginia, meanwhile, allowed limited forms of surrogate contracts but generally required a court's approval and supervision of the arrangement. Nevada law authorized surrogate contracts, but was vague as to whether the courts could enforce such agreements. The State of Washington prohibited such agreements if any money changed hands, but whether these contracts were enforceable was still unresolved.

Only two states, Arkansas and Florida, had taken steps by late 1993 to broadly permit some types of surrogate contracts. Arkansas had the most liberal law on the subject, although serious uncertainties remained. Like all states, Arkansas continued to outlaw the selling of babies, so that any exchange of money as part of a surrogate contract could cause serious legal troubles.

Florida, on the other hand, absolutely prohibited any exchange of money except to pay the mother's expenses. By late 1993, Florida also allowed the surrogate mother to void the contract up to seven days after birth and thus potentially to keep the baby, no matter what the contract said. Like Arkansas, however, Florida still had other laws that could cause serious legal problems for even the most carefully crafted surrogacy contract.

A wide array of legal strategies can be used to attack almost any surrogate contract, even in states that allow them. In many states, for example, fornication and adultery are still criminal offenses or are considered to be "against public policy." As a result, a surrogate contract with an unrelated woman could be deemed to be "immoral" and thus unenforceable. If the surrogate mother is married, the law in many states creates a very strong presumption that her husband is the father of any child born during the marriage. If the husband attempted to assert his paternal rights, it is not at all certain that the biological father who donated the semen could win in court.

Likewise, many potential surrogate mothers are unwilling to enter into contracts if they will not be paid in some form, even if only for medical expenses. However, every state prohibits the selling of babies. An unfriendly judge could interpret any exchange of money as a violation of these laws, except in a state that expressly authorizes payment of expenses. On the other hand, if no money is paid in support of the contract, some judges may be inclined to say that the contract is unenforceable because it lacks legal "consideration." Under standard contract law, an exchange of something of value is called consideration. Consideration is needed to create a valid contract.

Another serious problem exists for couples who live in states that either outlaw surrogacy contracts or have no clear law on the subject. Such couples may be inclined to try to enter into a contract in a state like Arkansas or Florida. However, sometimes these couples may not be able to take advantage of the law of another state unless they first establish legal residence there or have some other significant contact with that state. This could mean the couple might have to move to the state, find living quarters, and remain in that state until they can meet legal residency requirements.

Surrogate parenting is a highly risky and potentially expensive legal venture. Anyone wanting to enter into a surrogacy contract should at the very least seek out highly qualified attorneys to assist them—preferably attorneys with a demonstrated track record in surrogate parenting. In particular, any couple interested in taking advantage of another state's laws on this subject should first consult with a qualified attorney, preferably one licensed in the other state. Ask the attorney to determine whether a residency requirement exists.

Even then, there is no guarantee that the courts will enforce the contract should a dispute arise, no matter how thorough the lawyer has been. Many surrogate contracts in the United States have been completed successfully, usually because the surrogate mother does not attempt to question the contract's terms. However, if the surrogate mother decides to keep the baby and go to court, there is no guarantee *in any state* that her efforts will completely fail. Judges have been highly sympathetic to the complaints of surrogate mothers.

In any event, couples should never attempt to enter into a surrogacy contract in a state where it is prohibited. Some states have criminal penalties for anyone who violates the surrogate parent law. Very serious problems could be created even if the surrogate mother is completely cooperative.

Couples should be careful in states that have little or no clear laws on the subject. At best, a surrogate contract in those states is a gamble. Some judges may be inclined to enforce the contract, but others may not. Worse still, a couple in one of these states may end up in the unenviable position of becoming a "test case" as to whether a surrogate contract is legal in that state. Test cases often involve years of expensive lawsuits and emotionally draining appeals. Many people are unwilling to endure this kind of trouble.

Finally, surrogate agreements occasionally have been used by persons who either are single or who are involved in an unmarried relationship. Some single men, for example, have attempted to find a surrogate mother to bear children who will be handed over to the father's permanent custody. On occasion, homosexual couples have tried much the same. Obviously, the already serious problems associated with surrogate parenting contracts are only intensified in these situations. State legal systems have been generally hostile to surrogate contracts even for married couples. Unmarried people and those involved in unconventional relationships can only expect less favorable treatment.

b. GESTATIONAL SURROGATES

In recent years, medical science has begun to perfect the creation of test-tube babies. The procedure was originally devised for couples who could not get pregnant, but who nevertheless were able to produce healthy eggs and semen. Physicians were sometimes able to fertilize the mother's egg with the father's semen in a laboratory and then implant the resulting human embryo into the mother for eventual birth. A considerable number of couples have been able to bear children through this method. Today, hundreds of test-tube babies are successfully implanted each year in the United States.

However, physicians quickly realized that this test-tube procedure opened up another unusual possibility. Some women are able to donate a healthy egg for fertilization, but they are unable to carry the baby to term. However, in this situation it is possible to take the mother's egg and fertilize it with the father's semen, then implant the fetus in the womb of another woman who agrees to act as a "gestational surrogate." Sometimes couples have even used eggs or semen donated by someone else, with the resulting fetus then being implanted in another woman who agrees to carry the child to term.

This situation is different from surrogate parenting in that the host mother is not the biological mother of the child, but is merely carrying someone else's fetus to term. In one highly publicized case, a woman even agreed to be implanted with the fetus of her own grandchild because her daughter was unable to carry the fetus safely.

Significant legal problems continue to exist even in this situation. Many of the states that outlaw surrogate parenting have statutes so broadly written that they also prohibit gestational surrogacy agreements. However, at least one state — Florida — has enacted a law that treats gestational surrogacy completely differently.

In Florida, a contract for gestational surrogacy gives a couple far more legal rights than does a surrogate parenting agreement. The major requirements are that the woman who agrees to be the gestational surrogate must not be the biological mother of the child; the child must be the biological offspring of either a husband and wife legally married to each other, or at least one of them; and the wife must genuinely be unable to get pregnant. It is permissible for either the egg or the semen (but not both) to be donated by a third party, so long as the other requirements are met.

Under Florida law, both the married couple and the gestational surrogate must enter into a contract in advance. No money can exchange hands except to pay for reasonable expenses (including legal costs and medical expenses, which can be large). The couple must agree to accept the child no matter what impairments it might have. Finally, a court hearing must be held immediately after the child is born to make sure that all legal requirements have been met. Most important, there is no provision allowing the gestational surrogate to void the contract and keep the child, provided all other legal requirements are met.

The Florida law on this subject took effect in 1993. At the time of writing, no court case had yet arisen to challenge the new law. However, lawsuits are possible, including some that may challenge the law as unconstitutional for a variety of reasons.

As a result, anyone relying on the Florida law *cannot* be absolutely certain of their legal rights. The statute could still be declared invalid by a court.

Gestational surrogacy has been used in other states, though Florida is a leader in this area because it has a law making it legal. Obviously, a gestational surrogacy should not be attempted in a state where it is illegal. Even in states like Florida, an attorney's help is absolutely crucial in making sure that all legal requirements are met. Any mistake could result in great expense, embarrassment, and heartbreak.

Once again, some couples in other states may wish to take advantage of more liberal laws like the one in Florida. However, as a general rule, any couple choosing to do so should first consult an attorney in the other state. They should ask the attorney to determine whether they must establish legal residence in that state before entering into a contract. This is a possible problem that surrogate parents encounter as well.

c. SEMEN DONATIONS

Sperm banks, a service that stores donated sperm, are now in many major American cities. As a general rule, most semen donors are young men (often of college age) paid to donate sperm, and in return they sign agreements abandoning any claim either to the semen or to children that may be born because of their donation. A few states now require donors to undergo some sort of medical test, usually to detect venereal diseases or the AIDS virus. (Any woman receiving a semen implant *always* should make sure the donor has been tested. Ask *before* the semen is implanted.) Many donors also fill out questionnaires providing some information about themselves, their intelligence, health, and other factors that may be relevant to future mothers seeking artificial insemination.

Many sperm banks and similar clinics are reputable organizations that carefully comply with the law. However, there have been instances of abuse in the past. One notorious case involved a fertility doctor who added his own sperm to semen donations before implanting them in his patients. Some estimates said the doctor may have used this unethical and illegal procedure to become the biological father of as many as 75 children. Women have also contracted diseases from donated sperm, although this is less common now that medical testing of donations is standard practice among reputable sperm banks.

Many states have laws specifying that, under many conditions, a sperm donor abandons any right to claim that he is the legal father of a child produced with his semen. Nevertheless, there are usually certain legal requirements that must be met. Many states recognize that people sometimes engage in a kind of "informal" sperm donation — meaning that the mother-to-be either has sex with the donor, or the woman plants donated sperm in her body without a physician or sperm bank's help. Legally, an informal donation of this type is risky.

There have been several cases in the United States involving couples who engaged in some type of informal semen donation. On a few occasions when a child was produced, the biological father later tried to claim legal rights over the child. A number of courts have ruled that the father had a right to be the legal father unless the sperm was donated under a written agreement in which the father clearly waived his rights over the child. Sperm banks often see that such legal formalities are met, and attorneys can do the same. Nevertheless, a woman seeking to become pregnant through artificial insemination should keep in mind that the failure to observe these formalities may cause legal problems later on.

Legal disputes of this type can be especially bothersome if the woman is married to a man other than the semen donor. In all states, children born during a marriage are presumed to be the offspring of the husband. However, this presumption can sometimes be defeated by modern blood tests that are capable of proving who the father of a child is with great accuracy. If the donor can prove his fatherhood, he may be able to claim visitation and other rights over the child. At the very least, he may be able to involve the couple in a protracted, embarrassing, and costly lawsuit.

Many married couples seeking to have children through artificial insemination do not want the biological father to retain these kinds of rights. Couples should make absolutely sure that the semen donor has abandoned any rights he may have, and that he has done so *in writing*. Again, sperm banks should take care of this, but if you have any doubts, get a qualified attorney to help you. The expense involved in preparing a waiver for the donor to sign is minimal compared to the cost of a lengthy custody dispute after the child is born. Once again, preventive law is far better and far less expensive.

Once the biological father has validly waived his rights, any child born of artificial insemination almost always will be legally regarded as the mother's and, if she is married, as her husband's. If the mother is single, the law will generally recognize that the mother alone is the legal parent. A number of women who decide not to marry have given birth through artificial insemination and are very happy rearing their child alone. In many parts of American society, the earlier stigma of single motherhood has largely vanished.

Artificial insemination has become more common among women involved in nonconventional relationships, often with another woman partner. Again, the mother of the child almost always is regarded as the legal parent, and there is little the state can legally do to interfere. Sometimes a mother's live-in partner wants to adopt the child. A few adoptions of this type have succeeded, but many have not. The law in many states disfavors adoptions of this kind and often creates legal barriers that many women choose to avoid.

d. FROZEN OR STORED EMBRYOS, EGGS, AND SEMEN

The new reproductive technology has made it possible for human embryos, eggs, and semen to be frozen for future use. As you might expect, this development has resulted in novel legal problems. Cases have been brought involving either the ownership of frozen human embryos or the question of whether such embryos are "persons" entitled to legal rights. Likewise, there also have been disputes over the ownership of frozen human semen. In the years ahead, disputes of this type will become more common as reproductive technology grows more complex.

1. Frozen embryos

In the mid-1980s, the world first heard news of an unusual case involving a childless California couple who had died in a plane crash after employing the services of an Australian fertility clinic. The couple had experienced trouble becoming pregnant. As a result, the Australian clinic had taken eggs and sperm from the couple, fertilized them in a test-tube procedure, and then froze the embryos.

After the couple died prematurely, an unusual legal fight erupted. The issue was whether some effort should be made to implant the embryos in a surrogate mother so that any children could inherit the substantial estate left by the dead parents. The California court ruled that the so-called "orphan embryos" were not entitled to inherit the parents' property even if they were implanted in a surrogate mother. In sum, the embryos were not yet legally considered to be living human beings.

Yet another unusual case occurred in the late 1980s when an infertile couple sought help from a Virginia fertility clinic. They also engaged in a test-tube procedure that produced a frozen human embryo. The couple later decided to move to California and asked the Virginia clinic to transfer the frozen embryo to a clinic in San Diego, where they hoped the mother would be able to undergo a successful implantation. However, the Virginia clinic refused. When the couple sued, a court ruled that the frozen embryo was the property of the couple and had to be sent to the San Diego clinic.

Perhaps the most celebrated frozen embryo case of all took place in Tennessee in the early 1990s. A couple had frozen several of their own embryos after undergoing test-tube fertilization procedures. Before the wife could become pregnant, the couple's relationship soured and they agreed to divorce. However, the wife demanded that the frozen embryos be handed over to her so she could become pregnant herself or could donate the embryos to other childless couples. The husband strongly disagreed, because he did not want biological children brought into the world under these circumstances. Instead, he wanted the embryos destroyed.

The Tennessee court ruled in favor of the father. In doing so, however, the court established several important new rules of law. The court first noted that any state statute on the subject would control the question of who owns frozen embryos. Tennessee, however, had no such statute. In fact, the court noted that only Louisiana appeared to have a law on the subject. (The Louisiana law forbade the destruction of frozen embryos, requiring instead that they be made available to other couples if the biological parents no longer wanted them.)

Second, the Tennessee court said that since there was no state law, any contract the couple had entered about the embryos was binding. However, the couple involved in this lawsuit had entered into no agreement at all.

Third, the court said that several other factors must be considered if there is no state law and no contract. For example, the court said that one of the divorcing parents might be entitled to the embryos if there was proof that he or she could not have children any other way. Otherwise, the court said that the law would favor the parent who did not want the embryos implanted. Adults should not be forced to become biological parents against their will, the court said. As a result, the father won the case.

The dispute in Tennessee and the other frozen-embryo cases suggest that the law expects frozen embryos to be treated a certain way. As a general rule, the courts agree that the "parents" of frozen embryos can decide what will be done with those embryos unless state law says otherwise. However, if the parents cannot agree, a serious legal problem is created. Couples involved in creating test-tube frozen embryos should sign a written agreement saying exactly what will happen to the embryos if they ever disagree or if they divorce. If there is no written agreement, the law favors not allowing the embryos to be born unless one of the parents proves unable to have offspring any other way.

Generally, frozen embryos are not entitled to inherit property from the parents. Inheritance may be possible if a parent dies after the embryo is implanted in a womb, but probably not otherwise. Too many problems could be created if a frozen embryo could inherit property. The law in every state requires that a dead person's assets must become the absolute property of a living human being within a certain number of years. As reproductive technology advances, embryos possibly could be kept in frozen storage for years or decades.

This could mean that the dead person's property actually belongs to no living human being during this time. Moreover, the frozen embryo might not produce a living fetus even after implantation. On the whole, frozen embryos are unlikely to be recognized as "legal persons" for most purposes.

2. Frozen semen

Frozen human semen has presented distinct legal problems in recent years. One 1993 California case involved a man who was dissatisfied with his life and eventually committed suicide. Before he died, he deposited several samples of his own semen to be frozen at a local sperm bank. In his will, he left most of his property — including his frozen sperm — to his girlfriend. He hoped that his girlfriend would agree to be artificially inseminated and give birth to his children.

A lower California court concluded that semen could not be given away in a will but should be destroyed upon the donor's death. On appeal, the higher court disagreed. The California appeals court said that semen could be bequeathed like any other items of personal property. Moreover, the appeals court found that there was nothing illegal in an unmarried woman becoming pregnant with frozen sperm if the donor was dead, at least in California.

It is worth noting, however, that the courts do not consider human reproductive tissue, such as embryos or sperm, to be "property" in the same sense as an automobile or a house. The courts have generally found that there are definite limits on how reproductive tissue can be treated. All of the cases generally have found that the woman and man who donated the tissue have great control over it. But that control is not limitless. It is entirely possible that state laws could regulate the use of reproductive tissue. As a result, anyone involved in a dispute over embryos, eggs, or semen should check to see if there are state laws that will affect the dispute.

Finally, there have been cases where health care providers mistakenly destroyed stored human embryos that were awaiting transplant. Sometimes courts have allowed lawsuits in this situation. In 1985, a Pennsylvania court awarded $50,000 to a couple when a doctor destroyed the couple's eggs and sperm, which had been placed in a device to create a test-tube embryo. The court decided that the couple had a legitimate claim for mental suffering.

e. USING MEDICAL TECHNOLOGY FOR SEX SELECTION

The ability to create human fetuses outside the womb has created another unusual possibility — that couples can choose the gender of their baby in advance. There are now techniques to significantly (though not completely) separate "male" human sperm from "female" sperm. Through this means, a couple could have the husband's semen separated and then use the "appropriate" sperm to fertilize the mother's egg. This way, there is a much greater chance that the baby will be the gender they choose.

As medical technology advances, it may become possible for a couple to choose exactly which fetus they want implanted into the mother's womb. This would also allow the couple to select the child's gender. In fact, couples may be able to select a variety of other traits for their baby, too, perhaps choosing the embryo likely to be the smartest or most attractive. Some people have criticized this possibility as allowing "designer babies." Unquestionably, this practice raises serious moral and ethical questions that may result in new laws being passed to regulate the practice.

Gender selection can have medically useful functions, however. For example, the blood disorder hemophilia (where a person's blood cannot clot) is an inherited genetic disorder. Hemophilia is transmitted by the mother's genes, but only male children actually suffer from the disease in the vast majority of cases. Gender selection could be very useful if a mother knows that hemophilia runs in her family's blood line. The mother might choose to have only female children, avoiding the possibility of having a hemophiliac male child.

21
WHEN CAN SOMEONE SUE OVER BIRTH-RELATED PROBLEMS?

This century has seen great improvements in medical technology. Physicians can now prevent many birth-related problems that used to result in infant deaths. Today, such deaths are much rarer, even though the United States ranks relatively high among industrial nations for infant mortality. In any event, parents now have come to expect a healthy baby almost as if it were a "right."

That may explain the rapidly increasing number of birth-related lawsuits in recent decades. Throughout the United States, birth-related medical malpractice suits have risen so dramatically that some are calling it a crisis. In some states, a number of obstetrician-gynecologists have stopped assisting in childbirth because they have been sued so much or because their insurance rates were too high. Many state legislatures and assemblies have approved major reforms. Even then, the crisis seems to have continued.

Today, birth-related lawsuits involve legal issues unthinkable only decades ago. People have sued because their children were not born healthy. Some have sued because they became pregnant after a physician performed a sterilization procedure (such as a vasectomy) that somehow failed. Others have sued because an abortion procedure failed, perhaps resulting in the birth of a deformed or injured child. Still other people have sued because their physicians failed to warn them that their baby was likely to be born with a severe impairment or deformity.

There are many types of injuries associated with childbirth. Lawsuits have been brought for the following reasons:

- improper prenatal care,
- injury to the fetus during an examination,
- failing to properly vaccinate the mother against diseases that can injure the fetus (e.g., rubella), and
- botched deliveries.

If the health care provider's performance fell below the acceptable standard of care recognized by the profession, a lawsuit of this type will succeed. You must be able to prove that the provider did things that were unacceptable, or failed to do things considered to be standard procedure.

a. BIRTH-RELATED INJURIES

The most common types of birth-related injury in recent years are neurological problems or brain damage. A baby can be brain damaged if it was deprived of air for too long during or after birth. A child's brain can be so badly injured that it will never have a normal life. The most severely injured children often are profoundly retarded and must have constant care for the remainder of their lives.

The cost of providing such care can be large even in milder cases, and in the worst cases can be many millions of dollars. Malpractice suits also include claims for *intangible injuries* (e.g., pain and suffering). If the physician was reckless in causing the injury, juries also may be able to award huge *punitive damages* (awards of money designed to punish the misconduct). A few birth-related lawsuits have resulted in verdicts of tens of millions of dollars.

If you are a parent whose child has suffered *any* birth-related injury or has been born with a serious medical problem, you should immediately check to see if the attending physician committed malpractice. You should do this even if you aren't sure what caused the injury. Have an independent specialist examine your child and determine what caused the injury. Sometimes injuries are no one's fault. But at other times, the injury may have been the responsibility of the attending physician or other health care providers. On a few occasions, physicians and hospitals have tried to conceal the fact that they caused an injury to a newborn child.

If malpractice seems likely, you should contact an attorney who is trained in personal injury cases and, preferably, has experience in medical malpractice or birth-related lawsuits. Most attorneys will have an initial meeting with you at no charge. In some cases, an attorney may take a case on a contingent fee, meaning that no fee is paid unless the attorney wins the case. (Keep in mind, however, that you may have to pay the attorney's reasonable expenses, such as phone bills and travel. Always ask the attorney what expenses will be billed.)

A skilled attorney will conduct a "discovery." This means the attorney can get a court order requiring the physician, hospital, or other health care provider to hand over records, answer questions, and give sworn testimony. Through discovery, the attorney will be able to decide how strong the case is and how much money, if any, the health care providers should pay for the child's injury. Some attorneys will try to settle a case out of court, without conducting a trial. If damages are very great, however, a trial may be necessary to determine how much money is owed to whom.

Physicians and health care providers are very aware of the possibility of malpractice claims. Any physician involved in childbirth, however, should be especially careful in documenting every abnormality during a pregnancy, no matter how slight. All such abnormalities should be discussed with the parents wherever possible. Many birth-related lawsuits come about because parents were completely surprised by their child's impairment. This may lead the parents to conclude that everything was all right until the health care providers botched the child's birth.

Extensive medical tests are now done during every pregnancy. This includes relatively expensive procedures such as ultrasound, amniocentesis (taking a sample of amniotic fluid surrounding the fetus), and complex genetic testing. Many people have complained that this testing dramatically increases the cost of today's pregnancy care.

However, many physicians and health care providers use extensive testing on the advice of their lawyers. There is a widespread belief that the only way to prevent lawsuits is test for every possible medical problem, including some that may be rare or unlikely. In today's legal climate, "unnecessary" testing is a fact of life that seems unlikely to change.

b. BIRTH DEFECTS AND WRONGFUL BIRTH

Birth defects are something every parent fears. At one time, there was no way to detect birth defects in advance. As a result, women who became pregnant had no choice but to wait until the child's birth to learn if it would be healthy or if it would lead a limited life. Today, medical science can detect a variety of problems long before birth occurs, sometimes in the very early stages of pregnancy. Because of this early detection, lawsuits can be brought when a health care provider fails to properly perform tests to detect potential birth defects.

This type of lawsuit usually is called "wrongful birth." The name refers to the belief that parents properly warned about potential birth defects either could have avoided pregnancy or could have had an abortion. In other words, a birth has occurred only because a health care provider committed a "wrongful" or negligent act. Sometimes a wrongful birth lawsuit is filed because health care providers failed to conduct proper prenatal testing, such as failing to read test results correctly or failing to notify the parents of a problem. Other suits have been filed because the health care provider failed to perform any tests at all.

A successful wrongful birth suit will award the parents the money necessary to care for the child's birth defects. Damages of this type are hard to prove. In states where this type of suit is allowed, parents cannot sue for normal child-rearing costs, only for unusual costs associated with the child's birth defect. Determining the exact amount of these costs is difficult. Some states require that the jury assign a dollar amount to the value of the child's love or companionship, which is then deducted from the overall damages.

Wrongful birth cases are controversial, and some states limit them in a variety of ways. Nevertheless, it is possible for parents to sue a health care provider for a substantial amount of money if a child was born with a severe defect that was not properly detected. A few states even permit parents to sue for the entire cost of medical care and supervision throughout the child's life — a sum that could be enormous. Millions of dollars could be at stake.

Time is usually an important element in many wrongful birth cases. Sometimes children may be born with defects that are not immediately obvious but cause severe problems later in life. In a few states, parents may not be able to sue if they fail to file a lawsuit within a few years after the birth or sometimes within a few years after the bad medical advice was given. That means parents must make an active effort to learn whether their newborn has some genetic defect that a physician should have detected earlier.

If parents strongly suspect a birth defect of any kind, they should immediately consult with an attorney experienced in medical malpractice law. The attorney can refer them to experts who can establish whether the defect exists. In any event, an attorney has a professional duty to see that a lawsuit is filed before the legal deadlines expire. For children born with severe defects, proper legal advice could be the only means of getting sufficient money to pay for proper care.

Because more wrongful birth suits are being filed, doctors and health care providers have to make more "unnecessary" medical tests. Obstetricians today feel they must order potentially expensive prenatal genetic testing in almost every case. The obligation to test is even greater if there is any evidence that genetic problems run in a family's blood line. Wrongful birth suits, for example, are most likely to succeed if a couple already gave birth to a deformed child and a health care provider failed to take steps to prevent the same thing happening again.

Parents today must understand why their physicians want to order extensive and costly prenatal testing. This is the only real way health care providers can protect themselves from lawsuits and help deliver a healthy baby. While this is regrettable, it is a necessity imposed by the increasing tendency of Americans to sue each other over these problems.

c. WRONGFUL LIFE

In a few states, it is possible to file a suit for "wrongful life." This is similar to a wrongful birth suit, except that it is filed by the child or in the child's name. The object of this lawsuit is to compensate the child for future pain and suffering experienced because it was born with a birth defect.

Wrongful life suits have been even more controversial than wrongful birth. Many states do not permit wrongful life suits, while others say that all birth-related claims should be combined into the parents' wrongful birth lawsuit.

The criticisms of wrongful life are many. Some state courts refuse to permit a wrongful life suit on grounds that it undermines the value of the child's life. Wrongful life, in other words, treats the child's entire life as though it were an "injury" requiring compensation. A few states have said that it is impossible for a jury to determine the value of an impaired life against the "value" of never being born.

Few states permit wrongful life claims all by themselves. However, states that permit wrongful birth lawsuits sometimes allow the parents to sue for all damages associated with the birth defect. As a result, a skillful lawyer may be able to file a wrongful birth lawsuit that will accomplish the same objective as a wrongful life suit.

d. WRONGFUL PREGNANCY

Another type of birth-related lawsuit is sometimes called "wrongful pregnancy," although some states call it "negligent abortion." When a pregnant woman undergoes an abortion procedure that fails to eliminate the fetus, and later results in a live birth, this is a wrongful pregnancy. Sometimes a child born after a wrongful pregnancy suffers some injury or other problem caused by the failed abortion.

Wrongful pregnancy cases are rare. On the whole, abortions seldom fail to at least kill the fetus. Occasionally a botched abortion may result in infection or other medical problems for the mother, but these problems in themselves do not constitute a wrongful pregnancy if the fetus is dead. Rather, injuries to the mother would give rise to a completely different lawsuit for general medical malpractice.

e. WRONGFUL CONCEPTION

Another birth-related legal problem is called "wrongful conception." This can occur when parents go to a physician for sterilization or contraceptives, but become pregnant anyway. For example, the husband may have undergone a vasectomy that failed, or the mother may have undergone a tubal ligation that failed. Contraceptive drugs or devices may have failed. When that happens, couples have sued to recover the costs of aborting the fetus or, in rarer cases, of rearing the unwanted child to adulthood.

Most states have been very hostile to wrongful conception cases, except when the parents only seek the costs of an abortion. Since 1973, abortions have been widely available throughout the United States. Many judges believe that parents should not be allowed to sue for the costs of rearing a child when the mother could have aborted it. As a result, many judges may try to limit damages to the cost of the abortion.

However, in rarer cases, a substantial claim for damages could be made. For example, suppose the mother cannot safely undergo an abortion or suffers some horrible injury because of the abortion. In that situation, a wrongful conception case could be turned into a claim for substantial damages. If the mother died because of the wrongful conception, the claim could reach into the millions of dollars.

f. LAWSUITS FOR THE STERILIZATION OF A MINOR

At one time earlier in this century, the legal system was quite willing to authorize the sterilization of teenage children in certain circumstances. If the child was retarded or mentally ill, had reached puberty, and showed signs of uncontrollable promiscuity, sterilization was permitted. The justification was that sterilization was necessary to protect the morals and welfare of the child. However, other considerations often came into play.

Prior to World War II, many people seriously believed that retarded and mentally ill persons and some others should not be allowed to have children because they might pass on their disability to another generation. Adolf Hitler's monstrous program of exterminating "genetically inferior" persons brought a sudden end to this kind of thinking. After the end of World War II, sterilization of minors became more and more disfavored. Today, the procedure is unusual, though not unheard of. However, very rigid legal rules apply to all involuntary sterilizations.

First and foremost, it now is clear throughout the United States that involuntary sterilization of anyone — whether a minor or an adult — cannot be done without first getting permission from a judge. Judges on the whole have been increasingly unlikely to grant any such request. Since the 1970s, court decisions on sterilization of minors overwhelmingly refused to allow the procedure or else imposed restrictions so severe that there was no possibility of sterilization being authorized. States imposing these restrictions have included Alabama, California, Colorado, Delaware, Florida, Indiana, Maryland, Missouri, New Hampshire, New York, North Carolina, and Washington.

Only a very few reported court decisions have actually authorized sterilization of a minor, and these generally are not very recent cases. Two cases from 1983, one from Indiana and the other from New York, show what facts persuaded judges to authorize an involuntary sterilization at that time. (It should be stressed, however, that the law has changed significantly since 1983. There is no guarantee judges would agree with these cases today, even in Indiana or New York.)

In the Indiana case, the parents sought sterilization of a 12-year-old autistic child whose mental disability made her uncontrollable, combative, and self-destructive. The girl's physicians stated that the girl reacted violently to the sight of blood, and they feared what would happen when she began menstruating. Moreover, the evidence indicated the girl would remain profoundly retarded throughout her life and would never be able to make an informed decision about when and whether to become pregnant. Based on these facts, the Indiana court found that sterilization clearly was in the child's best interests.

The New York case was similar. A 14-year-old girl was seriously retarded and suffered painful medical problems as a result of abnormal menstruation. The girl's menstrual problems were so severe that she had to take to bed to convalesce. As in the Indiana case, the girl clearly would never be able to make an intelligent decision during her life about sexual matters and pregnancy. In light of these problems, the New York court authorized a partial hysterectomy, which had the effect of sterilizing her.

The common ground in these two cases was that the children had medical problems that clearly would be lessened by sterilization, and the girls would never be able to make an informed decision either to have children or to be sterilized. In other words, the reasons for sterilization went beyond a desire to protect the girls' morals or prevent them from passing on any genetic problems.

Nevertheless, there is no guarantee that courts today would authorize sterilization of a child even if there is a good medical reason to do so. In 1990, the U.S. Congress approved the Americans with Disabilities Act (discussed earlier in chapter 10). This new law imposes severe restrictions on any action that treats persons with disabilities unfairly, including minors who are retarded or mentally ill. As a result, judges today are even less likely to authorize sterilization of a child with disabilities.

There is another reason for caution. Children who have been sterilized have filed lawsuits after they became adults and discovered they could not have families. On the whole, the judge who authorized sterilization is usually immune from suit. Others, however, may not be. There is even a possibility that a sterilized child could sue the parent or other adult caretaker who requested the sterilization in the first place.

Another point should be considered. The courts have repeatedly said that people have a fundamental right to have children and families. Taking this right away is a very serious business indeed. It should never be done lightly. Anyone who is involved in attempting to sterilize a child, however good the reasons seem, should always use any other legal alternatives that exist, other than sterilization. Keep in mind that a sterilized child may later be able to sue, no matter how justified the sterilization seemed when it was done.

22
WHAT IS THE LEGAL STATUS OF THE UNBORN CHILD?

Perhaps the most significant and controversial issue involving children today is the legal status of the unborn. Of course, abortion is the major focus of the debate on this topic. Those who take a "pro-life" position have likened their cause to the 19th century movement to abolish slavery in the United States. Those who favor "pro-choice" view the issue as a paramount question of human rights and privacy. The two sides, in sum, have been unable to agree even on the nature of the issue. The debate is sure to continue in the years ahead.

The controversy over legal rights of the unborn, however, has spilled over into a variety of other issues as well. Pro-life groups have persuaded some lawyers, judges, and legislators to reexamine a variety of laws dealing with the unborn. Today, for example, one of the newest and most controversial kinds of lawsuits are those filed against abortion providers for allegedly causing various kinds of mental distress in their women patients. Likewise, other legal principles that deal with accidents and criminal attacks that injure an unborn child are being reexamined.

This chapter discusses several of the major legal issues that affect the unborn. The future course of the law in this area, however, is impossible to predict. The law dealing with the unborn is changing rapidly and sometimes dramatically throughout the United States. Court decisions can appear suddenly and can drastically alter the law without a moment's warning. Only one thing is clear: the controversy surrounding the law's treatment of unborn children is likely to rage well into the next century in unpredictable ways.

a. ABORTION

Few legal issues have divided the United States like abortion. People on both sides of the issue fervently believe in their causes. As a result, members of the two sides have sometimes attacked each other, sued each other, and occasionally committed crimes against each other as serious as murder. The rightness or wrongness of the opponents in this issue is beyond the scope of this book, as is the rightness or wrongness of abortion. These are moral questions. This book is concerned only with the legal issues.

1. Abortion law in general

Abortion law in the United States was drastically altered in 1973 by the United States Supreme Court's decision in *Roe. vs. Wade*. Prior to that decision, a substantial number of states either outlawed abortion altogether (typically with exceptions for medical emergencies, rape, or other unusual situations) or imposed severe restrictions. The *Roe* decision instantly overturned every one of these laws.

Roe rested on the Supreme Court's interpretation of the U.S. Constitution. Although the Constitution contains no provision expressly guaranteeing a right of privacy, the court held that a right of privacy had come into existence through the years as an "implication" of other parts of the Constitution. In turn, the court said that this right of privacy included the right of a woman *in some situations* to choose whether or not her body would become the vehicle for childbirth. That right necessitated some degree of access to abortions, the court said.

To determine when a woman had the right to an abortion, the court created a rather complicated method of analyzing the issue. The question, said the court, depends on which trimester of her pregnancy the woman is in. (A trimester is a third of the total term of pregnancy, or three months.) During the first trimester, the woman's right to an abortion always legally outweighs any right the state has in preserving the unborn child, according to the *Roe* decision. During the second trimester, the state is entitled to impose only reasonable restrictions designed to protect the health of the mother *if* she chooses to undergo an abortion.

The court then made a statement that has caused considerable legal confusion in recent years. According to *Roe*, the state can restrict or prohibit abortions altogether after the fetus reaches "viability" — in other words, when the fetus can live independently outside the mother's womb. In 1973, the court concluded that viability was only possible during the third trimester of pregnancy. This meant that state prohibition of abortion was legal only for the last three months of a pregnancy.

Since 1973, however, medical science has now reached the point where viability can occur earlier. To date, the full court has not yet considered whether the trimester system used by *Roe* must be changed. Some members of the Supreme Court have suggested that the question needs to be looked at again. Thus, there is a possibility that some future case will expand the time during which a pregnant woman can be forbidden to have an abortion.

Recently, another significant legal problem has come up. During the 1980s and 1990s, the U.S. Supreme Court was dominated by conservative members. Some of these have called for an out-and-out retreat from *Roe*, which would mean that each individual state could outlaw all abortions if it chose to do so. However, the full court has not endorsed this position.

In 1993, many people involved in the abortion issue believed that the appointment of Ruth Bader Ginsberg to the Supreme Court probably signaled at least a temporary halt to the possibility of the court overruling *Roe*. Nevertheless, the election of a conservative U.S. President in the years ahead could result in more conservative judges being placed on the court, increasing the possibility of *Roe* being reversed. Presidents appoint new members to the Supreme Court. Thus, a pro-life president could tilt the court in a new direction.

2. Minors and abortion

Perhaps the most troubling abortion-related problem has been the question of minors who want to abort their fetuses. This is an area of law that remains murky. The U.S. Supreme Court has said on several occasions that the states can require minors to obtain their parents' consent before getting an abortion. However, the court also said there must be exceptions to this general rule. Lawyers and judges alike, however, have strongly disagreed on exactly how these exceptions operate.

The main exception, according to the U.S. Supreme Court, is that minor girls must have some method of getting an abortion if their parents unreasonably withhold consent. Some parents may refuse consent without good reason or may even physically injure a girl who has become pregnant, the court suggested. As a result, states requiring parental consent also must have some sort of bypass mechanism. Typically, states have interpreted this to mean that a pregnant minor must be able to get consent for an abortion from an impartial state judge.

However, the devil is in the details, as many states have learned. The U.S. Supreme Court had suggested that one relevant fact is whether the minor girl is mature enough to consent to an abortion on her own. But judges and lawyers have strongly disagreed about what the word *mature* really means. There also has been disagreement over whether maturity alone is enough for a judge to grant permission.

In any event, the U.S. Supreme Court has allowed a variety of state laws on the subject to remain in effect. In 1993, for example, the court refused to overturn a Mississippi law that required the consent of both parents (wherever possible), or of a state judge if the minor is mature enough to make the decision or if an abortion is in the minor's best interests.

However, similar laws in other states have been struck down in lawsuits. In 1989, the Florida Supreme Court overturned a state parental consent law. It did so on a variety of technical grounds. Foremost, the Florida court found the law invalid because it did not allow adequate appeals of the case, did not adequately define what "maturity" meant, and did not give low-income minors legal counsel they might need.

The type of consent required for a minor's abortion varies considerably. Some states with parental consent laws strictly require consent by one or both parents, or a guardian if there are no parents. South Carolina, on the other hand, has permitted consent by a grandparent. Other states also create other exceptions that make their consent laws weaker.

Partly because of the legal controversy surrounding parental consent, some states have opted for a less strict approach. Several states do not actually require full-fledged parental consent, but that parents be notified that the child will receive an abortion. Typically, the parent, guardian, or other responsible adult must be notified at least 48 hours in advance (24 hours in some states). Sometimes notification must be in writing and sent by certified or registered mail.

While these notification laws are less strict than the consent laws, they still caused controversy. Pro-choice groups argue that parental notification laws actually give parents time to pressure their daughter or even file a lawsuit to stop the abortion. The effect may be the same as if parental consent were required.

The law on parental consent and notification is changing rapidly. Laws that are on the books in some states are sometimes suddenly changed by state lawmakers or by court order. However, by late 1993, states with some form of a parental *consent* law included the following states:

- Alabama
- Arizona
- California
- Indiana
- Kentucky
- Louisiana
- Maine
- Michigan
- Mississippi
- Missouri
- North Dakota
- Pennsylvania
- Rhode Island
- South Carolina
- Tennessee
- Wisconsin
- Wyoming

These states have some form of a parental *notification* law:

- Arkansas
- Georgia
- Illinois
- Kansas
- Maryland
- Minnesota
- Nevada
- Ohio
- South Dakota
- Utah
- West Virginia

In other states that do not have these laws, courts may fall back on the earlier legal requirement that parents had to consent to any medical procedure performed on a child. This could be true even if the state has no written law on the subject. However, a few states clearly give minors broad access to an abortion, with or without parental consent. By late 1993, these states included Connecticut and Florida.

There will be many more lawsuits dealing with parental consent and notification laws in the years ahead. Both sides in the abortion debate are well organized and well funded. There is no indication that the issue will fade away as a major problem in current American life.

Another point deserves mention. In those states requiring parental consent, parents may be able to sue abortion providers if the consent was not properly obtained. In theory, a suit could be filed for "battery" or even malpractice. However, cases of this type would involve complex issues of federal law that could result in years of delay and dispute. Such lawsuits also tend to become heavily politicized. If a state judge gave permission for the abortion, however, there would be very little chance a lawsuit could succeed.

b. RU 486 — THE "FRENCH ABORTION PILL"

In 1993, another abortion-related legal issue made headlines. That year, the new administration of President Bill Clinton announced that it would begin the process of certifying the so-called "French abortion pill" (also called RU 486) for use in the United States. The pill's first medical use here may be in providing treatment for certain forms of tumors or cancer, which may shrink or disappear when RU 486 is administered.

However, there is a possibility the drug may eventually be approved for use in inducing abortions within the first days or weeks after conception. A considerable number of women given the abortion pill spontaneously end a very early pregnancy without an abortion and sometimes without even needing medical supervision.

Whether the abortion pill will be available to minors, however, presents special legal problems. Many states allow young girls or girls of certain ages to give their own consent for family planning or pregnancy counseling services. In some of these states, the authorities may construe these laws to mean that such girls can be prescribed RU 486 without their parent's permission.

However, this may not be true in states that require parental consent or notification before a minor can receive an abortion. Courts may decide that RU 486 is the chemical equivalent of an abortion, meaning that the drug could not be prescribed unless the parental consent or notification requirement is met. If RU 486 is approved in the United States, it seems inevitable that lawsuits on this question will arise at some point.

c. ABORTION-RELATED LAWSUITS

Abortion has created more lawsuits than almost any political issue in American history. Every new state abortion law is inevitably challenged in court. Well-funded groups are often involved, and the case is taken from court to court over a period of years, until no further appeal is possible. A significant number of cases go all the way to the U.S. Supreme Court. However, abortion-related lawsuits are not always aimed at challenging the validity of state laws.

1. Abortion malpractice

An unusual new tactic in the abortion debate came to public attention in 1993. That year, several women filed malpractice lawsuits against the physicians who had performed their abortions. The suits did not claim traditional injuries such as a wrongful pregnancy. Rather, they said that their physicians had failed to warn them about the serious depression and other emotional difficulties that some women suffer. The lawyers representing these women argued that every abortion doctor has a duty to warn each patient about all possible problems, including emotional reactions, that might follow an abortion.

Lawsuits of this type are new and quite controversial. There is evidence that many of the suits are being supported by groups opposed to abortion, although this fact in itself does not mean the suits are unreasonable or lack merit. In fact, it is highly unlikely that the courts will say that these lawsuits are never permissible under any circumstances. Each case must be decided on its own merits, and some cases may result in a physician being held liable to pay damages.

Some women, who have no political agenda, have suffered genuine injury and were not adequately warned about the possibility by their physician. In the United States, the law says that no person should be subjected to any medical procedure without first giving "informed consent." This means that the patient must be given good warnings about all possible complications, sometimes including emotional problems, that could occur. The only thing new about these lawsuits is that the law of informed consent is applied in a way that could serve the goals of pro-life groups. Obviously, if lawsuits are likely because women suffer emotional trauma after an abortion, some physicians may be less willing to perform abortions.

Nevertheless, every case of this type involves complex legal issues resting ultimately on the meaning of the U.S. Constitution. The federal courts, including the U.S. Supreme Court, will ultimately have to decide when these cases are proper and when they are not. A reasonable guess at this point is that the courts will not allow such lawsuits to proceed if they are only meant to harass a doctor or serve some purely political purpose. But where a woman has genuinely suffered because of a lack of informed consent prior to an abortion, the lawsuit may be allowed to continue.

If you are a woman contemplating filing a lawsuit of this type, you should give serious thought to your reasons for doing so. The judge and jury who hear the case will require that you prove you suffered genuine emotional injuries because of having an abortion. A woman must present evidence from a psychiatrist or other mental health professional showing that she has suffered a real injury of substantial magnitude. Examples might include excessive depression or remorse.

In addition, some judges may require that the woman's mental problems result in a definite and provable physical ailment or injury, such as a suicide attempt, ulcers, or similar effects. This requirement is sometimes imposed on grounds that it is too easy to claim some "unseeable" emotional injury that may not exist. As a result, judges may want proof of something that can be seen and proven, such as an observable physical injury or ailment.

Abortion malpractice has caused great concern among pro-choice groups in the

United States. Some abortion providers believe it is unreasonable to require them to tell each patient of all of the possible emotional problems that might arise from an abortion. The list of such problems could be quite lengthy and might scare some patients away. Pro-life forces, meanwhile, argue that scaring some patients is precisely the point.

There can be little doubt that abortion malpractice cases are likely to have a definite impact on abortion providers. Some may even choose to leave the business for fear of being sued. Other providers may require their patients to sign a lengthy consent form that includes a detailed disclosure of possible emotional complications following an abortion. On the whole, requiring this kind of consent probably is a good idea, even if it has the effect of scaring away some patients. Any lawsuit — even an unsuccessful one — can be expensive and embarrassing.

2. Abortion racketeering

Yet another unusual legal problem related to abortion crept into the headlines in 1993. In December 1993, the U.S. Supreme Court heard the first case in which pro-life groups faced being charged with or sued for racketeering. Under federal law and in many states, racketeering or RICO laws have been enacted in an effort to root out organized crime. (RICO stands for "racketeer influenced and corrupt organizations.") However, these laws are so broadly written that they can be used against anyone engaged in a pattern of organized criminal activity. In early 1994, the court decided that RICO could be used against certain types of *criminal* acts directed at abortion clinics.

Some pro-choice groups filed a suit accusing the pro-life forces of being involved in just such a pattern. According to the suit, the pattern consists of continually blocking access to abortion clinics, vandalizing them, and attacking pro-choice volunteers.

RICO lawsuits could become a potent tool against many of the protest or civil disobedience activities aimed at abortion clinics.

RICO laws have been widely criticized for being too broad. In fact, many "common citizens" have been accused of racketeering simply because they committed two or more criminal acts that created a pattern. Many legal scholars have pointed out that RICO laws are enforced more against "plain vanilla" crimes than against organized criminal groups.

Nevertheless, the courts have shown a general tendency to allow broad enforcement of RICO laws in at least some situations. In an earlier case, the U.S. Supreme Court concluded that Congress deliberately decided to make the RICO law very broad. This was reaffirmed by the 1994 abortion case.

However, there are very serious legal problems involved in applying RICO to any type of activity involving legitimate political protest and free speech. The First Amendment of the U.S. Constitution guarantees the right to engage in this kind of speech. The courts may be unwilling to allow the RICO law to extend into purely political forms of protest or civil disobedience. Even then, the courts apparently will allow a RICO claim for a pattern of very serious crimes involving injuries to people, arson, or murder. The U.S. Supreme Court in other cases has said that a purely criminal motive is not free speech.

3. Accidents or negligence injuring unborn children

Until roughly the late 1930s, American courts almost always refused to permit lawsuits for injuries caused to unborn children. Until then, judges generally agreed that it was too hard to prove whether an accident involving a pregnant woman caused the death of her baby or a baby's birth defects. Given medical technology at the time, the judges' statements were probably true.

However, as medical science advanced, the old rule barring these lawsuits grew unjustifiable. As early as 1900, legal scholars criticized the rule as unreasonable. Then in 1939, California became one of the first courts to award a woman damages because of injuries caused to her child by a botched childbirth. By 1946, a District of Columbia court extended the rule to injuries caused even before childbirth. Changes rapidly followed in every state, and today lawsuits for prenatal injuries are possible throughout the nation.

Many cases arose because the mother suffered a physical injury or accident that affected the fetus. For example, a large number of cases involve pregnant women injured in automobile accidents. Some have involved a "slip and fall" accident caused by a slippery spot on the floor of a store. Virtually any kind of negligent physical injury to the mother can be grounds for a lawsuit if the fetus is injured. This can even be true if the fetus dies as a result of its injury.

Until recently, many states imposed an additional requirement on fetal injury lawsuits. A lawsuit was not possible unless the child was "quick" or "viable" — meaning that the child was capable of living outside the womb for at least some period of time, even if an incubator was necessary. This viability rule effectively meant that no lawsuit was possible if a fetus was injured during the early months of a pregnancy when the fetus could not possibly survive outside the womb.

However, the rule has been strongly criticized, and many courts have either rejected or ignored it. Medical science is so highly developed that the viability rule is dated. Some legal scholars have noted that American courts show a strong tendency to pay lip-service to the viability rule — until they actually confront a case involving a fetus injured in early pregnancy. Then the courts find some way to let the lawsuit proceed.

Any pregnant woman who suffers a serious injury that might have injured her baby should immediately consult her physician. If there is evidence of a fetal injury, the woman should contact a lawyer. Attorneys handling such cases should immediately begin documenting all facts about the injury. Often, the lawsuit will not be filed until the child is actually born or dies, at which point the true extent of the injury will be clear. Nevertheless, legal preparation should begin as soon as possible, even before the child is born.

4. Toxic injuries to unborn children

Another kind of fetal injury has gained wide publicity in recent years. Expectant women can be exposed to some chemical or other substance that is harmful to her fetus. Often, injuries of this type are called "toxic injuries" or "toxic torts." (Tort is the legal term for a wrongful injury.) Toxic injuries have become more common in the last half of the 20th century. There is every indication that these injuries will rise in the years ahead.

(a) Drug-related toxic injuries

Some of the most widely publicized cases have involved drugs given to pregnant women that caused their fetuses to have birth defects. The most notorious of these cases involved the tranquilizing drug thalidomide, which caused malformation of fetuses' limbs. Babies were born with arms and legs either missing or horribly shortened.

Diethylstilbestrol or DES, was a synthetic hormone given to pregnant women throughout the United States between 1941 and 1971. The drug produced no immediate problems in the children of these women. However, female children of DES mothers showed a markedly high incidence of certain types of cancer, which often struck 20 or more years after the children were born. Scientists later established that DES administered during a pregnancy created a very strong tendency for female children to develop these cancers later in life.

On the whole, the courts have shown an increasing willingness to allow lawsuits for drug-related toxic injuries. The policy underlying this attitude is simple: drug manufacturers produce these chemicals to make a profit, and so they should be required to bear the cost of any injuries caused by their business. The law in cases of this type is often complex, but lawsuits can result in multimillion-dollar verdicts against drug companies. Drug-related toxic injuries should be handled by skilled attorneys with experience in the field.

(b) The toxic workplace

Another kind of toxic injury involving unborn children has gotten considerable attention in the last two decades. It involves the so-called toxic workplace. Throughout the United States, women work in a variety of workplaces where hazardous chemicals or diseases are present and cannot be eliminated. For example, some manufacturing companies use chemicals that could be harmful to a fetus, even if the mother is unlikely to be affected. In other workplaces, such as hospitals, women can be exposed to diseases like rubella (also called German measles) that can cause birth defects in a fetus.

Beginning in the 1970s, the number of lawsuits involving toxic workplaces rose dramatically. Female workers often sued for damages to pay for the costs of caring for children born deformed because of their exposure to a toxic workplace. The courts saw little difference between these suits and cases involving other types of injuries to fetuses. By the 1970s, lawsuits of this type were well accepted throughout the United States.

Employers, however, reacted quite strongly to the rising number of lawsuits. Today, owners of many toxic workplaces have adopted "fetal protection policies." These are company regulations that try to regulate pregnant women working in a toxic setting. Sometimes the policy may even try to regulate all women of child-bearing age who may be working in a toxic workplace, whether or not they are pregnant or intend to have a baby. Some employers have argued that they cannot take the risk that a woman who is unknowingly pregnant may be exposed to dangerous toxins.

Fetal protection policies have been controversial. One study in 1980 indicated that fetal protection policies that year already had made it impossible for women to be considered as candidates for about 100,000 jobs nationwide. The figure was disturbing because fetal protection policies were not widely used in 1980. Today, some people believe that as many as 30 million American jobs involve exposure to substances or diseases that could harm fetuses.

Even some jobs traditionally dominated by women, such as nursing and child care, could possibly expose a fetus to harmful diseases such as rubella. If women of child-bearing age could be excluded from these jobs, then women in general could be placed at a serious disadvantage in the workplace.

For these reasons, many women have filed lawsuits, not because of injuries to a fetus, but because they believe their companies' fetal protection policies are an illegal form of sex discrimination. (Under federal law, employers cannot discriminate on the basis of gender, *including* pregnancy-related discrimination.) A considerable number of lawsuits have been successful, usually because employers did not draft their policies carefully enough.

As a broad rule, employers are most likely to run into legal trouble if they attempt to make decisions about a woman's reproductive health for her. Authoritarian attitudes often invite lawsuits.

In 1991, the U.S. Supreme Court ruled against an employer in a case involving women who wanted jobs in a workplace where they would be exposed to dangerous levels of lead. The employer's fetal protection policy forbade all women of child-bearing years from holding any job in the toxic workplace setting unless the women could prove they were unable to have children. On appeal, the Supreme Court found that the employer's policy was illegal and that the women could sue for gender discrimination.

The court reached this conclusion for several reasons. Foremost, the court did not like the fact that the policy applied only to women and had no real relationship to actual job performance. The court also believed that employers should let the women decide for themselves whether to work in a toxic setting. If the company properly warned women about the dangers involved, the court said, then the women could make up their own minds whether to expose themselves to the toxic workplace. Any woman who then gave birth to a deformed child would not be able to sue the employer because she already would have been warned about the problem.

Employers still have an obligation to warn their workers about toxic substances in the workplace. The failure to warn could deprive women of the ability to avoid pregnancy, resulting in the birth of a deformed or injured child. In turn, the employer could be sued for damages. However, once the warnings are given, the chance of a lawsuit succeeding is unlikely. The law long ago established that people cannot sue someone else if they knowingly decided to expose themselves to some hazard.

Lawsuits directed at fetal protection policies are complex and usually involve questions of federal law. Any women wishing to sue over a policy should consult a lawyer with experience in the field. Contact your state Bar association for the names of qualified lawyers (see Appendix 1).

d. CRIMINAL ATTACKS ON PREGNANT WOMEN

Criminal attacks on pregnant women sometimes create special legal problems. Of course, *any* criminal attack on *anyone* can result in prosecution. However, many states have special laws dealing with criminal attacks on pregnant women and their fetuses. Typically, these laws have much stiffer penalties than if the attack had been directed at someone who was not pregnant. In some cases, however, the attacker must actually know the woman was pregnant or must have been able to see the outward signs of pregnancy.

A criminal attack that kills a pregnant woman's fetus is a separate crime in some states. Georgia and Louisiana, for example, call this crime "feticide" and have strong penalties for it. Other states have similar laws, though most do not use the term feticide, but make the crime a variety of manslaughter or murder. Other states, including Minnesota and Illinois, have special criminal laws punishing persons who cause alcohol-related traffic accidents that result in the death of an unborn child.

In some states, a longstanding law says that murder or manslaughter is not possible if the victim was not alive to start with. In other words, a nonliving body cannot be murdered. A number of states still say that a fetus is not actually alive for purposes of murder and manslaughter laws until that fetus is "quick" or "viable" — meaning that it can survive outside the womb.

As a result, criminal attacks that kill a fetus early in pregnancy may not be a form of murder or manslaughter, though other criminal laws may apply. Feticide laws and similar laws may change this, however. In recent years, the controversy over abortion has resulted in many new laws that attempt to classify a fetus as a living human being either from the point of conception or after a definite period of time has elapsed. These new laws could make even the killing of a very young fetus a form of murder.

e. SEX SELECTION OF FETUSES

Another legal issue associated with abortion in recent years has been "sex selection" of fetuses. Medical technology today permits parents to learn quite early in a pregnancy which gender the fetus will be — boy or girl. In some instances, couples have chosen to abort because the fetus was not the "right" gender. Such decisions have outraged groups that feel that using abortion for gender selection is morally wrong.

At least one state — Pennsylvania — has outlawed abortion for gender-selection purposes. The U.S. Supreme Court has never directly addressed the legal issues involved, and at the time of writing, most states have not confronted the issue either.

There are serious practical problems involved in a law of this type however. If a gender-selection abortion is illegal, a couple would have little trouble inventing some other reason for wanting an abortion. Few doctors will try to determine whether gender-selection is the real motive. As a result, policing a gender-selection law may be virtually impossible.

The moral dimensions of gender selection will continue to be controversial. There are already indications in some other nations that gender-selection abortions are a common method of destroying female fetuses. A number of women's groups that favor abortion rights in general do not favor gender selection for this very reason. Thus, it is conceivable that even some pro-choice organizations may oppose gender selection achieved through abortions.

Finally, there may be some situations where parents choose to abort male fetuses for medical reasons. As noted earlier in chapter 20, some types of inherited diseases are transmitted only to males. An example is hemophilia, which almost never afflicts females. A couple who know they have a gender-linked genetic disorder such as hemophilia might choose to abort a fetus they know to be male. Such abortions are controversial, but they nevertheless may be legal in most states. (The Pennsylvania statute, however, appears to prohibit all abortions motivated by the fetus's gender, without exception.)

23
WHAT DOES THE LAW SAY ABOUT CHILDREN AND SUBSTANCE ABUSE?

Substance abuse has been a problem affecting children throughout history. Alcoholism has been a widespread problem in Western societies since humankind discovered how to cultivate the grape. Children have suffered because of their parents' alcoholism.

Substance abuse by children themselves is far more common today. The mind-expanding potential of drugs was popularized in the 1950s by the "Beat Generation." In the 1960s, the youth counterculture and Hippie movement virtually adopted drugs such as marijuana and LSD (the German abbreviation for lysergic acid diethylamide) as a centerpiece of their lifestyle. Popular writers, singers, and even college professors urged many youths to "tune in," and many did. In 1992, the United States elected the first President from this generation, Bill Clinton, who admitted trying marijuana, though he claimed he didn't inhale.

By the late 1960s, the downside of liberal drug use began to appear. Journalists and writers began reporting a variety of drug-related problems among many counterculture youth. The word "O.D." or "overdose" entered popular language at this time. Then in the early 1970s, the drug-related deaths of rock stars Janis Joplin and Jimi Hendrix first focused widespread public attention on drug-related problems in American youth.

Since then, drugs have remained a serious problem, though the "drugs of choice" often change according to popular fads. In the mid-eighties, for example, "crack cocaine" became popular — and created some of the most serious drug-related problems the United States has ever seen. Crack has spawned a massive amount of crime and ruined lives. "Crack babies" are born addicted to cocaine because of their mother's drug abuse. Crack is still popular in the nineties, though there is some evidence that both marijuana and LSD were making comebacks among college-age young people.

American attitudes toward drugs have taken peculiar historical swings. Prior to the early 20th century, drug abuse was also widespread, in part because the United States had virtually no laws regulating most narcotics. Cocaine and opium could be bought without a prescription, and even popular soft drinks contained small amounts of cocaine or other drugs.

The American Civil War was credited with creating a whole generation of opium addicts because war veterans who suffered injuries were commonly treated with opium or its derivatives. Few people understood the addictive nature of this narcotic at the time. Even heroin was originally invented as a cure for opium addiction, though people today understand that heroin is even more dangerous.

Starting roughly at the time of World War I, however, attitudes toward drugs began to change. The U.S. Congress passed a series of laws severely regulating most narcotics and generally forbidding their sale without a physician's prescription. By the time of the Great Depression, drug use was widely regarded as unacceptable and a problem only "bad" people had. This anti-drug sentiment remained strong in the United States until the 1950s, when the Beat Generation's lifestyle started to be popularized.

Nancy Reagan, the wife of President Reagan, used her position as First Lady in the eighties in a serious attempt to revive the anti-drug attitude of the thirties and forties. Her "Just Say No" campaign had some successes and may have helped change attitudes in some segments of American society. However, most people agree that the Nancy Reagan campaign was not widely successful among the classes of society in which drug abuse is most common. As an example, the problem with crack cocaine arose in the United States at virtually the same time Nancy Reagan's campaign was most active.

Nevertheless, there remains a possibility that American attitudes toward drugs will change again, as they have in the past. Already there are signs that use of illegal drugs is not as popular among college students as it once was. As these students graduate and assume positions of power, they may foster a new attitude toward drugs. However, it seems unlikely that the United States will ever completely eliminate the problem of drug abuse.

a. CHILDREN WHO ABUSE DRUGS

One of the curious aspects about American society is that some minors find it easier to get illegal drugs than legal substances such as alcohol. The reason is simple black market economics. Because alcohol is legally available and relatively inexpensive, there is virtually no black market for it. This is not true for illegal drugs. Drug dealers make huge profits on drugs such as crack cocaine, heroin, LSD, and marijuana. They have no scruples about selling to minor children if that is where they can make a profit.

As a result, illegal drug abuse among minor children remains a serious problem every parent must consider. Illegal drugs can pose special risks, moreover, because the dosages vary or the drugs may be tainted with toxic substances. A number of children have been killed by drugs that were unusually potent or were laced with poisons.

The most serious problems arise from continuous drug abuse and addiction. Drug-abusing children cannot compete successfully in school and may drop out of school in states where this is legal. Some children are arrested and get a criminal record that could cause future problems. Other children suffer from an increasingly strong addiction that wrecks their mental and physical health. Others die of an overdose or other complications.

Worse still, however, is the definite link between illegal drug abuse, promiscuity, and venereal diseases (including AIDS). Children who start using hypodermic needles to inject drugs run a serious risk of contracting dangerous or deadly infections. Many children have trouble getting "clean needles," and so they often share hypodermic needles with other abusers. If any one of them has a disease like AIDS or hepatitis, the infection can be spread through a contaminated needle. In fact, infected hypodermic needles are regarded as one of the easiest ways to transmit the AIDS virus to other people.

Diseases can be contracted in other ways associated with drug abuse however. Many children with drug problems become involved in promiscuous sex. There are a variety of reasons. Drugs may diminish the child's ability to "say no." Some children, particularly young runaways, are tempted to trade sex for drugs. In major American cities, young runaway girls — and occasionally even boys — may become trapped in a lifestyle in which drug abuse leads them into prostitution under the direction of "pimps" who are drug suppliers. Life can become hellish for these children.

Both state and federal law prohibits all of these illegal practices in the strongest terms. Both child prostitution and selling drugs to children are often punished by far more serious penalties than if only adults were involved. Many states, for example, have special criminal penalties for persons who sell drugs on or near a school. However, drug-abusing children also commit criminal acts. As with adults, every state and the federal government makes the possession of illicit drugs a criminal offense.

Every state has special "intervention" programs for these children. The goal is to help the child overcome drug-related problems and develop a drug-free lifestyle. Many of these programs have a significant success rate. Often, children who agree to participate in the programs are given a reduced penalty.

There are a few actions a parent or adult caretaker may wish to take when a child is arrested on drug-related charges. Juvenile judges often become concerned that the adult is not exercising sufficient control over the child. As a result, the judge may not be very lenient if the adult or child, or both, show signs of being uncooperative or belligerent. That type of attitude should be avoided at all costs.

Attorneys often suggest that parents immediately enroll the child in a certified drug rehabilitation program before the trial begins. This is a simple strategy that may impress the judge and result in a more lenient penalty. The judge, of course, should be told about the child's participation in the program and should receive reports from the child's counselors, especially if the reports are favorable.

This will convince some judges that the parent or guardian realizes the seriousness of the situation, has proper control over the child, and is taking sound corrective measures. If the child receives good reports from the rehabilitation program, the judge may be more inclined to give the child a less severe penalty. On the whole, enrolling the child in rehabilitation may be well worth the cost — and may help save the child from other problems that drug abuse can cause.

Sometimes a child may be arrested on drug charges that appear unfounded or improper. Children are especially vulnerable to illegal tactics, such as extracting a confession without proper warnings. When an adult sincerely believes the child is innocent or was arrested illegally, a criminal attorney should be consulted immediately. The attorney may be able to have the charges dismissed relatively quickly, saving the child any further legal problems. (For more information on children facing criminal charges, see chapter 11 of this book.)

b. CHILDREN WHO ABUSE ALCOHOL

Alcohol abuse has been a serious problem among young people in recent years. As noted earlier, children often find it harder to get alcohol than illegal drugs, but a significant number of children still succeed. Some youths steal their parents' alcohol or find a store that does not adequately enforce laws forbidding sales to persons under the age of 21. (Every state now prohibits the sale of alcohol to anyone who is 20 years old or younger; see chapter 12.)

Some of the most serious problems among young people are alcohol-related accidents. The most common involve young people driving motor vehicles while under the influence of alcohol. Injuries of this type sometimes result in death, but more often lead to the child's arrest on serious charges such as DUI (driving under the influence), DWI (driving while intoxicated), or DUBAL (driving with unlawful blood alcohol level).

Until 1980, the law regarded alcohol-related traffic offenses as relatively minor, but now every state treats the problem as a highly serious crime. The push to toughen drunk driving laws came from groups like Mothers Against Drunk Driving (MADD), which pointed to disturbing statistics about the number of people killed in alcohol-related traffic deaths each year. Prior to 1980, the number of young people killed or injured in such accidents was much higher than it is today, now that the drinking age has been increased and the laws toughened.

An adult caretaker of a child arrested on alcohol-related traffic charges should treat the matter very seriously. The problem is the same as if the child had been arrested on a drug charge. As noted above, judges may be far more lenient with a child who comes to court after enrolling in a rehabilitation program and cooperating with treatment. The adult may wish to find an alcohol treatment program and enroll the child in it immediately after the arrest.

Most states now operate a variety of alcohol treatment programs. These may include a general form of treatment or special programs specifically for people arrested for alcohol-related traffic offenses. Some programs of this type are offered by state-run clinics at a reduced cost. Any adult caretaker would be wise to find out about these programs and enroll the child in any that are appropriate.

A popular penalty for alcohol-related traffic offenses is "community service." Typically this means that the person guilty of the offense must donate a certain number of hours toward community-improvement activities. An example might be picking up litter along a highway.

If your child has been arrested, you should contact the local agency (usually the court probation office) that administers community service programs. You can find out the number of hours of community service usually required of children who commit alcohol-related traffic offenses. You can then enroll the child in the program for the same number of hours. When a child already has begun giving community service before the trial, the judge may be even more impressed that the adult and child are acting responsibly.

A separate criminal offense is when underage children possess alcoholic beverages. This offense is fairly minor, though some juvenile judges may be inclined to treat the offense as a sign of future trouble. Some judges may require the child to enroll in a rehabilitation program and perform community service. As a result, adult caretakers of such children may wish to make the child perform these activities even before going to trial.

For more information on children facing criminal charges, see chapter 12.

c. SUBSTANCE ABUSE BY PREGNANT WOMEN

With the increase in drug abuse in the 20th century and the continuing problem of alcoholism, the legal system has had to face another disturbing problem: substance-abusing women who are pregnant. In the 1980s and 1990s, the problem was most serious among women addicted to alcohol or cocaine, although some physicians say that even common drugs such as nicotine (received through smoking or eating tobacco) can cause health problems in fetuses. In a few highly publicized cases, obviously pregnant women have been denied alcoholic drinks in bars or restaurants.

Until quite recently, the legal system seldom intervened to make sure women were not harming their fetuses through substance abuse. In many cases, the woman's substance abuse was not done in public and was not even detectable until a child was born with health problems.

Many people feel that though these women are irresponsible, no one should intervene in such a private matter. This attitude, however, is showing signs of changing.

A number of states, including Arizona and Minnesota, now require that children attending the public schools must be taught about the effects alcohol and drugs can have on unborn children. Other states, including Maine, North Carolina, and Wisconsin require that all marriage license applicants be given a brochure describing this same information. Delaware, meanwhile, requires members of state-regulated health professions to advise pregnant women about the need to avoid substance abuse.

Beginning in November 1989, federal law requires special warning labels on all alcoholic beverage containers. The label must include information on the dangers of drinking and driving and that the fetuses of mothers who drink can suffer birth defects. In Arizona, California, Georgia, South Dakota, and the City of New York, state and local governments require that posters containing similar warnings be prominently displayed in businesses that sell alcohol.

The states have been much slower in attempting to pass special criminal laws outlawing substance abuse during pregnancy. Some bills in this general vein have been introduced in state legislatures and assemblies. On the whole, however, they have not won approval. The general lack of specific laws, however, has not always prevented the prosecution of some women.

1. Drug abuse by pregnant women

In several states, prosecutors have attempted a novel kind of criminal prosecution when children are born obviously addicted to an illegal drug such as cocaine. The State of Florida, for example, has had a few cases where addicted women were charged with illegally "giving" cocaine to their unborn babies via the umbilical cord. (Giving illegal drugs to someone else is a crime all by itself and may be subject to stiffer penalties if drugs are given to a child.) Other states have tried to prosecute the mothers under broad "child endangerment" statutes. Still other states have avoided criminal prosecutions, but have attempted to take children from the mothers on the grounds of child abuse or neglect.

Criminal prosecutions often have not been successful. In Florida, for example, the state's highest court ruled that the "drug gift" statute was not written so that pregnant mothers committed a violation just by using cocaine. Courts in other states (including Georgia and Michigan) have generally agreed, at least when the issue is "giving" a drug to a fetus via the umbilical cord. However, these courts have said that state legislatures or assemblies might be able to pass laws that make this a criminal offense.

Prosecutions for "child endangerment" caused by prenatal drug abuse have usually been unsuccessful. In many states, child endangerment laws do not say that the law applies to the unborn. Judges often say that criminal laws must be precise and that vague language is always interpreted in favor of the accused. As a result, state courts are unwilling to extend child endangerment laws to cover fetuses if state lawmakers did not do so. This has been true of some courts in Florida, New York, and Ohio.

However, prosecutions occasionally have succeeded when the mother is charged with different kinds of crimes. For example, several courts have allowed women to be convicted of the illegal possession of drugs because their infants were born with such drugs in their blood streams. Courts in Georgia and Massachusetts have allowed this type of prosecution, reasoning that the only possible source of drugs found in a newborn must have been the mother. However, a Texas court rejected a similar prosecution based on the special facts of the case.

Perhaps the most successful cases against drug-abusing mothers are not criminal, but involve proceedings for child abuse or neglect. Courts throughout the United States have shown a marked willingness to allow evidence of prenatal drug abuse in these cases. Judges generally say that mothers who repeatedly abused drugs during pregnancy are likely to do so after childbirth and are likely to be abusive or neglectful. However, these cases commonly involve clear evidence of abuse or neglect of other children or of the child *after* birth. Courts in Connecticut, Illinois, Maryland, and New York (among others) have agreed with this line of reasoning.

A somewhat novel case arose in Ohio involving prenatal drug abuse. As in many states, Ohio has special courts or judges who are in charge of matters affecting juveniles. An Ohio juvenile judge brought a pregnant woman into court on the grounds she was abusing cocaine and opiates. The juvenile judge then ordered the woman to undergo treatment and supervision to prevent further drug abuse. As grounds, the juvenile court said it had jurisdiction over the unborn fetus whose welfare was at stake. However, an Ohio appeals court disagreed and reversed the ruling. Appeals judges said that the juvenile judge did not have jurisdiction over either the fetus or the adult mother.

These cases show that prosecution of drug-abusing pregnant women is still new and uncertain. However, the fact that some prosecutions succeed opens the door for more. It also means that legislatures and state assemblies can pass criminal laws that specifically address prenatal drug abuse. In any event, drug-abusing mothers always risk the possibility of their children being taken away on the grounds of abuse or neglect. (Child abuse and neglect are discussed in greater detail in chapters 4 and 9.)

2. Alcohol abuse by pregnant women

Prenatal alcohol abuse is a widespread problem that has been studied in great detail. Scientists have determined that two kinds of problems can be caused by such abuse: fetal alcohol syndrome (sometimes called FAS) and fetal alcohol effect (sometimes called FAE). Fetal alcohol syndrome is the more serious problem, and is caused by excessive consumption of alcohol during pregnancy. The infant's symptoms can include low birth weight, mental retardation, and an abnormally small brain. Fetal alcohol effect involves less serious symptoms caused by less excessive consumption of alcohol during pregnancy.

Fetal alcohol syndrome occurs more frequently in some groups than others. In some impoverished minority groups, for example, the rate is as high as 2.6 cases of fetal alcohol syndrome for every 1,000 live births. The rate is only 0.6, however, for white middle-class mothers. Some researchers now believe that fetal alcohol syndrome is a leading cause of mental retardation. Also, there is a disturbing link between fetal alcohol syndrome and crime, caused in part by the increased lack of emotional control associated with the syndrome. An unusually large number of adults in prisons and on death rows suffered from fetal alcohol syndrome when they were born.

Prosecutors in the United States are unwilling to prosecute pregnant women for abusing alcohol. Any prosecution involves obvious problems. Alcohol is a legal drug that can be consumed in privacy, without detection. Moreover, physicians often do not immediately realize that an infant has fetal alcohol syndrome. Many of the defects caused by the syndrome are also caused by other medical factors or genetic problems. Sometimes it may be impossible to tell whether the child actually has fetal alcohol syndrome or some other condition.

In other words, prosecutors are less likely to file charges because they are less likely to win the cases. Many prosecutions of drug-abusing mothers have not succeeded, and so there is even less likelihood of winning a case involving only alcohol abuse. This is especially true in light of the fact that prosecutors generally only win drug-abuse cases when they charge the mothers with possession of an illegal substance. Such a prosecution is not possible for alcohol if the mother is 21 years of age or older.

However, the law has recognized for a very long time that evidence of alcohol abuse can indicate child abuse or neglect. As a result, the alcohol-abusing mother could still face the possibility of the state taking her child away on these grounds. Again, cases of this type are most successful where the mother's addiction has resulted in harm to the child, especially where the mother has become unable to provide necessary care.

3. Pregnant women who abuse other drugs

The bulk of the legal cases on prenatal drug abuse involve cocaine or alcohol, although mothers sometimes take a "cocktail" of other drugs as well. Obviously, addictive drugs such as heroin, morphine, or the newer artificial opiates like Dilaudid or Demerol probably would be treated much the same as cocaine. However, the same conclusions are less clear with less addictive drugs like marijuana, and even less so with legal drugs such as nicotine (in the form of tobacco or otherwise).

Marijuana abuse has sometimes become an issue in legal proceedings, typically when the state is charging a mother with child abuse or neglect. On the whole, however, a charge of abuse or neglect is likely to succeed only where the state can prove that a mother is actually harming the child or failing to provide necessary care. For that reason, marijuana use all by itself is seldom enough reason to take a child away from a mother, except where the mother has been thrown in jail or prison for possessing or selling marijuana and no other adult caretaker is available.

Tobacco use rarely becomes a legal issue. However, public attitudes about tobacco, and especially secondhand smoke, have changed dramatically in recent times. Before the 1980s, anti-smoking laws and rules were uncommon. Today they exist throughout the United States. The changing attitude toward tobacco may at some point result in pressure to create new laws dealing with pregnant mothers who smoke.

d. LAWSUITS AGAINST PREGNANT MOTHERS WHO ABUSED DRUGS

In chapter 22, the possibility of lawsuits because of prenatal injuries to a child was discussed. Such lawsuits have been accepted throughout the United States in at least some situations. As a result, there is a possibility that children could sue their mothers for injuries caused by prenatal drug or alcohol abuse. Obviously, young children are unlikely to know how to file a lawsuit. However, when children are taken away from addicted mothers, the adults who receive custody might be able to file a lawsuit on the child's behalf.

Insurance policies may be a strong incentive to file a suit for prenatal injuries caused by the mother's addiction. Many substance-abusing mothers lack money, often because they spent all they had on drugs or alcohol. However, some policies, especially homeowner's policies, will pay many thousands of dollars for negligent injuries caused by the policy holder. That could include the addicted mother, depending on exactly what her insurance policy says.

For more information on suits against parents, see chapter 9.

e. CHILDREN WHO TURN IN DRUG-ABUSING PARENTS

Another headline-grabbing legal issue in recent years has been children who help law officers arrest their parents for illegal dug use. Several of the cases have involved children who took part in drug-awareness programs presented by police agencies throughout the United States. After hearing vivid descriptions of the deadly properties of some drugs, these children voluntarily told the law officers that their parents used drugs. Many of these children said they did it because they did not want their parents to die.

Criminal defense lawyers almost always attempt to have these cases dismissed on grounds the children were tricked. The lawyers sometimes succeed, but usually only where the law officers engaged in some type of misconduct the judge finds highly improper. Some judges may dismiss the case if the law officers clearly told outrageous lies to a child, but a judge will not dismiss a case merely because a child believed things that are untrue. For example, illegal drugs do kill a substantial number of abusers. If children mistakenly assume their parents will die, that does not necessarily mean the police have told a lie or did anything illegal. Some judges may believe that parents who use drugs in front of their children knowingly run the risk the children will tattle.

Other legal problems can be created, however, if police use a child to gain admission to the parents' house. For example, the child may be the one who gives police permission to enter and search the house for drugs. The United States Supreme Court has not been entirely clear on whether this is proper. The law is fairly certain that any *adult* who lives in a house can give police permission to enter and search, even if that adult does not own the house. However, it is unclear whether permission given by a child who lives in the house is legal. Some judges may be inclined to say that police cannot rely on permission from very young children, though it is uncertain at what age a child is old enough to give permission.

If a judge says that the child could not give legal permission, then everything the police learned after entering the house cannot be used as evidence. This could include illegal drugs seized by the police. In the United States, police can search a person's house if proper permission is given. In the absence of proper permission, police must either have a warrant or there must be some pressing emergency requiring immediate entry of the house. In other words, police run a serious risk whenever they enter a house with only a child's permission.

f. CHILDREN OF ALCOHOLICS

In recent years, people throughout the United States have come to understand the special emotional problems suffered by children of alcoholic parents. Many such children believe they have been forced to grow up too quickly because of their parent's irresponsibility. Sometimes children of alcoholics actually assume responsibility for running the family; they get their own meals and raise younger sisters or brothers. Psychologists even speak of unique character traits children of alcoholics have because they have had to assume adult responsibilities.

The legal issues that affect alcoholic parents have been discussed in section **b**. However, one final point deserves mention. In many cities across the nation, support groups now exist to help children of alcoholic parents, including those who are still under age and those who are now grown up. Members of these groups say they have benefited from talking with other children of alcoholics about their problems. Your local community clinic or mental health center can put you in touch with a group in your area.

APPENDIX 1
RESOURCES

In the United States, each state, district, and territory has its own laws. There are a number of laws that are virtually the same everywhere, but other laws differ dramatically. As a result, each state government in the United States has its own court system, its own state agencies to administer laws, and its own system to regulate lawyers. Officials in one state usually have no legal authority anywhere else. Likewise, a lawyer in one state cannot practice law in any other state without that state's permission.

The fact that each state is so different, however, means that the rules are not always the same throughout the nation. Fortunately, most states and territories have adopted many of the same elements of government. Every state, for example, has a general child welfare agency. Each state also has its own Bar association, which is the agency that determines who can be a lawyer. In other words, people who need help on a child welfare issue or from an attorney usually can get help from the state agency or association.

The section below discusses agencies and associations that are generally the same throughout the United States and its territories. However, there may be differences in a few states or unique problems that occur only in one specific place. Readers who encounter a problem unique to their own state should contact one of their state agencies for assistance.

a. STATE OFFICIALS

Every state and territory has a governor, a system of courts, and an elected lawmaking body usually called a legislature or assembly. Of these three branches of government, elected lawmakers are the ones generally expected to provide general help to the people who have elected them. Lawmakers may go by the title "representative," "senator," "assembly member," or something similar. Anyone who is having a child-related legal problem may be able to get help from one of these lawmakers. This especially is true if the problem involves a dispute with a state agency.

b. STATE AGENCIES

Other major resources are the state agencies actually involved in providing children's services. Agencies exist throughout the United States to provide education to school children, to supervise child-welfare programs, to provide public assistance to needy families, and so forth. See the Appendixes for the names of various agencies. There may also be other agencies that can help you. Consult the government listings in your phone book to see what kinds of agencies exist in your area.

c. LEGAL AID ORGANIZATIONS

Many people cannot afford to pay for an attorney. As a result, programs have been established in many parts of the United States to give free legal advice and assistance. To qualify for legal aid, you must be able to prove that you cannot afford to pay for a lawyer. Contact your state Bar association to find out more about legal aid. See the list of state Bar associations in section **h**.

d. LAW SCHOOL CLINICS

Many law schools throughout the United States have civil and/or criminal clinic programs. The brightest senior law students are specially trained to give legal help to people who cannot afford a lawyer.

Anyone whose income falls below certain levels can usually apply for legal help from these clinics. Call the law school nearest you for more information.

e. COURT CLERKS

For some legal problems, people may be able to get help from the clerks who work at their local courthouse. Clerks cannot give you legal advice, but they can tell you how the legal process works, the types of forms that may be necessary in some situations, and so forth. Some clerks also can provide sample or blank forms for common types of legal problems, or may be able to refer a person to an attorney who is willing to help on a legal problem at a reduced cost. Phone numbers for court clerks can be found in the local government listings of the phone book.

f. COUNSELING SERVICES

Many state and local governments offer no- or low-cost counseling services for people with a variety of problems. Counseling can be for emotional troubles, financial planning, physical illness, or other problems. Anyone interested in learning about available services should contact their elected state official or call their local government information line.

g. PRO BONO ORGANIZATIONS

Many attorneys throughout the United States offer "pro bono" legal advice — meaning the client is charged little or nothing. This is usually done as a public service. You can get information on any pro bono organizations in your area from your state Bar association.

h. STATE BAR ASSOCIATIONS

Every state Bar association refers people to attorneys or organizations that may be able to help with a specific legal problem. This service can be especially helpful if you need an attorney who specializes in a particular field of law. A list of state bar associations is provided below.

Alabama State Bar Association
415 Dexter Street
P.O. Box 671
Montgomery, AL 36104
(205) 269-1515

Alaska Bar Association
510 L Street
No. 602
Anchorage, AK 99510
(907) 272-7469

State Bar of Arizona
363 N. First Avenue
Phoenix, AZ 85003
(602) 252-4804

Arkansas Bar Association
400 W. Markham
Little Rock, AR 72201
(501) 375-4605

State Bar of California
555 Franklin Street
San Francisco, CA 94102
(415) 561-8200

Colorado Bar Association
1900 Grant Street
No. 950
Denver, CO 80203
(303) 860-1115

Connecticut Bar Association
101 Corporate Place
Rocky Hill, CT 06067
(203) 721-0025

Delaware Bar Association
1225 King Street
P.O. Box 1709
Wilmington, DE 19899
(302) 658-5278

District of Columbia Bar
1707 L Street N.W.
Sixth Floor
Washington, D.C. 20036
(202) 331-3883

The Florida Bar
650 Apalachee Parkway
Tallahassee, FL 32399
(904) 561-5600

State Bar of Georgia
800 The Hurt Building
50 Hurt Plaza
Atlanta, GA 30303
(404) 527-8717

Hawaii Bar Association
1136 Union Mall
Ninth Floor
Honolulu, HI 96813
(808) 537-1868

Idaho State Bar
P.O. Box 895
Boise, ID 83701
(208) 342-8958

Illinois State Bar Association
424 S. Second Street
Springfield, IL 62701
(217) 525-1760

Indiana State Bar Association
230 E. Ohio Street
Fourth Floor
Indianapolis, IN 46204
(317) 639-5465

Iowa State Bar Association
521 E. Locust
Des Moine, IA 50309
(515) 243-3179

Kansas Bar Association
1200 Harrison Street
Topeka, KS 66612
(913) 234-5696

Kentucky Bar Association
514 W. Main Street
Frankfort KY 40601
(502) 564-3795

Louisiana State Bar Association
601 Street Charles Avenue
New Orleans, LA 70130
(504) 566-1600

Maine State Bar Association
124 State Street
P.O. Box 788
Augusta, ME 04330
(207) 622-7523

Maryland State Bar Association
520 W. Fayette Street
Baltimore, MD 21201
(301) 685-7878

Massachusetts Bar Association
20 West Street
Boston, MA 02111
(617) 542-3602

State Bar of Michigan
306 Townsend Street
Lansing, MI 48933-2083
(517) 373-9030

Minnesota State Bar Association
514 Nicollet Mall
Suite 300
Minneapolis, MN 55401
(612) 333-1183

The Mississippi Bar
643 N. State Street
Jackson, MS 39202
(601) 948-4471

The Missouri Bar
326 Monroe
Jefferson, City MO 65102
(314) 635-4128

State Bar of Montana
46 North Main
P.O. Box 577
Helena, MT 59624
(406) 442-7660

Nebraska State Bar Association
635 S. 14th Street
Second Floor
Lincoln, NE 68508
(402) 475-7091

State Bar of Nevada
201 Las Vegas Boulevard
Suite 200
Las Vegas, NV 89101
(702) 382-2200

New Hampshire Bar Association
112 Pleasant Street
Concord, NH 03301
(603) 224-6942

New Jersey State Bar Association
1 Constitution Square
New Brunswick, NJ 08901-1500
(908) 249-5000

State Bar of New Mexico
121 Tijeras Street N.E.
Albuquerque, NM 87102
(505) 842-6132

New York State Bar Association
One Elk Street
Albany, NY 12207
(518) 463-3200

North Carolina State Bar
208 Fayetteville Street Mall
Raleigh, NC 27611
(919) 828-4620

State Bar of North Dakota
515½ E. Broadway
Suite 101
Bismark, ND 58502
(701) 255-1404

Ohio State Bar Association
1700 Lake Shore Drive
Columbus, OH 43216
(614) 487-2050

Oklahoma Bar Association
1901 North Lincoln
Oklahoma City, OK 73105
(405) 524-2365

Oregon State Bar
5200 S.W. Meadows Road
P.O. Box 1689
Lake Oswego, OR 97035
(503) 620-0222

Pennsylvania Bar Association
100 South Street
P.O. Box 186
Harrisburg, PA 17108
(717) 238-6715

Puerto Rico Bar Association
P.O. Box 1900
San Juan, PR 00903
(809) 721-3358

Rhode Island Bar Association
115 Cedar Street
Providence, RI 02903
(401) 421-5740

South Carolina Bar
950 Taylor Street
P.O. Box 608
Columbia, SC 29202
(803) 799-6653

State Bar of South Dakota
222 E. Capitol
Pierre, SD 57501
(605) 224-0282

Tennessee Bar Association
3622 Westend Avenue
Nashville, TN 37205
(615) 383-7421

State Bar of Texas
1414 Colorado
P.O. Box 12487
Austin, TX 78711
(512) 463-1400

Utah State Bar
645 S. 200 East
Suite 310
Salt Lake City, UT 84111
(801) 531-9077

Vermont Bar Association
P.O. Box 100
Montpelier, VT 05601
(802) 223-2020

Virginia State Bar
707 E. Main Street
Suite 1500
Richmond, VA 23219
(804) 775-0500

Virgin Islands Bar Association
P.O. Box 4108
Christiansted, VI 00822
(809) 778-7497

Washington State Bar Association
500 Westin Building
1001 Sixth Avenue
Seattle, WA 98121
(206) 727-8200

West Virginia State Bar
2006 Kanawha Blvd. E.
Charleston, WV 25311
(304) 558-2456

State Bar of Wisconsin
402 W. Wilson Street
Madison, WI 53703
(608) 257-3838

Wyoming State Bar
500 Randall Avenue
Cheyenne, WY 82001
(307) 632-3737

APPENDIX 2
PRIVATE CHILD WELFARE ORGANIZATIONS

ABA Center on Children and the Law
1800 M Street, N.W.
Washington, DC 20036
(202) 331-2250

Action for Child Protection
4723-C Park Road
Charlotte, NC 28209
(704) 529-1080

Adam Walsh Child Resource Center
11911 U.S. Highway 1
Suite 301
North Palm Beach, FL 33408
(407) 775-7191

AIDS Resource Foundation for Children
182 Roseville Avenue
Newark, NJ 07107
(201) 483-4250

American Humane Association Children's Division
63 E. Inverness Drive
Englewood, CO 80112-5117
(303) 792-9900

Americans for International Aid
435 Wavetree
Roswell, GA 30075-2928
(404) 552-0129

Association of Administrators of the Interstate Compact on the Placement of Children
c/o American Public
Welfare Association
810 First Street N.W.
Suite 500
Washington, DC 20005
(202) 682-0100

Association of Child Advocates
1625 K. Street N.W.
Washington, DC 20005
(202) 554-4747

Believe the Children
P.O. Box 77
Hermosa Beach, CA 90254
(213) 379-3514

Catholic Charities USA
1731 King Street
Number 200
Alexandria, VA 22314
(703) 549-1390

Catholic Guardian Society
1011 First Avenue
New York, NY 10022
(212) 371-1000

Center for the Support of Children
5315 Nebraska Avenue N.W.
Washington, DC 20015
(202) 363-5923

Child Abuse Institute of Research
P.O. Box 1217
Cincinnati, OH 45201
(513) 351-8005

Child Abuse Listening & Mediation
P.O. Box 90754
Santa Barbara, CA 93190-0754
(805) 965-2376

Child Find of America
P.O. Box 277
New Paltz, NY 12561
(914) 255-1848

Child Welfare Institute
1265 Peachtree Street, N.E.
Suite 700
Atlanta, GA 30309
(404) 876-1934

Child Welfare League of America
440 First Street N.W.
Suite 310
Washington, DC 2000
(202) 638-2952

Children of Alcoholic Parents
23425 Northwestern Highway
Southfield, MI 48075
(313) 353-3567

Children of the Americas
P.O. Box 140165
Dallas, TX 75214-0165
(214) 823-3922

Children's Defense Fund
25 E Street N.W.
Washington, DC 20001
(202) 628-8787

Children's Foundation
725 Fifteenth Street N.W.
Suite 505
Washington, DC 20005
(202) 347-3300

Children's Healthcare is a Legal Duty
P.O. Box 2604
Sioux City, IA 51106
(712) 948-3500

Children's Rights of America
655 Ulmerton Road
Suite 4-A
Largo, FL 34641
(813) 587-122

Child Welfare League of America
440 Fist Street N.W.
Number 310
Washington, DC 20001
(202) 638-2952

Citizen's Committee to Amend Title 18
P.O. Box 936
New Hall, CA 91321
(805) 298-2261

Clearinghouse on Child Abuse & Neglect Information
P.O. Box 1182
Washington, DC 20013
(703) 385-7565

Coalition for America's Children
1710 Rhode Island Avenue N.W.
Fourth Floor
Washington, DC 20036
(202) 857-7829

Committee for Children
172 Twentieth Avenue
Seattle, WA 98122
(206) 322-5050

Defense for Children International—USA
21 S. 13th Street
Philadelphia, PA 19107
(215) 569-8850

Find the Children
11811 W. Olympic Boulevard.
Los Angeles, CA 90064
(310) 477-6721

Foundation for Texas Children
5807 Wellington Drive
Austin, TX 78723
(512) 928-4312

Grandparents Anonymous
1924 Beverly
Sylvan Lake, MI 48320
(313) 682-8384

Grandparents/Children's Rights
5728 Bayonne Avenue
Haslett, MI 48840
(517) 339-8663

International Child Resource Institute
1810 Hopkins
Berkeley, VA 94707
(510) 644-1000

International Society for Prevention of Child Abuse & Neglect
1205 Oneida Street
Denver, CO 80220
(303) 321-3963

Kevin Collins Foundation for Missing Children
P.O. Box 590473
San Francisco, CA 94159
(415) 771-8477

Legal Services for Children
1254 Market Street
Third Floor
San Francisco, CA 94102
(415) 863-3762

Looking Up
P.O. Box K
Augusta, ME 04332
(207) 626-3402

Medical Network for Missing Children
67 Pleasant Ridge Road
Harrison, NY 10528
(914) 967-6854

Missing Children of America
P.O. Box 670-949
Chugiak, AK 99567
(907) 248-7300

Missing Children Help Center
410 Ware Boulevard
Suite 400
Tampa, FL 33619
(813) 623-5437

National Association for Native American Children of Alcoholics
P.O. Box 18736
Seattle, WA 98118
(206) 322-5601

National Association of Public Child Welfare Administrators
c/o American Public Welfare Association
810 First Street N.E.
Suite 500
Washington, DC 20005
(202) 682-0100

National Black Child Development Institute
1023 Fifteenth Street N.W.
Number 600
Washington, DC 20005
(202) 387-1281

National Center for Missing & Exploited Children
2101 Wilson Boulevard
Suite 550
Arlington, VA 22201
(703) 235-3900

National Child Support Advocacy Coalition
P.O. Box 420
Hendersonville, TN 37077-0420
(615) 264-151

National Committee for Prevention of Child Abuse
332 S. Michigan Avenue
Suite 1600
Chicago, IL 60604
(312) 663-3520

National Child Support Enforcement Association
400 N. Capitol Street N.W.
Washington, DC 20001
(202) 624-8180

National Committee for Prevention of Child Abuse, Idaho Chapter
P.O. Box 6032
Boise, ID 83707
(208) 336-4780

National Council on Child Abuse & Family Violence
1155 Connecticut Avenue N.W.
Suite 300
Washington, DC 20036
(202) 429-6695

National Network of Runaway & Youth Services
1319 F. Street N.W.
Washington, DC 20004
(202) 783-7949

National Safe Kids Campaign
111 Michigan Avenue N.W.
Washington, DC 20010-2970
(202) 939-4993

Odyssey Institute Corporation
5 Hedley Farms Road
Westport, CT 06880
(203) 255-4198

Orphan Foundation of America
1500 Massachusetts Avenue N.W.
Number 448
Washington, DC 20005
(202) 861-0762

Parents Against Molesters
P.O. Box 3557
Portsmouth, VA 23701
(804) 363-2549

Parents Anonymous
520 S. Lafayette Park Place
Suite 316
Los Angeles, CA 90057
(213) 388-6685

Parents Anonymous of Pennsylvania
2141 N. 2nd Street
Harrisburg, PA 17110
(717) 238-0937

Parents Anonymous of Delaware
124-D Senatorial Drive
Wilmington, DE 19807
(302) 654-1102

Parents Anonymous of Florida
P.O. Box 4295
Tallahassee, FL 32315-4295
(904) 488-5437

Parents Helping Parents
535 Race Street
Suite 140
San Jose, CA 95126
(408) 288-5010

Society for Young Victims,
Missing Children Center
66 Broadway
Paramount Plaza
Newport, RI 02840
(401) 847-5083

Society for Young Victims of Indiana
3430 W. Maryland
Evansville, IN 47712
(812) 425-1628

United Nations Children's Fund (UNICEF)
3 United Nations Plaza
New York, NY 10017
(212) 326-7000

Vanished Children's Alliance
1407 Parkmoor Avenue
Suite 200
San Jose, CA 95126
(408) 971-4822

APPENDIX 3
PRIVATE CHILD WELFARE ORGANIZATIONS FOR MISSING CHILDREN

Adam Walsh Child Resource Center
11911 U.S. Hwy. 1
Suite 301
North Palm Beach, FL 33408
(407) 775-7191

Child Find of America
P.O. Box 277
New Paltz, NY 12561
(914) 255-1848

Find the Children
11811 W. Olympic Boulevard
Los Angeles, CA 90064
(310) 477-6721

Kevin Collins Foundation
for Missing Children
P.O. Box 590473
San Francisco, CA 94159
(415) 771-8477

Medical Network for Missing Children
67 Pleasant Ridge Road
Harrison, NY 10528
(914) 967-6854

Missing Children of America
P.O. Box 670-949
Chugiak, AK 99567
(907) 248-7300

Missing Children Help Center
410 Ware Boulevard
Suite 400
Tampa, FL 33619
(813) 623-5437

National Center for Missing
& Exploited Children
2101 Wilson Boulevard
Suite 550
Arlington, VA 22201
(703) 235-3900 or
(800) 843-5678

Society for Young Victims,
Missing Children Center
66 Broadway
Paramount Plaza
Newport, RI 02840
(401) 847-5083

Society for Young Victims of Indiana
3430 W. Maryland
Evansville, IN 47712
(812) 425-1628

Vanished Children's Alliance
1407 Parkmoor Avenue
Suite 200
San Jose, CA 95126
(408) 971-4822

APPENDIX 4
STATE CHILD LABOR AGENCIES

Alabama
Industrial Relations Department
Industrial Relations Building
Montgomery, AL 36130
(205) 242-5386

Alaska
Labor Standards & Safety Division
Department of Labor
P.O. Box 107021
Juneau, AK 99510
(907) 264-2452

Arizona
Industrial Commission
800 W. Washington
Phoenix, AZ 85007
(602) 542-4411

Arkansas
Labor Standards Administrator
Department of Labor
Room 100
10421 W. Markham
Little Rock, AR 72205
(501) 682-4501

California
Labor Standards Enforcement Division
Department of Industrial Relations
30 Van Ness Avenue
San Francisco, CA 94102
(415) 557-3827

Colorado
Division of Labor
Department of Labor & Employment
1120 Lincoln Street, 13th Floor
Denver, CO 80203
(303) 894-7530

Connecticut
Occupational Safety
& Health Director
Department of Labor
200 Folly Brook Boulevard
Wethersfield, CT 06109
(203) 566-4550

Delaware
Department of Labor
820 N. French Street
Sixth Floor
Wilmington, DE 19801
(302) 571-2710

District of Columbia
Child Labor Administrator
DC Public Schools
415 Twelfth Street, N.W.
Room 1209
Washington, DC 20004
(202) 724-4260

Florida
Department of Labor
& Employment Security—
Child Labor
Florida Capitol Complex
Tallahassee, FL 32399
(904) 488-3131

Georgia
Child Labor Section
Department of Labor
148 International Boulevard
Suite 276
Atlanta, GA 30303
(404) 656-3613

Hawaii
Child Labor Administrator
Labor & Industrial Relations Department
830 Punchbowl Street
Room 340
Honolulu, HI 96813
(808) 548-4071

Idaho
Labor & Industrial Services
277 N. Sixth Street
Boise, ID 83720
(208) 334-3950

Illinois
Department of Labor
1 W. Old State Capitol
Room 300
Springfield, IL 62720
(217) 782-6206

Indiana
Bureau of Child Labor
Department of Labor
402 W. Washington Street
No. W 195
Indianapolis, IN 46204
(317) 232-2676

Iowa
Division of Labor Services
Department of Employment Services
2000 E. Grand
Des Moines, IA 50319
(515) 281-3606

Kansas
Employment Standards
& Labor Relations
Department of Human Resources
512 W. Sixth
Topeka, KS 66603
(913) 296-7475

Kentucky
Director of Employment
Standards & Mediation
The 127 Building
U.S. 127 S.
Frankfort, KY 40601
(502) 564-2784

Louisiana
Office of Labor
P.O. Box 94094
Baton Rouge, LA 70804
(504) 925-4221

Maine
Bureau of Labor Standards
Department of Labor
State House Station #45
Augusta, ME 04333
(207) 289-2015

Maryland
Division of Labor & Industry
Department of Licensing & Regulation
501 Street Paul Place
Baltimore, MD 21202
(301) 333-4179

Massachusetts
Office for Children
10 West Street
Boston, MA 02111
(617) 727-8900

Michigan
Bureau of Employment
Standards
P.O. Box 30015
Lansing, MI 48909
(517) 322-1825

Minnesota
Labor Standards Division
444 Lafayette Road
Street Paul, MN 55101
(612) 297-3349

Missouri
Division of Labor Standards
Department of Labor
& Industrial Relations
P.O. Box 449
Jefferson City, MO 65102
(314) 751-3403

Montana
Division of Labor Standards
Standards Bureau
Capitol Station
Helena, MT 59620
(406) 444-2723

Nebraska
Labor Law Compliance
Program Manager
Department of Labor
1313 Farnam
State Office Building
Omaha, NE 68102
(402) 595-3095

Nevada
Labor Commissioner
505 E. King Street
Room 602
Carson City, NV 89710
(702) 687-4850

New Hampshire
Department of Labor
95 Pleasant Street
Concord, NH 03301
(603) 271-3171

New Jersey
Department of Labor
John Fitch Plaza
CN-110
Trenton, NJ 08625
(609) 292-2323

New Mexico
Labor & Industrial Division
1586 Pacheco Street
Room 105
Santa Fe, NM 87501
(505) 827-6875

New York
Department of Labor
Campus, State Office Building
Albany, NY 12240
(518) 457-2741

North Carolina
Wage & Hour Division
Department of Labor
4 W. Edenton Street
Raleigh, NC 27601
(919) 733-2152

North Dakota
Department of Labor
State Capitol
Fifth Floor
Bismark, ND 58505
(701) 224-2661

Ohio
Minimum Wage & Minors Division
Department of Industrial Relations
2323 W. 5th Avenue
Columbus, OH 43266
(614) 644-2239

Oklahoma
Division of Employment Standards
Department of Labor
4001 N. Lincoln Boulevard
Oklahoma City, OK 73105
(405) 528-1500

Oregon
Wage & Hour Division
Bureau of Labor & Industries
State Office Building
Third Floor
Portland, OR 97201
(503) 229-6486

Pennsylvania
Bureau of Labor Standards
Department of Labor & Industry
Labor & Industry Board
Room 1305
Harrisburg, PA 17120
(717) 787-4670

Puerto Rico
Department of Labor
& Human Resources
505 Munoz Rivera Avenue
Hato Rey, PR 00918
(809) 754-5353

Rhode Island
Division of Labor Standards
Department of Labor
220 Elmwood Avenue
Providence, RI 02907
(401) 277-2734

South Carolina
Department of Labor
P.O. Box 11329
Columbia, SC 29211
(803) 734-9603

South Dakota
Division of Labor & Management
Department of Labor
Kneip Building
Pierre, SD 57501
(605) 773-3681

Tennessee
Department of Labor
501 Union Building
Nashville, TN 37243
(615) 741-0851

Texas
Department of Licensing
& Regulation
P.O. Box 12157
Austin, TX 78711
(512) 463-5522

Utah
Division of Anti-Discrimination
& Labor
Industrial Commission
160 E. 300 S.
Salt Lake City, UT 84111
(801) 530-6921

Vermont
Department of Labor & Industry
7 Court Street
Montpelier, VT 05602
(802) 828-2286

Virginia
Department of Labor & Industry
13 S. 13th Street
Richmond, VA 23219
(804) 786-2377

Virgin Islands
Department of Labor
P.O. Box 890
Christiansted, VI 00820
(809) 773-1994

Washington
Department of Labor & Industries
406 Legion Way
Olympia, WA 98504
(206) 753-3487

West Virginia
Division of Labor
State Capitol Complex Building 3
Charleston, WV 25305
(304) 348-7890

Wisconsin
Division of Equal Rights,
Industrial Labor, & Human Relations
P.O. Box 7946
Madison, WI 53707
(608) 266-0946

Wyoming
Division of Labor Standards
Department of Employment
Herschler Building
Cheyenne, WY 82002
(307) 777-7261

APPENDIX 5
STATE CHILD SUPPORT ENFORCEMENT AGENCIES

Alaska
Child Support
Enforcement Division
Department of Revenue
550 W. 7th, Suite 310
Anchorage, AK 99501
(907) 263-6277

Arizona
Division of Family Support
Department of Economic Security
1717 W. Jefferson
Phoenix, AZ 85007
(602) 252-0236

Arkansas
Department of Human Services
P.O. Box 3358
Little Rock, AR 72203
(501) 682-8417

California
Child Support Program
Department of Social Services
944 P Street, MS 9-010
Sacramento, CA 95814
(916) 323-8994

Colorado
Child Support
Enforcement Bureau
Department of Social Services
1575 Sherman Street
Third Floor
Denver, CO 80203
(303) 866-5994

Connecticut
Child Support
Enforcement Bureau
Department of Human Resources
1079 Asylum Avenue
Hartford, CT 06106
(203) 566-3053

Delaware
Child Support Enforcement Division
Health & Social Services Department
1901 N. DuPont Highway
New Castle, DE 19720
(302) 421-8356

Florida
Department of Health
& Rehabilitative Services
Child Support Enforcement
1317 Winewood Boulevard
Tallahassee, FL 32399
(904) 488-9900

Georgia
Office of Child Support Recovery
Department of Human Resources
878 Peachtree Street
Fifth Floor
Atlanta, GA 30309
(404) 894-5087

Hawaii
Child Support Enforcement
Department of the Attorney General
680 Iwilei Road
Honolulu, HI 96817
(808) 587-3700

Idaho
Child Support
Enforcement Bureau
450 W. State Street
Boise, ID 83720
(208) 334-5710

Indiana
Child Support Division
IGC-S, W360
402 W. Washington
Indianapolis, IN 46204
(317) 232-4894

Iowa
Bureau of Collections
Department of Human Services
Hoover State Office Building
Des Moines, IA 50319
(515) 281-5767

Kansas
Child Support Enforcement
Social & Rehabilitation Services
Department
300 S.W. Oakley
Biddle Building
Topeka, KS 66606
(913) 296-3237

Kentucky
Child Support
Enforcement Division
275 E. Main Street
Frankfort, KY 40601
(502) 564-2285

Louisiana
Office of Child Support
Enforcement
P.O. Box 94065
Baton Rouge, LA 70804
(504) 342-4780

Maine
Child Support Enforcement
Department of Human Services
State House Station 1
Augusta, ME 04333
(207) 289-2886

Maryland
Child Support Enforcement
Department of Human Resources
311 W. Saratoga Street
Baltimore, MD 21201
(301) 333-3981

Massachusetts
Child Support Enforcement
Department of Revenue
141 Portland Street
Cambridge, MA 02139
(617) 727-4200

Michigan
Office of Child Support
Department of Social Services
1406 Grand Tower
P.O. Box 30037
Lansing, MI 48909
(517) 373-7570

Minnesota
Child Support Enforcement Division
Department of Human Services
444 Lafayette Road
Street Paul, MN 55155
(612) 296-2499

Mississippi
Division of Child Support
Enforcement
P.O. Box 352
Jackson, MS 39205
(601) 354-6844

Missouri
Child Support
Enforcement Division
P.O. Box 1527
Jefferson City, MO 65102
(314) 751-4301

Montana
Child Support
Enforcement Division
Department of Social &
Rehabilitation Services
P.O. Box 5955
Helena, MT 59604
(406) 444-4614

Nebraska
Enforcement Services Division
Department of Social Services
Nebraska State Office Building
Fifth Floor
Lincoln, NE 68509
(402) 471-9390

Nevada
Human Resources
2527 N. Carson Street
Carson City, NV 89710
(702) 687-4128

New Jersey
Division of Economic Assistance
Department of Human Services
Quakerbridge Road
CN 716
Trenton, NJ 08625
(609) 588-2361

New Mexico
Child Support Enforcement
Human Services Dept.
P.O. Box 25109
Santa Fe, NM 87504
(505) 827-7200

New York
Child Support Enforcement Office
Department of Social Services
1 Commerce Plaza
P.O. Box 14
Albany, NY 12260
(518) 474-9081

North Carolina
Child Support Enforcement
Division of Social Services
100 E. Six Forks Road
Raleigh, NC 27609
(919) 571-4120

North Dakota
Child Support Enforcement Division
Department of Human Services
State Capitol
Bismark, ND 58505
(701) 224-3582

Oklahoma
Child Support Enforcement Division
Department of Human Services
2409 N. Kelly, Annex
Oklahoma City, OK 73111
(405) 424-5871

Oregon
Support Enforcement Division
Justice Department
100 Justice Building
Salem, OR 97310
(503) 378-4879

Pennsylvania
Child Support Enforcement Bureau
Department of Public Welfare
P.O. Box 8018
Harrisburg, PA 17105
(717) 783-8729

Rhode Island
Department of Children & Families
610 Mt. Pleasant Avenue
Providence, RI 02908
(401) 861-6000

South Carolina
Department of Social Service
1535 Confederate Avenue
Columbia, SC 29202
(803) 734-5760

South Dakota
Division of Child Support Enforcement
Department of Social Services
Kneip Building
Pierre, SD 57501
(605) 773-3641

Texas
Child Support Enforcement Division
Office of the Attorney General
P.O. Box 12548
Austin, TX 78711
(512) 463-2181

Utah
Office of Recovery Service
Department of Human Services
120 N. 200 W.
Salt Lake City, UT 84103
(801) 538-4400

Virginia
Division of Child Support
Enforcement
8007 Discovery Drive
Richmond, VA 23299
(804) 662-7671

Virgin Islands
Division of Paternity & Child Support
Justice Department
GERS Complex, 2nd Floor
Street Thomas, VI 00802
(809) 774-5666

Washington
Office of Support Enforcement
Department of Social & Health Services
712 Pear Street S.E.
M/S: HJ-31
Olympia, WA 98507
(206) 586-3520

West Virginia
Department of Child Advocacy
State Capitol
Charleston, WV 25305
(304) 348-3780

Wisconsin
Division of Economic Support
Department of Health & Social Service
1 W. Wilson Street
Madison, WI 53703
(608) 266-3035

Wyoming
Division of Self-Sufficiency
Department of Family Services
Hathaway Bldg., 3rd Floor
Cheyenne, WY 82002
(307) 777-6849

APPENDIX 6
STATE CHILD SERVICE AGENCIES — GENERAL SERVICES AND CHILD ABUSE AND NEGLECT PROGRAMS

Alabama
Bureau of Family & Children's Services
64 N. Union Street
Montgomery, AL 36130
(205) 242-9500

Alaska
Family & Youth Services Division
Department of Health & Social Services
P.O. Box H
Juneau, AK 99811
(907) 465-3170

Arizona
Division of Children, Youth, & Families
Department of Economic Security
1717 W. Jefferson
Phoenix, AZ 85007
(602) 542-3981

Arkansas
Division of Children & Family Services
Department of Human Services
P.O. Box 1437
Little Rock, AR 72203
(501) 682-8770

California
Department of Social Services
744 P. Street
Sacramento, CA 95814
(916) 323-2888

Colorado
Division of Family & Children's Service
Department of Social Services
1575 Sherman Street
Second Floor
Denver, CO 80203
(303) 866-3672

Connecticut
Children & Youth Services Department
170 Sigourney Street
Hartford, CT 06105
(203) 566-3536

Delaware
Department of Services
for Children, Youth & Families
1825 Faulkland Road
Wilmington, DE 19805
(302) 633-2500

District of Columbia
Family Services Administration
Department of Human Services
First & I Street, S.W.
Room 215
Washington, DC 20024
(202) 727-5947

Florida
Division of Children, Youth, & Families
Department of Health
& Rehabilitative Services
1317 Winewood
Building 8, Third Floor
Tallahassee, FL 32399
(904) 488-8762

Georgia
Division of Family & Children Services
Department of Human Resources
878 Peachtree Street
Fourth Floor
Atlanta, GA 30309
(404) 894-6386

Hawaii
Department of Human Services
810 Richards Street
Suite 400
Honolulu, HI 96813
(808) 548-6123

Idaho
Division of Family
& Children Services
Department of Health & Welfare
450 W. State Street
Boise, ID 83720
(208) 334-5700

Illinois
Department of Children & Family Services
406 E. Monroe Street
Springfield, IL 62701
(217) 785-2509

Indiana
Division of Families & Children
Family & Social Services Administration
302 W. Washington
IGC-S, E414
Indianapolis, IN 46204
(317) 233-4451

Iowa
Adult, Children & Family Services
Department of Human Services
Hoover State Office Building
Des Moines, IA 50319
(515) 281-5521

Kansas
Youth Services
Department of Social
& Rehabilitation Services
Smith-Wilson Building
300 S.W. Oakley
Topeka, KS 66606
(913) 296-3284

Kentucky
Division of Family Services
Department of Social Services
275 E. Main Street
Frankfort, KY 40601
(502) 564-6852

Louisiana
Office of Community Services
Department of Social Services
P.O. Box 44367
Baton Rouge, LA 70804
(504) 342-4000

Maine
Child & Family Services
Department of Human Services
State House Station 11
Augusta, ME 04333
(207) 289-5060

Maryland
Child Welfare Services Office
Department of Human Resources
300 W. Preston Street
Baltimore, MD 21201
(301) 333-0208

Massachusetts
Department of Social Services
150 Causeway Street
Boston, MA 02114
(617) 727-0900

Michigan
Office of Children & Youth Service
Department of Social Services
300 S. Capitol
P.O. Box 30037
Lansing, MI 48909
(517) 373-4506

Minnesota
Department of Human Services
Fourth Floor
658 Cedar Street
Saint Paul, MN 55155
(612) 297-2673

Mississippi
Division of Family & Children's Services
P.O. Box 352
Jackson, MS 39205
(601) 354-6661

Missouri
Children's Services
Division of Family Services
Broadway Building, Box 88
Jefferson City, MO 65103
(314) 751-2882

Montana
Department of Family Services
48 N. Last Chance Gulch
Helena, MT 59601
(406) 444-5902

Nebraska
Division of Human Services
Department of Social Services
P.O. Box 95026
Lincoln, NE 68509
(402) 471-9308

Nevada
Children & Family Services
505 E. King Street
Carson City, NV 89710
(702) 687-4400

New Hampshire
Children & Youth Services
Department of Health & Welfare
Hazen Drive
Concord, NY 03301
(603) 271-4451

New Jersey
Division of Economic Assistance
Department of Human Services
Quakerbridge Road
CN 716
Trenton, NJ 08625
(609) 588-2361

New Mexico
Children's Bureau
Human Services Dept.
P.O. Box 2348
Santa Fe, NM 87504
(505) 827-8439

New York
Department of Social Services
40 N. Pearl Street
Albany, NY 12243
(518) 474-9475

North Carolina
Division of Social Services
Department of Human Resources
325 N. Salisbury Street
Raleigh, NC 27603
(919) 733-3055

North Dakota
Children & Family Services
Department of Human Services
State Capitol
Bismarck, ND 58505
(701) 224-4811

Ohio
Family & Children's Service Division
Department of Human Services
51 N. High Street, 3rd Floor
Columbus, OH 43266
(614) 466-8783

Oklahoma
Department of Human Services
P.O. Box 25352
Oklahoma, City OK 73125
(405) 521-2778

Oregon
Children's Services Division
Department of Human Resources
198 Commercial Street S.E.
Salem, OR 97310
(503) 378-4374

Pennsylvania
Division of Children,
Youth & Families
Department of Public Welfare
P.O. Box 2675
Harrisburg, PA 17105
(717) 787-4756

Puerto Rico
Children's Services
P.O. Box 3349
Santurce, PR 00904
(809) 725-0753

Rhode Island
Department of Children & Families
610 Mt. Pleasant Avenue
Providence, RI 02908
(401) 861-6000

South Carolina
Division of Children & Family Services
P.O. Box 1520
Columbia, SC 29202
(803) 734-5670

South Dakota
Department of Social Services
Kneip Building
Pierre, SD 57501
(605) 773-3227

Tennessee
Department of Human Services
111 Seventh Avenue N.
Nashville, TN 37243
(615) 741-1820

Texas
Department of Human Services
P.O. Box 149030
Austin, TX 78714
(512) 450-3080

Utah
Division of Family Services
Department of Human Services
120 N. 200 West
Fourth Floor
Salt Lake City, UT 84103
(801) 538-4004

Vermont
Division of Social Services
Department of Social
& Rehabilitation Services
103 S. Main Street
Osgood Building
Waterbury, VT 05671
(802) 241-2131

Virginia
Department of Social Services
8007 Discovery Drive
Richmond, VA 23229
(804) 662-9236

Virgin Islands
Department of Human Services
Barbel Plaza South
St. Thomas, VI 00802
(809) 774-0930

Washington
Children & Family Services Division
Department of Social & Health Services
Office Building # 2
M/S: OB-41
Olympia, WA 98504
(206) 586-8654

West Virginia
Social Services Bureau
Division of Human Services
1900 Washington E.
Building 6
Charleston, WV 25305
(304) 348-7980

Wisconsin
Bureau of Children,
Youth & Families
Department of Health & Social Services
P.O. Box 7851
Madison, WI 53707
(608) 266-6946

Wyoming
Division of Youth Services
Department of Family Services
Hathaway Building, 3rd Floor
Cheyenne, WY 82002
(307) 777-6095

APPENDIX 7
MAJOR GOVERNMENT AGENCIES INVESTIGATING MISSING, KIDNAPPED, AND EXPLOITED CHILDREN

a. FEDERAL

FBI
10th & Pennsylvania Avenue N.W.
Washington, DC 20535
(202) 324-4245
(202) 324-2606

U.S. Department of Defense
Office of Family Policy, Support & Services
4015 Wilson Boulevard
Suite 903
Arlington, VA 22203
(202) 696-4555

U.S. Customs
Pornography Tipline
1301 Constitution Avenue
Room 3136
Washington, DC 20229
(202) 566-2101
(800) 843-5678

National Center for the
Analysis of Violent Crime
Quantico, VA 22134
(703) 640-6131
(800) 634-4097

U.S. Dept. of Justice
Child Exploitation & Obscenity Section
Washington, DC 20530
(202) 514-5780

Office for Victims of Crimes
633 Indiana Avenue N.W.
Washington, DC 20531
(202) 307-5983

Office of Child Support
Enforcement
370 L'Enfant Promenade S.W.
Washington, DC 20447
(202) 401-9267

Administration for Children,
Youth & Families
330 C Street S.W.
Washington, DC 20201
(202) 245-0102

National Center on Child Abuse
& Neglect
P.O. Box 1182
Washington, DC 20013
(202) 245-0586

b. STATE

Alabama
Alabama Missing Children Bureau
P.O. Box 1511
Montgomery, AL 36102
(205) 242-4207
(800) 228-7688 (in state)

Arizona
Arizona Dept. of Public Safety
P.O. Box 6638
Phoenix, AZ 85005
(602) 223-2158

Arkansas
Arkansas Missing Children
Services Program
323 Center Street # 400
Little Rock, AR 72201
(501) 682-5028
(800) 482-8982 (in state)

California
California Missing Persons
P.O. Box 903417
Sacramento, CA 94203
(916) 739-5114
(800) 222-3462 (in state)

Colorado
Colorado Bureau of Investigation
690 Kipling, Suite 3000
Denver, CO 80215
(303) 239-4251

Conneticut
Missing Persons Unit
294 Colony Street
Bldg. 9, 3rd Floor
Meriden, CT 06450
(203) 238-6688
(800) 367-5678 (in state)

Delaware
Delaware State Police
P.O. Box 430
Dover, DE 19903
(302) 739-5883

District of Columbia
DC Missing Persons
1700 Rhode Island Avenue N.E.
Washington, DC 20018
(202) 576-6771

Florida
Missing Children
Information Clearinghouse
P.O. Box 1489
Tallahassee, FL 32302
(904) 488-5224
(800) 342-0821 (in state)

Georgia
Georgia Bureau of Investigation
P.O. Box 370808
Decatur, GA 30037
(404) 244-2554
(800) 282-6564

Illinois
Illinois State Police
I SEARCH
500 Iles Park Place
Springfield, IL 62718-1002
(217) 524-6596
(800) 843-5763 (in state)

Indiana
Indiana State Police
309 State Office Building
100 N. Senate Avenue
Indianapolis, IN 46220
(317) 232-8310
(800) 831-8953

Iowa
Division of Criminal Investigation
Wallace Office Building
Des Moines, IA 50319
(515) 281-7963
(800) 346-5507 (in state)

Kansas
Kansas Bureau of Investigation
1620 S.W. Tyler Street
Topeka, KS 66612
(913) 232-6000
(800) 572-7463 (in state)

Kentucky
Kentucky Missing Child
Information Center
1240 Airport Road
Frankfort, KY 40601
(502) 227-8799
(800) 222-5555 (in state)

Louisiana
Clearinghouse for
Missing & Exploited Children
P.O. Box 3318
Baton Rouge, LA 70821
(504) 342-4008

Maine
Maine State Police
36 Hospital Street
Augusta, ME 04333
(207) 621-1297
(800) 452-4664

Maryland
Center for Missing Children
1201 Reisterstown Road
Pikesville, MD 21208
(301) 799-0190
(800) 637-5437

Massachusetts
Missing Persons Unit
Massachusetts State Police
West Grove Street
Middleboro, MA 02346
(800) 447-5269 (national)
(800) 622-5999 (in state)

Michigan
Michigan State Police
714 S. Harrison Road
East Lansing, MI 48823
(517) 336-6680

Minnesota
Bureau of Criminal Apprehension
1246 University Avenue
Saint Paul, MN 55104
(612) 642-0610

Mississippi
Mississippi State Hwy. Patrol
P.O. Box 958
Jackson, MS 39205
(601) 987-1599

Missouri
Missing Persons
State Highway Patrol
P.O. Box 568
Jefferson City, MO 65102
(314) 751-3313 ext. 178

Montana
Missing Persons Clearinghouse
Dept. of Justice
303 N. Roberts Street
Helena, MT 59620
(406) 444-3817
(800) 332-6617 (in state)

Nebraska
Nebraska State Patrol
Box 94907
Lincoln, NE 68509
(402) 479-4002

Nevada
Crime Prevention Coordinator
401 S. 3rd Street
Suite 500
Las Vegas, NV 89101
(702) 486-3420

New Hampshire
New Hampshire State Police
P.O. Box 235
West Ossipee, NH 03890
(603) 271-1166
(800) 852-3411 (in state)

New Jersey
Missing Persons Unit
P.O. Box 7068
West Trenton, NJ 08628
(609) 882-2000 ext. 2895

New Mexico
NCIC Section
Dept. of Public Safety
P.O. Box 1628
Santa Fe, NM 87504
(505) 827-9187

New York
Missing & Exploited
Children Clearinghouse
Executive Park Tower
Albany, NY 12203
(518) 457-6326
(800) 346-3543 (in state)

North Carolina
Division of Victim
& Justice Services
116 W. Jones Street
Raleigh, NC 27603-1335
(919) 733-3718
(800) 522-5437

North Dakota
Clearinghouse for
Missing Children
P.O. Box 5511
Bismarck, ND 58502
(701) 224-2121
(800) 472-2121 (in state)

Ohio
Missing Child Education Program
65 S. Front Street
Columbus, OH 43266-0308
(614) 466-6830
(800) 325-5604 (in state)

Oklahoma
State Bureau of Investigation
P.O. Box 11497
Oklahoma City, OK 73136
(405) 848-6724

Oregon
Missing Children Clearinghouse
107 Public Service Building
Salem, OR 97310
(503) 378-5775
(800) 282-7155 (in state)

Pennsylvania
Missing Persons Unit
1800 Elmerton Avenue
Harrisburg, PA 17110
(717) 783-5524

Rhode Island
Missing & Exploited Children Unit
P.O. Box 185
N. Scituate, RI 02857
(401) 647-3311 ext. 237
(800) 544-1144 (in state)

South Carolina
Missing Persons
Information Center
P.O. Box 21398
Columbia, SC 29221
(803) 737-9000
(800) 322-4453 (in state)

South Dakota
Division of Criminal Investigation
500 East Capitol
Pierre, SD 57501
(605) 773-3331

Tennessee
Bureau of Investigation
P.O. Box 100940
Nashville, TN 37210
(615) 741-0430

Texas
Dept. of Public Safety
P.O. Box 4143
Austin, TX 78765
(512) 465-2814
(800) 346-3243 (in state)

Vermont
Vermont State Police
103 S. Main Street
Waterbury, VT 05676
(802) 244-7357

Virginia
Missing Children's Clearinghouse
P.O. Box 27472
Richmond, VA 23261
(804) 674-2026
(800) 822-4453 (in state)

Washington
Missing Children Clearinghouse
P.O. Box 2527
Olympia, WA 98504
(206) 753-3960
(800) 543-5678 (in state)

Wyoming
Division of Criminal Investigation
316 W. 22nd Street
Cheyenne, WY 82002
(307) 777-7537

c. **CANADA**

Royal Canadian Mounted Police
Missing Children's Registry
P.O. Box 8885
Ottawa, Ontario
Canada   K1A 0R2
(613) 993-1525

OTHER TITLES IN THE SELF-COUNSEL SERIES

PLEASE, LISTEN TO ME!
Your guide to understanding teenagers and suicide
by Marion Crook

Teenage suicide can be prevented — do you know how?

Suicide is one of the leading causes of teenage death. Social and peer-group attitudes toward suicide make nearly every teenager susceptible, but there *are* steps you can take to help your son or daughter deal with the pressures and the temptation to consider suicide as a solution. $9.95

This book speaks practically and sensitively to the most important issues surrounding teenage suicide and helps parents answer s questions such as:

- How do I tell if my teenager is considering suicide?
- How do I talk to my teenager about suicide?
- What aspects of our family life may be influencing what my teenager thinks about suicide?
- Where do I look for help for my teenager and my family?
- Why should I worry — my teenager *seems* normal?

NO-GIMMICK GUIDE TO MANAGING STRESS
Effective options for every lifestyle
by E.J. Neidhardt, B.Sc., M.D., M.S. Weinstein, Ph.D., R. Psych., and R.F. Conry, M.S., Ph.D.

Learning to unwind and enjoy has physical, emotional, and spiritual benefits. This book provides six of the most effective ways to reduce the stress in your life — simple, proven techniques to relieve both physical and mental tension. It covers general health and well-being, personal planning skills, communications skills, quieting, and progressive relaxation training. A no-gimmick, commonsense approach to managing day-to-day and chronic stress. This is an illustrated workbook that enables you to set goals and measure the results.

The book is authored by three top researchers in the field of stress. Dr. Joseph Neidhardt is a specialist in health screening and psychosomatic illness, Dr. Malcolm Weinstein is a consulting psychologist experienced in occupational and organizational stress analysis, and Dr. Robert Conry is a professor at a leading Canadian university and a specialist in individual assessment and program evaluation. Here they pool their experience and deliver the best ways to eliminate the unhealthy stress in your life — simple, effective techniques that go right to the root of the problem. $11.95

FAMILY TIES THAT BIND
A self-help guide to change through Family of Origin therapy
by Dr. Ronald W. Richardson

Create a better life for yourself. Most people's lives are complicated by family relationships. Birth order, our parents' relationship, and the "rules" we were brought up with can affect our own self-esteem and future relationships with spouses, children, and other family members. Now the Family of Origin theory and techniques recently developed and successfully used by family therapists can help you find different and better ways of dealing with family relationships. This easy-to-read, practical book explains how families function and what you can do to change the way you act in your family and with other important people. Step-by-step exercises show how to apply the principles to your own situation and develop a more positive approach to all aspects of your life. $8.95

Contents include:
- How families work
- You never talk to me — closeness and distance among family members
- You're not better, just different — dealing with differences
- How to be true to yourself and still have friends
- Triangles in relationships
- Who's on first? — Birth order and gender position in the family of origin
- Doing the work — The steps in doing family of origin work

BIRTH ORDER AND YOU
How your sex and position in the family affects your personality and relationships
by Dr. Ron Richardson and Lois A. Richardson, M.A.

Are you the oldest, middle, or youngest child in your family? Are you a leader or a follower? An introvert or an extrovert? Your position in the family has a far-reaching effect on the way you experience the world — it is a cornerstone of your personality. With insight and accuracy, this book shows you the way to a greater understanding of your friends, family, and yourself. Some of the topics covered are: $7.95

- Why birth order matters
- How the sex of your siblings affects your personality
- Introducing birth order position and sex
- Oldest children
- Youngest children
- Middle children
- Only children
- Twins
- Exceptions and variations: Factors that alter the usual birth order pattern
- Parenting your children of different birth orders
- Siblings as a psychological resource

A CARE-GIVER'S GUIDE
Practical solutions for coping with aging parents or a chronically ill partner or relative
by Jill Watt

It's normal to be concerned about your chronically ill partner, relative, or elderly parent. Although you want to do what is best for your loved one, you are faced with practical problems and emotional dilemmas. With the help of this book, you can establish priorities and work toward a positive and meaningful relationship with your care-receiver, whether you choose to care for your relative in your home or not.

The book explores a variety of care-giving arrangements. Worksheets help you assess your specific situation so you can manage your time and monitor your own well-being. $11.95

Its answers questions like —

- How will I feel toward the care-receiver?
- What are the financial considerations of being a care-giver?
- What adjustments will I have to make in my home?
- When should I ask for help from family, friends, and professionals?
- How do I choose medical support for the care-receiver?
- When is it time to consider moving the care-receiver into an outside care facility?

ADOPTING YOUR CHILD
Options, answers, and actions
by Nancy Thalia Reynolds

You think you would like to adopt. But you've heard about long waiting lists, intimidating investigations into your private life, and outrageous costs.

It doesn't have to be that way. This book can lead you to the adoption of your choice — whether that be of an infant through a private, independent arrangement, a special needs child through a public agency, an international adoption, or some other plan suited just for you. Non-traditional options are also examined, and checklists and worksheets help prospective parents devise a strategy to keep their plans on track. $12.95

Some of the issues addressed are —

- How are adoptive families different from birth families?
- Why do I need to be an advocate?
- What are the legal requirements for adoption?
- How do I avoid illegal adoption and fraud?

Each chapter includes a Resource Guide and Tips with specific leads and information.

THE SOUL-SEARCHER'S GUIDE TO THE GALAXY
Figuring out life's challenges from housework to sex to global warming
by Douglas Todd

- Would you steal to feed your hungry kids?
- Is there such thing as a just war?
- Who does the housework in your home?

This book is designed to help you explore your attitudes, define your beliefs, and focus your views.

Douglas Todd, who was recently named the best religion reporter at any secular newspaper or magazine in North America, asks readers to take stock of their inner values and discover the things that really count in their lives.

Todd offers views on issues ranging from sex to civil disobedience, animal rights to political correctness. He takes the reader through the whole human experience with his thought-provoking and insightful (but never dogmatic) comments.

Each chapter begins with a quiz to get the readers thinking about their values and goals. But don't look for an answer key. There are no right or wrong responses. Todd's goal is to help you sort through the fog created by life's questions and help you feel better and more confident about the beliefs you hold and decisions you have to make every day. $9.95

ORDER FORM

All prices are subject to change without notice. Books are available in book, department, and stationery stores. If you cannot buy the book through a store, please use this order form. (Please print)

Name _____

Address _____

_____

Charge to: ❑ Visa   ❑ MasterCard

Account Number _____

Validation Date _____

Expiry Date _____

Signature _____

❑ Check here for a free catalog.

Please send your order to:
Self-Counsel Press Inc.
1704 N. State Street
Bellingham, WA 98225

YES, please send me:

_____ copies of **Please, Listen To Me!,** $9.95

_____ copies of **No-Gimmick Guide to Managing Stress,** $11.95

_____ copies of **Family Ties That Bind,** $8.95

_____ copies of **Birth Order and You,** $7.95

_____ copies of **A Care-Giver's Guide,** $11.95

_____ copies of **Adopting Your Child,** $12.95

_____ copies of **The Soul-Searcher's Guide to the Galaxy,** $9.95

Please add $2.50 for postage & handling. WA residents, please add 7.8% sales tax.